Museums at the Crossroads?

Museums at the Crossroads?

Essays on Cultural Institutions in a Time of Change

Jack Lohman

ROYAL **BC** MUSEUM
Victoria, Canada

Published by the Royal BC Museum, 675 Belleville Street, Victoria, British
Columbia, V8W 9W2, Canada.

Edited, designed and typeset by Gerry Truscott.
Typset in Minion Pro 11/15, with Gill Sans headings.
Editorial assistance by Amy Reiswig.
Index by Carol Hamill.

Front cover art and design by Ping Zhu.
Full cover design by Stuart Wootton (form-creative.ca).
Printed in Canada by Friesens.

MIX
Paper from
responsible sources
FSC® C016245
www.fsc.org

Library and Archives Canada Cataloguing in Publication

Lohman, Jack, 1958-
Museums at the crossroads?: essays on cultural institutions in a
time of change / Jack Lohman.

Includes bibliographical references and an index.
ISBN 978-0-7726-6698-7 (pbk),   978-0-7726-6726 (cloth)

1. Lohman, Jack, 1958-. 2. Museums – Social aspects. 3. Museums
– Educational aspects. 4. Museum architecture. I. Royal BC Museum
II. Title. III. Title: Essays on cultural institutions in a time of change.

AM7 L64 2013   069   C2013-980081-6

Contents

For Helen Hamlyn and Rupert Hambro
with thanks for their inspiration.

Preface

In 2002, on my last day in South Africa as CEO of Iziko Museums of Cape Town, while en route to the airport, I was involved in a car crash. My luggage, containing not only my personal effects but my collection of mementos and much treasured laptop were, in an instant, destroyed. I had lost three years of work and writing.

My close friend and chairman of the board of Iziko, Colin Jones, collected me from the site of the accident. As we sat lamenting the broken pieces of my life in South Africa, strewn alongside the highway, he pulled from the debris a note to me from President Thabo Mbeki thanking me for my work. Mr Mbeki had been the first president of the new South Africa to set foot in the old South African Museum and had written on the occasion of his visit: "The discovery of our past is a journey to a more human future. Your valuable work gives us the possibility to do both."

He had come to see the famous Bushman diorama in the natural history museum, which I had officially closed, pulling down the shutter on the embarrassing and shameless tableau of indigenous people "in the wild" and village scenes depicting various tribal groups. Narrow and dimly lit, the tableau had been a favourite of tourists brought in groups by white tour guides and had held a morbid fascination for generations of school children. In the nearby cultural history museum, the story of "white" civilization made the lesson of racial contrast all too clear. The diorama was a lingering insult to the new South Africa. For a moment the closure made world news. In the transformation taking place in the country toward a shared future, the museum was transforming the way in which people saw themselves in the past. His note has since accompanied me on my travels, a daily syrup of immense personal meaning reminding me of the mission driving my work.

The writing and the speeches in this volume were compiled after my period as chief executive officer of Iziko Museums of Cape Town, when I accepted the position of director of the Museum of London, professor in museum design at the Bergen National Academy of the Arts and, later, CEO at the Royal BC Museum. They speak for themselves as standalone pieces. They are all honest reflections and speak from the heart. I have refrained from rewriting them. They are included here not to sound off some arrogant intelligence but rather to point to a relationship with the world and the excitement of international work. Taken together, the essays constitute a state of readiness to reflect on those issues left behind in times of rapid social change.

The layout of the book is not chronological but thematic. Transformation and cultural change are its central themes and always implicit. Beneath, there is a sense of responsibility I carry personally to celebrate history and share it, an inner conviction that museums, among all that we do, can and should play this role in the societies and world of which we are part. The ingredients of the essays and speeches were all supplied by the issues, locations and the museums that make up the landscapes of my professional life. I have not always felt optimistic about the projects I have undertaken around the world, but my stand on facing the toughest challenges in museums has always been unequivocal. No museum is perfect and museum transformation takes time. The time to change, however, is always now and this requires the institutional acquisition of confidence and the courage to embrace change and put our skills and resources to work for the benefit of those we serve.

I would like to express my deep thanks to all those I have worked with in Cape Town, Bergen, London, Warsaw, Victoria, Doha, Addis Ababa, Kigali, Cairo, Bogota and Pristina. I am particularly grateful to Dr Colin Jones, now director of a new museum in Doha, who saved my life that day and has since been a colleague and companion on the sometimes hazardous but always exciting road along which we are all, in some way, travelling.

Victoria, August 2013

Collaboration as Strategy

I presented this paper at the British Columbia Museums Association (BCMA) annual conference in Kamloops, October 2012. I was greatly buoyed by the questions from the conference floor that followed my address and have taken those with me into the dynamic of other writings on British Columbia.

In November 1884, a man with the rather unlikely name of Newton H. Chittenden submitted an *Official Report of the Exploration of the Queen Charlotte Islands* to the government of British Columbia.[1] He had been hired by the chief commissioner of Lands and Works to survey Haida Gwaii (then called the Queen Charlotte Islands) and describe what he found. His report is, in its fashion, anthropological. He describes potlatches and dancing, religion and food, habits of dress and behaviour among "the Hydah" – that "very remarkable race of people" as he calls them. He was, as so many of us are, particularly won over by Haida carving. So he decided, like many a tourist supporting the local economy, that he would like one to take home. "Desiring to possess some small article of Hydah manufacture," Chittenden wrote enthusiastically, "I gave a young Indian jeweller a two-and-a-half dollar gold piece at nine o'clock in the morning, with instructions to

---

1. Chittenden 1884.

make from it an eagle. Before one o'clock the same day, he brought me the bird – so well-made that not many jewellers could improve upon it."

Chittenden was a fascinating character. At 70, he was the subject of a feature article in the *New York Times*, living out his days in New Jersey and starting each morning with a 20-kilometre walk before breakfast, dressed with post-modern abandon in a sombrero and sturdy corduroy trousers. In 1910, he was still every inch the explorer.

And the story of his Haida gold eagle fascinates me. He didn't spend his money: he transformed it. He was not picking up evidence: he was commissioning a work of art, one so refined that "not many jewellers could improve upon it". His 1884 report on the Haida is (as you might expect) full of top-down attitudes that make us cringe today. But something else is also going on. Newton Chittenden was trying to see what's there. He was trying to hear what the poet Susan Musgrave once called "the sound of nobody listening".[2] He may have been colliding with a culture he knew little about, but he was also connecting. And he may have provided a path for us today.

You could say – if we don't press too hard on the point – that Chittenden collaborated with his Haida carver. It's somewhere in there, with all those unspoken transactions between the two of them. Why an eagle? Why the emphasis on speed of execution? Who impressed whom here – the man who flashed his shiny gold piece or the man who shifted its shape? It is a matter not so much of whose but of what story we decide to narrate. Choosing what story we tell is, of course, something that all museums across the world have to ask, and not only ask at the start, but keep asking themselves. At my museum – the Royal BC Museum – the story is so well told, so comprehensive, that it almost engulfs itself: man and nature, landscape and population, the long past and the shifting future. As the story of British Columbia, it's wonderful, and wonderfully done, as its nearly half a million annual visitors can attest. But what's excluded here? What stories could the museum tell? Or any museum?

I want here to suggest some starting points for change at the Royal BC Museum, but my concern is less with the particular case than its

---

2. Musgrave 1977, pp. 124–25.

implications for all of us. City or regional museums, or themed museums, are often so keen to master their histories that everything that doesn't fit is muscled out. And any modern museum that has fixed its story is – if we're completely honest – only a jazzed-up version of those dusty museums of bygone days, with their stuffed cases and unchanging displays. Museums are, by definition, about containment. But maybe we need to turn them inside out and create not just access, but a genuine openness to other voices, other ways. We need – and the metaphor should be applied widely – to bring in to the museum what doesn't belong.

One of my favourite museums is Te Papa in New Zealand. It's a strik-ing building that overlooks the harbour in Wellington. What I like about it is that it manages to create an *experience* for the visitor – not through bells and whistles, flashing lights and whatever the museum equivalent of a rollercoaster might be (a very fast escalator, perhaps). No, it creates a sat-isfying experience by taking visitors inside a fully imagined, sympathetic environment. At Te Papa, the approach, the building, the collections, the displays, the programming seem of a piece. The museum gives you some-thing solid and noteworthy – it's certainly not amorphous – but it is also open to what you bring to the experience. The colours alone make me feel good. They seem to make sense of where I am and what might have gone on there. Without seeming homogeneous or monoglot, everything at Te Papa is speaking together.

Easier to achieve, you might say, if you're looking over a sun-filled harbour in New Zealand. But Te Papa's openness picks up on something recently noted in the *World Cities Culture Report 2012*, a survey of the cultural life of a dozen world cities from Shanghai to Mumbai, Johannes-burg to São Paulo. The report notes that infrastructure – the hard build of bricks, mortar and the odd Corinthian column thrown in to let us know we are entering the temple of Culture – is by no means the only measure of cultural effectiveness. Cultural activity (festivals, street life, pop-up events) is, the authors write:

> an increasingly important driver of a city's appeal to residents and
> businesses alike. In this domain, the gap between the older, richer
> cities and those of the emerging economies is smaller, and on some
> of these indicators the emerging cities outscore the older cities – in

part, because they are often larger. These wider measures of vitality and diversity suggest that the world cities are more balanced cultur- ally than simple counts of, say, museums would indicate.[3]

It's an interesting point and affects a number of issues, from how museums will have to rethink themselves within such active cities, to how we will compete with changing types of cultural attraction. It also affects how we set about our own cultural advocacy: to the public, to potential funders and to government. In Canada, as in many countries, the model is increasingly moving away from a dominant national policy toward a more localized and autonomous cultural sphere,[4] so one way in which museums will thrive is by plugging into the informal cultural activity around them. Museums are rarely comfortable doing this. They usually have very big doors with very strong locks to keep the world out. But as Te Papa shows, openness can become a way of working.

And if the result of collaborating with the wider culture is greater vital- ity, diversity and cultural balance – to use the terms of the *World Cities Culture Report* – so too is the geographical extension of that engagement: not just drawing energy from the cities where we are, but creating new synergies with other cities and towns, other regions and countries. Part of the Royal BC Museum's mandate is province-wide, and this covers a number of areas: advising on collections and conservation, sending loans and travelling exhibitions, mentoring and training museum colleagues. *Aliens Among Us* – a fascinating look at the 4000 natural species that have come (like many of us) to live in BC – started life as a successful Royal BC Museum exhibition. It is now travelling to nine museums across the prov- ince over a two-year period: from Nelson to Kitimat, Penticton to Prince George. It's an excellent way to raise the profile of the provincial museum and its partners, and to collaborate on new programs of engagement for

---

3. BOP Consulting 2012, p. 57.

4. For a short summary of this changing approach, see McNeil Bertrand 2010. See also Slaby 2008: comparing arts advocacy networks in Sweden, Australia, USA and UK, Slaby notes the difficulties of creating coherent bodies to influence national policy in Canada.

young people, adults and others across the region. But is it enough? It feels like one tenuous thread across a province that occupies 10 per cent of Canada's land surface. With an area of 95 million hectares, British Columbia is larger than France and Germany combined. If this is our cultural Trans-Canada Highway, we need to get more traffic moving along it!

Indeed, I want to extend this looking out even further. Collaborating can seem a bit like holding hands on a first date. Very safe. Very cosy. Sure, let's connect. But frankly, I want a few cultural sparks to fly too. I want some real difference, not just complementarity. We shouldn't be afraid of it. The most popular music downloaded from iTunes is often a mash-up of artists and songs, old and new, samples and remixes. It's what I want for museums. Some days, just like in the real world, I want my culture to collide.

The Canadian writer Jack Hodgins wrote a wonderfully entertaining novel called *The Invention of the World*. The boarding house he describes on Vancouver Island is, in its zany way, a kind of west coast museum of characters and ideas, a living cabinet of curiosities. The boarding house proprietor Maggie – the novel's equivalent of me, if you will – knows exactly what she's got. As Hodgins writes:

> She had a perfect set-up. She had this land, opened up to the whole
> wide strait along this edge as if there were no real borders on her
> world ... a solid base from which to rise.[5]

Standing outside my museum, looking out over the water, I know how she feels. The landscape inspires me to infinite possibilities. But if I'd like to encourage not just mine but all museums to open up, look outward and make more connections, I think museums also (particularly in times of economic difficulty) need to look inward, to make sure they have "a solid base from which to rise". We have to start by collaborating with ourselves.

One way we can do this is by keeping our permanent galleries fresh. Think of Newton Chittenden. Think of the moment he and the Haida carver meet. That's the feeling we need to get into our public spaces. It's something more than precious objects or helpful information or re-enactment. It's a kind of sympathetic awareness and imaginative power that we

---

5. Hodgins 1977, p. 46.

need to build into the museum experience. If I don't feel it, no amount of text or impressive display is going to make me feel it.

It's not a question of externals either – of big shot architects or glamorous imported exhibitions. It's about reinventing what we have. If we rethink it, so will the public. We sometimes know our own collections so well that we only see the catalogue we've inherited: here are the fixed categories, here's what we have, here's what we say about it. It may all be very worthy. But the world around us is changing all the time. What people do, what they think, what interests them is constantly on the move. Coming from London, I know how exhausting this can be! But what power was there, once we found ways to bring it into the museum. Get out into British Columbia, and you can see mighty rivers converted into electricity. That's our model. We have to transform history into light. We have to be as wide and open to the skies as the Peace River. We have to be hydroelectric.

I am not about to set up a new income stream for the museum by taking on BC Hydro. But I do want to suggest two ways in which we can generate power from our collections. One is by celebrating the individual. There is an understandable push to get as much of our collections on display as we can. It's a laudable instinct, especially when the public are frustrated that everything we hold isn't out for them to see. They want it all! But selection is one of our greatest assets. Of course there are times we want to show variety, development; quantity can be impressive at times. But think of some of your most powerful experiences of art or nature. Is it not the single artwork whose very uniqueness is enhanced when it appears alone? Is it not the apparition of a solitary Mule Deer, still and watchful at the forest's edge? If our displays can achieve the force of concentration, think what we can do with them. Rather than engulf the visitor, we can get them to ricochet from one great event to the next, so that they come away not just remembering a landscape or culture, but enchanted by the droll coral-striped beak of a single Tufted Puffin, or the towering authority of a Kwakwaka'wakw totem pole.

So powerful is the unique that it needn't restrict itself to the obviously beautiful. Puffins and totem poles are easy sells – but we need to dig deeper. At the Royal BC Museum we are about to display one of British Columbia's earliest land treaties. Signed in the 1850s by the governor of Vancouver Island James Douglas, the treaty is just the sort of cultural moment we saw with Newton Chittenden on Haida Gwaii – and one with much greater long-term effects. This is the moment, there, on the page, stuck with bits of bark and other material, when the representative of the British crown colony seals the deal with representatives of Vancouver Island's First Nations. It looks like connection; it feels like collision; it certainly wasn't collaboration.

It is a legal document, really; a bill of sale; a text we could reproduce online or on the wall. But how potent it is, that physical bit of paper. Everyone in Canada lives on the result. And it was until recently tucked neatly away in the museum archive.

I love archives. They are the closeted glories of the museum world, and we do not do enough with them. There have always been too many gilded teacups and worthy portraits to put on show. But if we stop looking and start seeing, what riches lie hidden there? And this brings me to my second approach to recharging the museum from within. We have to communicate our assets. It's not just the collections, but the archives themselves – all that history and research – that need to be better known. We need to get learning programs that delve in and create new approaches, new topics for us. We need to stop talking at the young and start asking them what they want to know. We need to digitize, not only so that we can speak to the world, but so that the world can speak to us. Te Papa has a Soundings Theatre and *Te Marae*, a place where all can stand and all can belong. That's what I want for my museum. A warm welcome for those who are arriving, and a sense that everything – the collection, the archives, the visitors, the staff – belongs. I want so much collaboration that we stop using the word "collaboration".

Across British Columbia you will find three UNESCO world-heritage sites. It is an impressive number, and if you get a chance to explore them, they will remind you of an essential attribute of the past and present culture here on the west coast: that we always see ourselves in relation to the mountains and the forests and the sea. As Jack Hodgins' heroine Maggie understood looking out from her Vancouver Island boarding house, British Columbia is not so much at the edge of the world as on the cusp of it – as if, as Hodgins says, "there were no real borders on her world".

And that's how I want the Royal BC Museum to be: on the threshold of the world. Open to its currents. Ready to extend an invitation to all. Any museum can be that – intellectually, in terms of vision. But here in BC the land and the ocean are much more than a picture postcard backdrop. They colour everything, shape every experience. Find me a visitor who hasn't marvelled at the Rocky Mountains behind, the Pacific before, trees so wide you can't see past them. That's the scale of experience here, that's daily life, and unless the Royal BC Museum finds its analogy to this, it is never going to match the power and beauty, the expressiveness of what surrounds it.

Taking Shape:
Knowledge as Museum Display

This is a keynote address I presented at the University of British
Columbia's annual Research Day in March 2013. The theme of the day
was "Infrastructures of Knowledge: Mediating Memories, Representing
Relationships, Framing Futures", a subject broad enough to draw in
museums.

There probably aren't many who haven't read or plan to read Esi Edugyan's
wonderful novel, *Half-Blood Blues*. Nominated for the Man Booker Prize
and a Governor General's Award, it won the 2011 Giller Prize for fiction.
It tells the story of a group of black musicians before and after the Second
World War – from the jazz clubs of pre-war Berlin, to occupied Paris, to
the rainy streets of modern-day Baltimore. The novel hasn't much to do
with Canada. But Edugyan – based in Victoria – allows herself one very
Canadian joke. The protagonist Sid, desperate to get his cab driver to stop
gabbing, is asked where he lives:

> "Not London England," I said. "London Ontario. In Canada."
>
> The cabbie's eyes sort of glazed over. Canada kills any conversa-
> tion quick, I learned long ago. It's a little trick of mine.[1]

---

1. Edugyan 2011, p. 35.

Well, it's not just Canada. If it's any consolation, museums too have this silencing effect on people. High vaults and cupolas rarely encourage chat. From the start, the entire design of museums appears to have had the sole intention of imposing silence and awe on the visitor. Reverence was demanded – though in many cases less for the objects of the past than for those rich and oh so admirable people who put them there. There's a perfectly good reason we all know the Getty as "the Getty".

What this silence tells us is that museum spaces – and perhaps, by extension, all public spaces – are already mediated. They exercise their influence before anyone has seen or done anything inside them. It's easy to forget. Many imagine the museum to be an empty container, something like a large piece of tupperware in which you can place lots of cultural tidbits that need preserving. More recently, the architectural brilliance of many contemporary museums has been designed to work with the collection inside and communicate key messages. One thinks immediately of Daniel Libeskind's powerful Jewish Museum in Berlin, with its jagged light, its blocked corridors, its narrowing perspectives. The building is the content it intends to display (or in the case of the Holocaust, notates architecturally a loss and a terror the museum is unable to display).

But even here, before we get to understand the specific meaning intended by a Libeskind or a Frank Gehry, the building exerts its force upon us. We approach, we admire, we quite literally "look up" – and we begin already in a position of silent veneration.

I want to start with the building because museums can focus a little narrowly on the words they use to explain things. And yet how collections are displayed, and the buildings that house them, are just as important as any caption or text panel set nearby. It's a mistake no visitor ever makes. The building is the first thing that has an impact on their experience. But we professionals become so accustomed to our environment that we forget the influence it wields.

There are of course many approaches one might take. Libeskind's Jewish Museum is deliberately polemical: it shouts, it shakes you up. It's an argument in architecture that grabs you by the lapels as you pass through. Some people may not like this, but one aspect of it we might agree on: a sense of awe is not in itself bad. I want people to feel the drama and excitement of culture. Museums are inspiring and need to feel that way. Part of the appeal of a museum like the Royal British Columbia Museum is its pleasing situation. You could say the building honours the land as much as the stories inside do. What you learn in the building is, in the best cases, reinforced by the environment in which you learn it.

So 18th- and 19th-century museums, even the most daunting, were onto something with their awe-inspiring facades. They announced that something important was going on inside. Creating an oppressive silence may no longer be what we want from them, but silence in itself is no bad thing. As a forum for welcoming discussion, it makes the museum space all the more engaging to visitors. There's something to be said for leaving room for others to speak. Silence is also an opportunity.

Acknowledging this shifting tension between insistence and opportunity in the space itself is, I would argue, one of the ways museums can reframe themselves for the modern visitor. And it's not just the bricks and mortar that determine how museum spaces work. Let me give you an example. One of the new voices in museums in the 21st century is that of technology. Museums increasingly provide independent digital pathways through their galleries – headset tours, QR access points, audio- and video-guides. These digital directives are both highly determined (since the museum usually provides the content) and yet highly undetermined, for the visitor can put together any number of journeys through the collection. As more digital content is made available to them, growing numbers of visitors are doing so, and that is only likely to increase.

With ever larger numbers of headsets covering ever larger numbers of ears, a new type of museum space – or perhaps a new definition of that space – is about to emerge, where each visitor moves entirely on their own, doing their own thing. It's highly tailored and admirably free in the choice it offers. But perhaps now is the moment, before it is utterly embedded in our visitor environment, to ask: do we want the museum experience to be completely autonomous? Are we creating a less mediated experience with more choice, or an unchallenging exercise in self-absorption?[2] Does too

---

2. Compare Reynolds 2011, pp. 118–19, on the iPod's narrowing of social

much choice mean you only encounter what already interests you? Is this selection, or is it shopping?

"Encounter" may be the key word here. In trying to be flexible and move away from a dominant curatorial voice, in trying to open up their spaces and not over-determine matters for visitors, museums risk losing any sense of dialogue. So keen are we not to impose meanings that we risk retreating into silence. Instead of engagement, we have escape. Instead of community, we have solitude. It's the risk of a de-centred approach to the museum, and I think it's probably not what people want when they gather in a public space such as a museum.

My concern really is that in fearing how we, the museum guardians, frame the history, knowledge, archives and collections we hold, we mustn't imagine some innocent state where no mediation is possible. The worst thing we could do is become tentative and passive. We have instead to understand clearly the implications of what we are doing and seize the museum framework as part of our expressive potential. The building, as I've argued, is one such frame that can encourage and suggest, from a general sense of inspiration and scale of importance, to a more specific, thematic set of meanings. The museum's intellectual scaffolding must also find a strong foothold between the open-ended and the absentee. We can't change the collections every two minutes, but we can invigorate the intellectual life of the museum quite easily with new topics, new approaches.

Take language, for example, as a way into a museum collection. Abstract concepts are not the usual approach to objects, where the materiality of our displays tends to skip away from the intangible when we explain them. We remain rooted to the material past. But if museum objects represent points of contact with the groups of people who made

---

experience: "iPod fans always go on about how the machine is like having your own personal radio station. Exactly: the iPod is Radio Me, where there's no nasty surprises and the program magically knows what you want to hear. Which means it's the opposite of the radio, which is a medium for surprise, for connection with people you might have nothing else in common with, for creating strange social alliances."

or encountered them, language too in all its varieties is a very potent representation of those same communities.

But is language of much use as a museum topic, where people come to look at things? When you walk into the Smithsonian's National Museum of the American Indian in Washington, DC, one of the first things you will see – and you can hardly avoid it – is a wall of video screens. This welcome wall greets visitors in no less than 150 Native American languages. You are showered in the indigenous languages of the Americas. It's wonderful – and it also immediately makes a very useful intellectual point: no museum, even one as powerful as the Smithsonian, is ever going to be able to present to you that many cultures in one building in one afternoon. Even to understand a select few with the correct weight and feeling, you need to place them in the context of these many missing languages and cultures. The welcome wall is a clever device: you start your museum visit by seizing in a very quick and graphic fashion just how much there is to know, and then you make your selection. And it does that not with objects, but with a more abstract, yet contiguous idea ... about language.

The Royal BC Museum is embarking on its own display of First Nations languages in British Columbia. The project is one of the first ventures to emerge from a joint memorandum of understanding between the Museum and the First Peoples' Cultural Council. It is the latest in a long history of rewarding collaborations between the museum and British Columbia's First Nations.

Such collaboration expands the Museum's voice to include the voices of other contributors, particularly those with first-hand experience and knowledge of cultural practice. It fills the silence with sound and enables a more multi-dimensional approach to how we display First Nations cultures to our visitors. But this exhibition is more ambitious. Like the Smithsonian's welcome wall, it aims to bring the uncontainable into the museum container. For us, it is not just a question of First Nations languages, but of the world views they represent – about land and water, family and social structures, moral values and ways of life. Paradoxically, it is language that often gives us access to the unspoken, or as is often the case in First Nations languages, to the unwritten. With language as our focus all kinds of new questions arise. What place do we give in history to the unregistered? How do we preserve the undefined and the uninscribed? What might we be missing if we ignore it? As the writer Robert Kroetsch puts it in a collection of essays entitled *The Lovely Treachery of Words*, we are finding that (in his words) "the unnaming allows the naming. The local pride speaks. The oral tradition speaks its tentative nature, its freedom from the authorized text."[3] We are learning that language gives us access to information that objects alone (and the histories that surround them) might not convey.

One of the exhibition's goals is to show that not everything can be translated into other languages, and it is here perhaps that we find ourselves at the heart of our most cherished beliefs. Such concepts are the hardest to articulate, the source of every culture's myths and originary tales, its deepest thinking. They are of the essence of who we are. As Northrop Frye wrote in his study of the Canadian imagination, our "myths are expressions of concern, of man's care for his own destiny and heritage, his sense of the supreme importance of preserving his community."[4] Lose the language in which to express such beliefs, and you lose that very bond that ties a community together. Preserving such languages is one reason we want to put on this exhibition.

I cite this example as an instance of how an innovative lens such as language can re-present the collection and the knowledge it represents. Change the prism, and you change the content. No one imagines it is practicable or desirable to keep altering museum displays as times and fashions change. But what you can do is reintroduce them, suggest new frames or angles, new starting points for thinking about what is, and isn't, there.

Language is one idea for recontextualizing the collection intellectually. But there is no getting away from the fact that museums are filled with things. Unlike the academy, where the horizon of knowledge extends as far as scholarly minds wish to travel, museum knowledge is embedded in objects themselves. I can travel with them, but they make for a very heavy trunk.

The shape of things is, of course, their great power. The pleasure of museums is that knowledge is embodied. History is palpable – we ask you

---

3. Kroetsch 1989, p. 32.
4. Frye 1971, p. 194.

not to touch, but the reality of the past is there, before your eyes, in any handmade pot or curiously fashioned piece of jewellery.

What we say about objects and how we present them is highly influential. You could rewrite and redesign the exact same collection and end up with radically different museums. But even more compelling of late, as a means of reframing the collection, are the prospects of bringing different collections together – physically, intellectually, electronically.

One of the special exhibitions we have planned at the Royal BC Museum is on gold rushes. It's an exhibition about movement and looks at one of the founding activities that went into making British Columbia the place it is today: bringing people and influences, turning this particular stretch of land and water into a dreamscape of wealth and personal prosperity. It's a very BC story. Or is it? One of the ways of breaking out of the parochialism of museum knowledge is to imagine the same exhibition put on elsewhere. What does an exhibition on gold rushes look like in California, or Australia? Why not bring those elements in? We'll never really understand British Columbia's place in the world unless we see how other regions were shaken by the same adventures. We hope the exhibition will do just that, by drawing on collections from as far away as China and Australia, Britain and the southern United States.

My larger point is that collections can move, physically and, increasingly, digitally. They're not static, and what we've already said about them can change. One of the Royal BC Museum's great projects is a planned Atlas of British Columbia. It's a kind of giant digital museum that will bring together archives and collections from across the province, including those of private collectors. It's an attempt to recombine dispersed knowledge and make it available to everyone for free, however remote their location. We could never hope to bring this material together physically, but digitization has meant not just that information can be stored, but that astonishing new possibilities for intelligent archiving and comparative research are arising. It's such an exciting moment for museums, libraries and archives, and will, among its many effects, send us back to the physical collections, asking new questions, needing to make new descriptions, pursuing new scientific and other investigations.

What this joining up of physical collections demands is a freedom from the traditional boundaries of museum and archival work. Those can be disciplinary boundaries, or the boundaries of agreed thought. They are sometimes the boundaries of professional culture, which so easily become ossified as a high-minded but unyielding set of protocols. There are few things more discouraging for a young curator full of fresh ideas than being told in no uncertain terms, "This is how we do things." The only appropriate response, it seems to me, is "Change!"

These boundaries are also, in a very conventional sense, regional. When we bring collections together, we are going to have to let down our guard. We need to open the museum up if we are to ensure that knowledge remains vital, comprehensive and relevant. You can't just stay in your place, working quietly in your corner. You need to travel; you need to look out; you need to let outside influences in. The Atlas of British Columbia that we're proposing will include as many dispersed artifacts and records that we can find, including those from abroad. The exhibition on gold and gold rushes will draw on everything from Chinese immigrant histories to trade routes across America. In both cases, understanding British Columbia involves engaging not just with the province but with the world.

Even a topic such as language in British Columbia needs to break out of its provincial encyclopedia. In an age when people are bouncing images and music across the world, where even the US President learns the moves to Gangnam Style (not very well, according to his wife), museums need to be international, and keep an international perspective.

Allow me to finish with a short passage from Audrey Thomas's novel *Intertidal Life*, which is set on Galiano Island.

> Alice ... took out a small book called *A Spanish Voyage to Vancouver*. Since coming to the island she had been interested in the Spanish exploration of the northwest coast.... The island has a Spanish name, as did some of the others in the archipelago, and it amused her to think of these Spanish captains coming through Porlier Pass.... All those men sailing the oceans of the world ... did their wives ... hang on their tales of Indians and waterfalls, strange ceremonies and strange sights, the way Desdemona hung on the words of Othello? What if

women had been the explorers?.... Imagine a ship of women then, trained in the use of all those wonderful instruments – quadrants, chronometers, the azimuth compass – knowing how to steer by the stars, knowing the difference between an artificial horizon and a real.[5]

It's a brilliant passage. Thomas reminds us that in case we forget, BC's imaginative heritage connects to everything from early navigational instruments developed in China and the Middle East to Shakespeare's *Othello*. And reading her reminds me that we need, when trying to frame the past or future, to keep our perspective wide. If an exhibition at the Royal BC Museum is going to talk about languages in the province, we will point out Kwakw'ala, Nisga'a, Tlingit, Halkomelem ... there is a long list of languages to discuss. And one of them is Spanish.

---

5. Thomas 1986, p. 15. The book Alice Hoyle is reading is by Josef Espinosa y Tello (1763–1815).

The Professional Museum: Who Needs It?

The Swedish Museums Association was quite prescriptive in the themes they wished me to cover in my keynote address at their annual general meeting in Stockholm in March 2004. This paper was the culmination of a relationship that had started 10 years earlier, when I worked with the Riksantikvarieämbetet, the Swedish National Heritage Board. Nanna and Lars Cnattingius kindly looked after me and later provided the memorable opportunity of visiting the island of Gotland.

I would like to begin by talking about the bad old days. In 1964, an influential article was published in the *Museums Journal* entitled "The Fault is in Ourselves"[1] – quoting Shakespeare's *Julius Caesar*, of course: "The fault, dear Brutus, is not in our stars, but in ourselves, that we are underlings"[2] (our first clue that it is High Culture, indeed, that we are discussing). In this article, the former Public Relations Officer at London's Victoria & Albert Museum, Charles Gibbs-Smith, struck a sharp blow against the museum world. The majority of museum curators, he wrote, "patronise, resent,

---

1. Gibbs-Smith 1964, pp. 227–29.
2. *Julius Caesar*, I.ii.140-1.

despise, dislike or even hate the public". He did not mince his words. He went on with great vitriol and verve to label much of the curatorial retreat behind "research" as phoney (a strangely streetwise word for the double-barrelled Gibbs-Smith). Why should a museum, he asked, hide behind all the standard academic armour of technical language and obscure reference? Why should curators retreat behind the lofty and cool erudition of their specialized discourse? What was the point of all their learning?

"They seem," he wrote, "terrified of talking with affection or enthusiasm about a painting or sculpture or piece of magnificent furniture." Was it for fear of appearing vulgar or common (a terrible sin in England, you know)? Of losing their status as serious scholars? Was it just easier for them to ignore the public? Or is this attack an early indication of that moment in history when things were about to change, when the old culture of the learned amateur was about to give way to a broader, more professional view of the role a museum curator might play?

It is a culture we are still living with today, though one in constant debate with the newly professional museum and its contemporary ideals. The old "shut the doors and keep the public out" idea – and we have all of us heard this fogeyish approach that the museum or gallery would be perfect if it weren't for having to let the public in – is the legacy museums live with. And though it may be a disappearing culture in institutions, it is one which still has to be overcome in the public eye. Addressing new audiences is difficult in part, because no matter what measures we take as professionals, the old sense that museums are not for the likes of us lingers. The aristocracy of knowledge is just that: a set of closed gates, psychological as much as physical. There is no point throwing open those gates and welcoming a public who simply feel they do not belong, that they are as much curiosities (as they march down the corridors of cases and displays) as any monkey's paw or zebra skin. The professional museum cannot just thrive on good intentions: it needs to know what it's about.

Most European museums grew, of course, out of private collections. The whole idea of their belonging to a private space (rather than a public one) still hangs about them. This remains true not only of the royal collections of France and Germany, for instance, that can now, by a sleight of hand, be thought of as the nation's (the royals themselves in some sense belonging to the state, or at least these days, to the heritage industry). But it is also true of the great collections of private individuals.

And those private collectors are, as Kenneth Hudson has pointed out in his fascinating *A Social History of Museums*,[3] often very private indeed. Though often accused of acquisitiveness – a kind of showy one-upmanship in acquiring the best objects that marked many of their business careers – these collectors may have been less interested in conspicuous consumption than in a somewhat old-fashioned idea (to our minds, at least) of the consolations of art.

Statements by famed lovers of art, such as Grenville Winthrop (whose astonishing collection is now at the Fogg Art Museum in Harvard), New York's Henry Clay Frick and others, confirm the *Citizen Kane* idea of a solitary man surrounded by the reliable, unchanging objects of his devotion. Such treasure houses constituted a place for private contemplation, a quite intimate, somewhat idolatrous love affair with the objets de préférence, the precious jewels, the rare statuary. They are for the owner's pleasure, no one else's. As the celebrated Armenian collector Calouste Gulbenkian once said, when asked to show his collection: "Would I admit a stranger to my harem?"[4]

Objects gathered in such a way acquire a mystique, a special sense of their rare value. And we almost still believe in the magic that adheres to our precious objects, though it is worth noting that it is not inherent in them and that we need not hold onto all of them in quite the fearful way we do. One of the ways in which museums in the past became inaccessible was by turning the quite normal process of buying a painting or a Chinese vase into something recherché and mysterious, governed by those in-the-know pretty much exclusively for those in-the-know. Acquisitions made by the Uffizi Gallery, say, in Florence were based upon, until the 19th century at least, open debates among the artists, patrons, dealers, purchasers and so

---

3. Hudson 1975. Gibbs-Smith's article is elaborated at length in Hudson's striking polemic, as are several other instances of historic museum experience cited in this essay.

4. Hudson, p. 5.

forth. But after that, the museum economy (an idea to which I will return) became a much more closed affair.

Couple this newfound mystique with the removal of objects from their places of origin and you can see how museums became places, quite literally, of pedestals, where those who knew what to buy for the good of the nation venerated their magnificent finds (members of the public were welcome to come and watch, preferably in silence and certainly from an appropriate distance). Cults of the rare were thus put in place by museum staff: objects were better the older they were, the more remote their source, the stranger their cultural origin. There was a certain satisfaction in showing how weird other cultures were and, by extension, how sound our own.

Things have changed. Once we had treasure houses; now we have sites of multiculturalism. Once we had collections kept safe for higher-level study; now we have programs designed to increase public access and learning. When Pope John Paul II met Yasser Arafat at the recently opened the International Nativity Museum in Bethlehem in the West Bank, the press photos circulated round the world. As the Pope made a plea for peace and expressed his wish that the Palestinians might find a homeland, so museums showed their modern function as sites of reconciliation and international importance.

The days of fusty educational institutes – for such was the impression most museums gave, and a few, dare I say, continue to give – are past. Museums did once understand the importance of their architecture: their fat columns and lofty pediments boasted their importance to the nation, and the grand stairs that led to many of the collections reminded the visitor that culture was not available at street level; to reach it, one had, painfully, step by step, to ascend to the higher glories.

But it is only in recent times that issues of design and display have been truly addressed. The Museum of London, for instance, when it redesigned its 19th-century *World City* galleries shook Imperial London out of its wooden Victorian cases and produced a set of galleries that are fresh, open and alive for the modern visitor. The walls came down, the sightlines were made clear across the vast sweep of the galleries and the courtyard garden next to them. And with everything from great wheels of industrial manufacture to entire hansom cabs and cars on open display atop long unadorned plinths, the visitor can practically step into the past. With the objects unimpeded and so present, they can almost reach out and touch the power of the past for themselves. (We prefer it if they don't, but they could, because we wanted to make the past as immediate as possible to the visitor.)

And all this is not just for entertainment but to reveal what the International Council of Museums (ICOM) defines as the core function of the museum: to "communicate and exhibit, for purposes of study, education and enjoyment, material evidence of people and their environment".[5] Interestingly, ICOM's definition itself has changed in line with what we might see as the rise of the professional museum. It used to see museums conserving "objects of cultural value". But whose culture? And who was placing the value where? And why just precious objects? The questions have changed today, and to meet them, to present meaningful "evidence of people and their environment", museums require a dedicated staff of trained professionals.

Museums and galleries in England were once run by "keepers". Rarely has a job title been more accurate. They were the first curators, guarding and "keeping" the treasures safe and in good condition, often by allowing the public as little access to them as possible. Over time, as museums shifted from places frequently dominated by talented, often highly committed amateurs, the professions began to weigh in: the anthropologists, the conservators, the historians. The approach may have remained fundamentally conservative – to preserve and care for the collections – but the nature of the institutions began to change. Today museums require a fleet of competent players who can address a raft of other issues that face museums today, from raising the museum's profile in the press to raising money for programs or even new or refurbished buildings.

The great European international exhibitions held in Paris, London and so forth in the 19th century are in part responsible for this change in attitude and staffing. It was their huge expositions that began to provide

---

5. ICOM 2004, para. 1. See page 133 for a more complete definition.

new models for professionalizing the museum. As world capitals competed to put on the best display ever, for the first time serious discussions were made about transport for the public, access, numbers, letting in the light, the height of cases, how to animate displays. Even toilets! – which anyone who runs a modern museum knows are at least one of the meetings one has to have. The English euphemism "to spend a penny" as a shorthand for going to the lavatory originated with that magnificent temporary museum, the Great Exhibition of 1851 held at London's Crystal Palace. Banks of toilets had to be installed for the Great Exhibition in order to deal with the huge numbers of visitors from around the globe. And the cost to use them? Well, you had to spend a penny.

When connoisseurs gave way to curators, and collectors made way for directors, the professional museum was born. And with it, a shift of focus away from the guardians of the collections themselves toward the public who might actually benefit from seeing them. Old roles now have new components. Curators are expected to speak not simply to their colleagues (though they must do that too, for their research is an invaluable resource for the museum) but to the public, to funders, to staff who might require appropriate briefings on a recent discovery, a new purchase, a forthcoming exhibition. It isn't that museums must become in any way less centres of knowledge: they must deploy that knowledge differently. Professionalizing the museum is in part taking the resource of its expertise out of the library and into the world.

New roles have emerged alongside the revolutionizing of the old:

- Museums need to attract audiences – and require marketing teams to do so.
- Museums need to reach new communities (a particular issue in London where more than 300 languages are spoken) – and require specialist liasion officers to do so.
- Museums need to meet a complicated array of issues to do with money and financial responsibility – and require fundraisers and financial advisors to do so.

Such jobs are a far cry from the gentle amateurism of the past, and with them has come a new model of employee: trained to perform key tasks, experienced often in several institutions, set on a particular career path that may have more to do with their specialist skills than with the museum field itself. And this is no bad thing. Loyalty is no longer a question of working your way up from the post room, but of committing to specific projects and making sense of issues that may be much larger and more diverse than the specific concerns of the institution itself. The new professionals within the museum are much better at placing their organization in the real world, that outside context – economic, socio-political, international – in which they have to compete in the 21st century.

And of course the rise of museum advisory bodies and training programs reflects this. Existing staff require training to meet the ongoing specialist demands of their jobs. Increasingly there are short courses run to fill strategic gaps in expertise. And indeed, one can now in many parts of the world earn a degree in museum studies.

Such courses include essential areas for the modern museum – team-building, fundraising, design, marketing. They set essential levels of professional standards and professional demeanour (not always a strong point for museums in the past). Key concepts emerge from such training and governing bodies, including ethical policies (as we shall see), allocating resources effectively and strategies of evaluation. The point is no longer to rush at things and get them safely in a box, but to examine the processes that best use our resources (since we cannot do everything) and to evaluate honestly the effectiveness of our projects as part of our professional responsibility: we must never be content to rest on the praise we receive!

In Britain, the National Museums Directors Council has become a key factor and support of what is now sometimes termed the museum industry. And we mustn't shy away from such terms. By making connections among museums, the NMDC has been streamlining museum advocacy. Duplication, poor planning, competition and other issues show a lack of cooperation, perplex the public, damage the reputation of museums and make them look unprofessional. Most of London's principal galleries open their major international art exhibitions within weeks of one another. Why don't they spread them out and maximize their publicity, impact and audiences? Because no one has sat down and asked them to do so.

The British government has allocated £70 million over a four-year period to create a new cooperation among museums, calling this program Renaissance in the Regions. It has created nine regional hubs to bring the specializations and interests of smaller museums together under one umbrella and achieve some of the profile (and privilege) of the larger museums. The Museum of London leads the London hub and will thus position itself as a key player in London's cultural life – the aim is to reconfigure the entire museum scene in the capital. The days of gathering clay pipes and Roman coins from the shoreline of the Thames may not quite be over, but they have certainly given way to a larger vision of the role museums can have not as the nation's attic, but as cultural leaders.

So what's the point of professionalism? On Tuesday, December 7, 1784, at 11 am, a bookseller from Birmingham visited the British Museum. William Hutton was one of a small group who'd managed to purchase tickets to the still fairly new institution, and his experience was not good. As he and the others were marched hastily through gallery after gallery, Hutton asked

> whether there were none to inform us what the curiosities were as we went on? A tall genteel young man ... who seemed to be our conductor, replied with some warmth, "What! Would you have me tell you everything in the Museum? How is it possible? Besides, are not the names written upon many of them?" I was much too humbled by this reply to utter another word. The company seemed influenced; they made haste and were silent.

Hutton went on to complain, in a memorable phrase:

> If I see wonders which I do not understand, they are no wonders to me. Should a piece of withered paper lie on the floor, I should, without regard, shuffle it from under my feet. But if I am told it is a letter written by [King] Edward the Sixth, that information sets a value upon the piece, it becomes a choice morceau of antiquity, and I seize it with rapture.[6]

---

6. From *The Life of William Hutton, Stationer, of Birmingham, Written by Himself*, quoted in Hudson, pp. 8–9.

Hutton's tour of the British Museum lasted 30 minutes. He came away, in his own words, "completely disappointed". The unprofessional museum? Partly. We are here back in the bad old days. But the story reminds us that we are not mausoleums of choice morceaux, but that we exist to communicate histories to the public:

- to inform them, yes;
- to entertain them, sometimes;
- but to be relevant to them, always.

And to do this, the museum must exist in the world. Indeed it already does, though it has often (and again, we can see the origins of this in its genteel past) pretended its superiority to worldly matters. But it simply isn't so. One of the points made in Mark Sandberg's fascinating recent study of turn-of-the-century Scandinavian waxwork museums is that museums create their own markets, in this case for a panoply of real and fake artifacts used to support a vogue for highly naturalistic displays of early life in Sweden, Denmark and Norway.[7] We return to the question of the museum economy I referred to earlier. In Britain, four out of five top tourist attractions are museums. Museums need to be less naive about the role they play economically, and the power they have.

Kenneth Hudson, with characteristic forthrightness, states: "collectors are essentially robbers and destroyers. It makes little difference whether the collector is Andrew Mellon or the Metropolitan Museum of Art. There is simply too much of everything."[8] It is one of the reasons why a museum's collecting policy must include two elements: one that restricts acquisitions – since there is, as Hudson says, simply too much of everything – and one that deals with disposal or deaccession. It is in the latter area that some of the thornier issues of our time arise. What are the obligations of museums toward their objects? What are their obligations toward those from whom such objects were taken? What are their obligations, if any, toward an idea of the nation's treasures? As Edward Alexander has argued:

Collections management certainly includes out-go, as well as in-flow. The difficulty here, however, is that a museum is a kind of

---

7. Sandberg 2003.
8. Hudson, p. 12.

public trust and that deaccession and disposal of objects can lead to public criticism. Even the boards of museums that accept no public funds occupy a trusteeship relationship that is subject to some state supervision.[9]

It is here the question of museum ethics becomes a key one for the professional museum. For my museum – the Museum of London – ethics are paramount and require a strong sense of leadership. One of the first policies I put in place as director was a 14-point set of guidelines for the sensitive and appropriate display of human remains. The Museum of London has over 17,000 human remains, the third largest such collection in the country. And this is not merely a short-term set of principles. Ethical treatment of highly sensitive collections – and few could be more sensitive than actual bodies, many of which have been seized from their very graves, with little regard for their sacred burial, religious practice or descendants' wishes – absolutely requires a long-term strategy to examine why these remains continue to be held, the purpose they serve, and how that purpose relates to a possibly higher one of restitution of them to their places of honour.

The answers are not easy, nor must our approach to them be simplistic. To this end, I set up a Human Remains Working Group as part of a new Centre for Human Bioarchaeology. Their questions are in part scientific. The nine human osteologists found, for example, evidence of hitherto unknown epidemics in London's history in their studies of historical pathology. There is good work still to be done here, and a comprehensive database will soon share the group's knowledge with the world. But its approach to the remains will remain an ethical one, so that the museum becomes not a mass grave but a place, potentially, of research without possession.

In all of this, political correctness is essential. The professional museum becomes no better than its conservative forebears if (just as the curators of old hid behind their superior learning) it retreats behind the caution, the safe haven, of its very professionalism. Our responsibility is not simply to our new standards of behaviour. Our responsibility is to those whom we

9. Alexander 1979, p. 134.

can benefit with our new behaviour. We need to act: ethically, responsibly and, yes, politically.

Such politics are in part a question of staff development, of professionalization. The Museum of London now has a Diversity Manager (as part of its new professionalism) to help the museum deal with the complexities of the Race Relations Act. They are there to give voice to previously unheard communities, to form successful liaisons with outside bodies and advisory groups, to raise issues of race within the museum itself, even when – especially when – it is inconvenient to hear them. The job is necessary, and it is political. It does not merely pay lip service to present-day concerns over diversity and multiculturalism. It acts on those concerns. It responds to them. We need, as professionals, to give such jobs their own remit and respect that remit. We may not always like the results, but that's the whole point: if we merely wanted to act out the forms of social inclusion, we need not hire a Diversity Manager at all. The same issues apply to all forms of "otherness" that museums need to address. Whether it is providing elevators for the disabled or including representations of gay and lesbian Londoners, we need to get on and do it. Without apology. With the confidence of our new role as social leaders.

And it is as a social leader that the professional museum needs to see itself. Its place is not a small, dusty corner of the archive: it is a public stage, a world platform. Two weeks ago Britain launched a *Manifesto for Museums*. It argues not for the insularity of museums but for their participation in "the world's culture and achievement.... [Museums] stimulate creativity and enrich the cultural, social and economic life, not only of our nation, but of the whole world."

The effects we have can come about in different ways. By digitizing our collections, we can make them available to a vast international audience who might never otherwise see them. By getting our collections out of their stores and onto trucks and planes, we can tour them round the world. We can, as the British Manifesto makes plain, through cultural diplomacy contribute substantially to international relations. The Tate and Victoria & Albert Museum's work in Iran; the British Library in Egypt; the British Museum in Iraq have all seen the United Kingdom and other European countries exploit their expertise and resources to assist the geopolitical crisis that is in part a war on culture. The Museum of London has recently had a team of Iraqis visit to discuss the repair and conservation of objects damaged in the recent Iraq War. It is important to remember that ICOM was set up just after the Second World War in 1946 at the same time as UNESCO. We must recognize our heritage as peacemakers and partners to other countries. We must remain at the forefront of cultural reconciliation.

The professional museum must have, in addition to an ethical stance, a foreign policy. Having for so long represented outside cultures on their behalf, it must now provide a space for those cultures to represent themselves. It is one thing to begin to encourage communities to have their own museums, but quite another to offer them a chunk of the patrimony itself. But that's what they need and deserve. Not token museums in the corners of their boroughs, but an open access to the displays and texts and resources of the nation's institutions. In a country like Britain, this foreign policy applies to immigrant communities old and new, to former colonies, to countries whose treasures rest uneasily in the marble halls of Western wealth – to the entire world, in fact, with whom any museum can establish a relationship and dialogue.

I would like to end with an anecdote told by the American anthropologist and museums studies professor Christina Kreps, whose recent study, *Liberating Culture*, looks at non-western models of museums and curatoral practices:

> One day, I arrived at the Museum [Balanga in Borneo] in time to see the staff preparing a float for a parade commemorating Indonesian Independence Day.... Staff members were busily carting objects out of the museum to create a display on the back of a truck. The display was designed to represent a traditional Dayak mortuary ceremony known as a tiwah. Large brass gongs had been arranged on the bed of the truck along with five-foot-tall wooden figures known as sapundu. An antique ceremonial cloth was being nailed onto the side of the truck, while two other workers were giving the only masks in the museum's collection a new coat of paint. Observing these actions, I was confronted with the dilemma of whether or not

to intervene in the staff's activities. As a person trained in "proper" and "professional" museum practices, I felt compelled to inform the workers about the potentially damaging effects of their actions on the objects. When I expressed my concerns to one staff member, who was wrestling a sapundu onto the truck, he turned to me with a perplexed look and said: "Oh, it doesn't matter. There are lots of them in the villages."[10]

Our notion of the sanctity of objects – of keeping them and preserving them, not using or renewing them – may have more to do with Western materialism than cultural insight. We need to learn from other cultures not just how to deal with their objects, but how to deal with our own. We may have to look to a remote part of Borneo to see what exactly our professional museum is worth.

---

10. Kreps 2003, p. 30.

Challenges for Today's Museums Functioning in a Mass Culture

This lecture was originally given in Polish at the National Library in Warsaw in March 2008 to mark my inauguration as Chairman of the National Museum in Warsaw. Professor Dorota Folga-Januszewska, then acting director of the National Museum provided the title and theme. Tomasz Merta, then Secretary of State for Culture, kindly introduced me to the audience.

In the 2006 Hollywood film *Night at the Museum*, Larry, played by Ben Stiller, discovers something strange in New York's Museum of Natural History.[1] He's hired as a night watchman, and it's all looking pretty sleepy and straightforward ... until suddenly there's a mighty crash – the mammoths, the Tyrannosaurus Rex skeleton, the lions and zebras come alive at night, and it's up to Larry to keep them in order until the museum reopens the next morning. Even the tiny dioramas – once so beloved of museums – come to life: miniature Mayans build a temple in one corner, Romans do battle, the Wild West is tamed by the great railway that united America from coast to coast.

---

1. The film's fictional museum is based on the American Museum of Natural History in Manhattan.

The movie's appeal is wide-ranging – I particularly like the scene where visitor numbers suddenly pick up! And it goes to the heart of something we are all drawn to in museums: the wonder of the exhibits. The fantasy of museum objects coming alive is an extension of the imaginative process that actual museums so powerfully provoke. To understand the past, to be moved by it, you have to engage your imagination to animate the swords and sceptres, the crosses and cradles that are shown to you. Museums are places of enchantment – provided we can get people inside.

Enchantment is not a bad word to keep in mind as we examine the challenges facing museums today. It can sometimes seem as if museums are given two choices. On the one hand, they can adopt a traditionalist position: they can ignore what's happening around them and get on with doing what they've always done, regardless of visitor figures or adverse criticism. On the other hand, museums can modernize, though at some risk of turning themselves into theme parks, with bells and whistles, light shows and lots of buttons to keep the children occupied so they don't have to look at any boring old maps or dusty flint-axes.

Faced with an ever-hurrying popular culture, it can sometimes seem as if there is no successful middle ground for museums – either you stop and become old-fashioned, or you rush ahead and become over-technologized.

But we need to examine more closely the relationship we have to this mass culture that museums are so often rushing toward or reacting to. To understand it is to pinpoint the quality of its influence – and our possible response to it.

Perhaps the most immediate threat posed by mass culture (if it is a threat – and I shall return to this later) is that it sets a new challenge for museums as *attractions*. One of the great qualities of popular culture is its appeal, and if museums are to win the struggle for audiences, they need to understand that appeal and know when – and when not – to compete with it.

Traditional cultural institutions will suffer from this question if they see themselves at the losing end of change, as if the museum were something fixed and solid being slowly eroded by modern shifts of behaviour and interest, as if museums themselves were incapable of change. If our concept of a museum is lodged at some point in the 18th century, or even worse, in the 19th century, when that air of the mausoleum begins to hang about the place, we will not stand a chance when faced with the rapid changes in society.

As cultural leaders, all of us can see what needs to be done: we have to shift the elephant. It's not that we can't see the need for change, or even the direction it might take. It's finding a way of shifting the mammoth beast from what it was – and that includes how it was built, what it holds, how we work inside it – to what it might be for today's and tomorrow's audiences.

So how do we ensure that we stay relevant? How do we operate as attractions? What methods can we use to shift the beast and improve the quality of the visitor experience today? Let me suggest a few.

Fundamental to the way museums present themselves is the architecture of their buildings. Exciting architecture can generate a sense of importance to visitors. A compelling building can become a draw in itself. We may be suspicious of such a competitive pull, but it is not a diversion. Frank Gehry's crumpled Guggenheim Museum in Bilbao has created a new level of economic prosperity for the Spanish city. And when such architecture is outstanding, it supports the meanings of the collection it houses. Gehry's building makes reference to the industrial forms of Bilbao's past, its factories and wharves. China's new Capital Museum in Beijing has created a gateway to its collection using a temple structure immediately identifiable to local Chinese, while in no way detracting from the building's avant-garde modernity.

Indeed, one can go further and argue that a museum building does not merely support but can create a powerful cultural argument. One thinks of Libeskind's Jewish Museum in Berlin, where one's very passage through narrowing corridors and darkened towers encapsulates the experience of both the collection that's there and (perhaps more tellingly) the collection that's not, the lost artifacts which can never be retrieved and displayed. It is a building that needs to, and does, communicate what W.G. Sebald has called "the ambience of total destruction".[2]

One of Britain's best and brightest young architects argues strongly for the representational importance of new architecture. David Adjaye

---

2. Sebald 2003, p. 46.

was born in Tanzania, but grew up in multicultural modern Britain. As he describes it, "I've had to negotiate culture being a Christian boy in a Muslim country, then an African boy in north London.... I was born negotiating."[3] His critics are quick to praise the polymorphous influence of his buildings. They are, writes one:

> informed by an eye that has looked hard and seriously at dwellings, building styles, forms, materials and traditions in north and east Africa, the Middle East and Japan, absorbing and assimilating ideas without ever falling into a studied vernacular.[4]

When we are examining the possibilities of our museum buildings – and we must be attentive to the varied international contexts in which we now work – it is the contemporary mix of an architect such as Adjaye that may best speak to our increasingly diverse and world-drawn audiences.[5] One of our own central negotiations must be between the specifics of our own cultural study (the very reason for our particular museums) and the widest possible communication of those meanings. And smart buildings help.

The building, of course, is not enough, and the luxury of a new structure is not always possible. Indeed there may be a compelling argument for preserving the cultural history enshrined in a period building, not least for the sense of national pride and value such a building can project.[6]

But inside, the design opportunities are wide-ranging and exciting. I

3. Quoted in Hall 2005, p. 11.

4. Hall, p. 11.

5. Adjaye's work includes the design of cultural institutions and museums. In October 2007, his luminous new building for the Museum of Contemporary Art opened in Denver, Colorado. His recent highly topical buildings in London include the Stephen Lawrence Centre in Deptford. This is architecture at the centre of representation and cultural debate. The building commemorates the brutal murder of a black teenager, and has already been attacked by racist vandals.

6. Buildings such as the elegantly restored Józef Mehoffer House of the National Museum in Krakow are a case in point, as is the domestic history preserved in London's Geffrye Museum, housed in a row of 18th-century almshouses.

haven't the space here to discuss the great sweep of advances in museum design in recent decades, but many will be familiar to you. As expectations have grown, so have attitudes toward what we permit in the museum space. Technological advances have enabled a spectrum of new ways of engaging the visitor, from soundscapes of oral history (the voices of the past quite literally coming to life) to personally engaging interactive displays. But let's look briefly at a few instances of good practice that suggest certain principles we can draw on to shape whatever design elements we choose.

The National Museum of Australia (NMA) in Canberra is a significant touchstone for me. It has provided some rich inspiration in pioneering museums as collections of subjects rather than objects. Increasingly, museums like NMA deal with the holding of subjects, or more precisely, holding people in conversations about subjects of importance to their personal and societal cultural identity. These subjects need to be curated with as much care and sensitivity as precious and rare objects. Some of these subjects are concerned with owning the past, however painful or difficult, facing the present with all its challenges of living with increasing tensions between global and national interests, and shaping a shared yet diverse future with all its unpredictability. Design has been used to create a museum experience that speaks both to those whose history is being staged and to those who are new to it.

David Chipperfield's extension to the Anchorage Museum in Alaska is an inspiration in glass and steel. The principal exhibition, *Living Our Cultures, Sharing Our Heritage*, promotes clarity, warmth and depth of the subject by including voices of indigenous people. There is a sense here that they are included in the process of co-creation.

Such issues are particular to each museum. But the larger point holds: that museum design, both inside and out, can create a quality visitor experience by considering the politics and protocols of its audience.

Regardless of the appeal of consumer culture and cyberspace, people will come to museums if we frame our collections well. And if we do so, we have a double advantage. All the tricks and tools of modernity can be ours, and we still have our real objects, in all their historical potency and mystery, their enchantment. In a recent article entitled "A Museum is not an iPod", English writer Kathryn Hughes reminds us:

> There is something irreplaceable and unique about visiting a bricks-and-mortar museum in real time, rather than gutting its content electronically from home.[7]

What is irreplaceable is the collective experience a museum can offer, where one's response is enhanced and expanded by those of others, and the sheer joy of material things. There was a wonderful description of this experience in a review of some Indian miniature paintings displayed at the British Museum in 2007:

> Of course, we sit for many hours in front of screens scanning images. But those images are not also things. One butts eagerly against the glass cases in which this exhibition is housed partly because one's pleasure in the density of the pigments, the delicacy of the brush-marks – everything that makes them things as well as pictures – tells of an element missing from our own visual diet.[8]

The great strength of museums has always been that they looked inward: gathering, studying, preserving the past. Today they need to use the wealth of that material to reach out to audiences and grab hold of them. Design and technology, public events and learning programs all create new approaches to our traditional collections. Audiences will always be hungry for real treasures. Museums come alive provided the experience of them is not a historical impediment, blocked by unhelpful descriptions and dull presentation, but instead makes sense to modern viewers.

To view museums as attractions is important. Yet to do so succumbs in large part to the paradigm of *competition* that mass culture poses.

But the role of museums is much wider than vying with shopping malls and swimming pools to provide leisure for the family on a Sunday after-noon. And it is in these larger considerations that the balance begins to shift toward understanding the absolute importance of museums in times of rapid social change.

One key area where museums are growing is in terms of leadership. Some may balk at the professionalization of museums, but improved skills

---

7. Hughes 2007.
8. Campbell 2007, p. 27.

are exactly what the cultural sector requires if it is to succeed on the larger platform of the modern world.

The issue is partly an internal one: we are not producing the right sort of leaders to carry our organizations forward. The need for leadership training is becoming clearer. The development of museum studies courses reflects this, as do more recently focused programs such as the UK's Clore Leadership Program (now broadening its intake internationally) or the Getty's Museums Leadership Institute. As the Getty Foundation states, there is a pressing need to provide "a strategic perspective to the increasingly complex issues facing today's museums".

And the issues are complex. National identity. Economic influence. Social improvement. Museums have often turned their backs on *contemporary* society, while paradoxically trying to explain the importance of *past* societies. It is a misplaced luxury, and one we no longer have or want. If mass culture is drawing audiences away, we need to show that we are relevant to them now.

One way of doing so is by making the most of our collections. Enchantment is one thing, but it doesn't deal with the logistical issues of getting people and objects to connect. This is one area where good direction comes in.

In London, there is now a museums hub to coordinate work across institutions. It is not surprising that museums often feel beleaguered when they are so often working in isolation. The hub was set up to create a Renaissance in the Regions program. The Museum of London acts as a leader to share collections, knowledge and programming among a group of local museums, so that each has a greater impact than it might standing alone.

In eastern Europe, the prospects for such coordination are tantalizing. We can see in Poland a real rise in the importance of museum culture. Polish history, Polish collectors, Polish monuments – these are being rightly brought forward and celebrated.

But imagine the prospect of not just a Polish museum, but a transnational collection that could move and be seen by millions of people. I'm not speaking of ownership here, in a literal sense, but of a shared resource that culturally belongs to everyone.

Mass culture poses a threat when we ourselves behave narrowly. If we can shake off the mindset that wants to lock things up safely for posterity, that thinks in terms of the storeroom and the safe, then curators and museum staff can become *facilitators* of collections and the knowledge that surrounds them. By distributing our collections more widely, and by encouraging and supporting different communities to interpret collections in ways that are meaningful to them, museums can jointly create a cultural space that is both personal and universal. And once museums are so richly meaningful, they are far from being at risk. They show, in fact, that culture is essential to lead the way for social development and a better world.

Such is the leadership we must lay claim to. In London there is no point in trying to narrow down some particular definition of the city and locking it up in a museum. The whole point is that London, like so much of our globalized society, indeed like all of our countries, is constantly changing – and the Museum of London has a responsibility to come up with ways of capturing that change and responding to it.

Take immigration. The Eurozone has created new patterns of migration one can hardly keep up with from day to day. Globally, the patterns of power and development are shifting enormously, and the traditional prominence of certain cultures is altering. IBM has identified the BRIC countries as it calls them – Brazil, Russia, India and China – as the four most important emerging economies, with population growth and economic development predicted to proceed at twice the rate of Europe's. Goldman Sachs has identified the N11 countries, the Next 11, that show the most promising outlooks for investment and future growth based on macroeconomic stability, political maturity, openness of trade and investment policies, and quality of education. Those countries are Bangladesh, Egypt, Indonesia, Iran, Mexico, Nigeria, Pakistan, Philippines, South Korea, Turkey and Vietnam.

I mention these not to offer you personal advice on financial investment, but to shake up our categories of engagement. Relevance is about anticipating the world's impact not just internationally, but locally, since these social revolutions affect all of us. If we as museums are specialists in cultural understanding, then leading the debate on social change is where we need to position ourselves.[9]

Earlier I made the point that museums can be isolated. Discussions about the fate and function of museums often make it seem as if they inevitably existed apart from everything else in society. You can see how this thought arises: the rare suit of damascened armour, the Old Master madonna and child, the 4000-year-old Chinese jade – such objects are special and justly displayed in all their solitary beauty. Preservers of such masterpieces, museums seek to inhabit a similar identity as unique places.[10]

But in an age of mass culture, where none of us is unencumbered by a small pile of electronic gadgets (each with their own charger!) and children spend increasing amounts of their time online, that specialness of museums can seem outmoded. But does that mean that museums are irrelevant?

---

9. A report commissioned from AEA Consulting for the National Museum of Australia identifies the importance of the global contexts in which museums work today: "World-class museums have also generated visibility by adapting to the global marketplace – often simply by operating internationally. Competitive strategies to secure corporate sponsorships, acquisitions for their collections, high-calibre volunteers, and cultural tourists are now conducted in an international arena, and the world's great museums benchmark themselves internationally and are proactive in generating visibility and buzz among a global audience and a global constituency of opinion-formers. From developing satellite facilities abroad (Guggenheim Bilbao, Berlin, Venice), to brokering exclusive exhibition partnerships (the V&A and the Museum of Fine Arts San Francisco) to crafting innovative, deeper international strategic alliances (the Louvre and the High Museum, Atlanta), world-class museums are conscious of the need to be visible internationally and to undertake high-profile, carefully crafted initiatives that will garner and sustain institutional visibility."

10. The argument is not so straightforward, of course, for such special objects themselves are often representative of mass culture (our museums are as full of "typical" objects as rarities). Grand works of high art are also fascinated by and connected to the larger cultures out of which they emerge: an urban genre painting of a crowd in a railway station by W.P. Frith, uniquely impressive as it may be, may tell us more about 19th-century life in London than a surviving piece of Victorian ironwork.

I recently gave a tour of the Museum of London in Polish. There is a large Polish community in London, and I hoped that 20 or 30 might show up – a good size for a weekend talk. When 450 people crowded into the museum's foyer, I not only had a logistical problem (running museum events is never easy!), but a thrilling proof of the hunger for culture that exists not just in London, but in every city.

And indeed it is here, in this desire, this hunger, that I find the opposition between mass culture and museums untenable. In a globalized society, mass culture is not a threat, for we are all part of a mass culture now, from museums to Muji. Our mistake is in failing to recognize the fact. Museums are, par excellence, mass culture: they have their rich collections, the international weight of their scholarship and research, their libraries and archives. They have diversity and comprehensiveness. What popular culture offers is not a threat to museums, but an exciting opportunity to rethink our self-presentation. Instead of bemoaning virtual games or consumer mentalities, we should be asking ourselves: What is the museum equivalent of a music video? What is the emailable museum? The textable museum? How do we take our strengths and connect once more with new audiences?

It may sound silly, but our embarrassment at such ideas shows that these divisions are being drawn by the old guard, not by the watchers of YouTube and MTV. Young audiences especially are open to everything they can get their hands on. They want to upload, download, video-clip the world. They want to carry it round in their pockets. And it's not just them. In countries like the UK, televised history programs are among the most highly watched. When the eminent historian Simon Schama leaps across a Roman rampart near Avignon on the television, is it so different from watching a Janet Jackson video?

I'm teasing, of course. But the serious point is that these cultures overlap, and within ever-changing technological forms the same desires and needs are at play: to understand our pasts, to know more about the world, to see things that are new to us.

It is here that our attitudes are crucial. We need to be accessible. We need enlightened direction. It is an idea that the great museum director

Stanislaw Lorentz himself would have understood. As he once said, "Collections are stores that only become museums when they are enlightened by scholars and cultural leaders." In effect, museums need, as in the film I began with, animation. Otherwise they are inert "stores", as Lorentz says.

When a mainstream film like *Night at the Museum* celebrates a large, lovable, traditional museum, it is a sign that museums are not so far off the radar of public interest. They are not just yet ready for the dust heap and it would be a mistake to see them as such.

Museums are places of leadership, where the very forces that shape social change can be discussed and polemicized. Edward Said once wrote that he first experienced Palestine as history and cause – by talking to his aunt.[11] This is exactly what museums do: raise awareness of the world by telling individual stories of the past. By doing so, and by ensuring an awareness of the relevance of the work we do, we can set the tone for a cultural argument that encompasses all the communities of the world. Our challenge, perhaps our only threat, is to keep our thinking larger than the walls that surround us.

11. Said 1999, p. 119.

Getting Out into the World
– and Staying There

In working toward the Olympics for London in 2012, Jude Kelly, artistic director of the South Bank Centre, and I often found ourselves sharing a platform encouraging arts organizations to go out into the world to create relationships, rather than expect the world to simply come to us. This paper is one such instance when I addressed museum professionals in May 2010 in the lead-up to the games.

At almost any moment, somewhere in the world an exhibition of Magnum photographs is being shown. Magnum has been, of course, one of the great gatherings of world talent, since its starry founding in 1947 by Robert Capa, Henri Cartier-Bresson, George Rodger and David Seymour. It is an independent collective of international photographers (the founding four were Hungarian, French, English and Polish). Its interest has been in world news and the personal lives we don't always witness underneath the public reporting: from Capa's groundbreaking look at life behind the Iron Curtain in the late 1940s to Cartier-Bresson's coverage of India at the time of Gandhi's assassination. Magnum photographs have been, and continue to be, 60 years later, justly celebrated.

I introduce Magnum not by way of promotion, but to raise a certain idea about culture and the world, for Magnum perfectly represents both a cultural possibility we can be proud of – and a missed opportunity. The possibility is evident: that a cultural form such as photography can go out and lay claim to the world as its true subject. It can raise the profile of countries needing international attention. As journalism, it can depict the heartbreak and heroism of *people*, not just offer a facts-and-figures analysis of *populations*. Photography – in exhibitions, published in newspapers and magazines, available to millions on the web – is immediately persuasive as almost no other art form can be.

And its approach is international – or is it? We celebrate Magnum's presence in the toughest of war-torn principalities, at the brave face of environmental catastrophe and inhuman strife. We want to know what Magnum has to tell us.

But something remains of the traveller, the colonizer, the cultural tourist in all of this. In Magnum's founding work we have not a Hindu nationalist view of Delhi in 1948, but a Frenchman in India. George Rodger was no Tunisian documenting the inside story *for Africans* of Rommel's retreat, but an Englishman racing across the continent, snapping shots of that "other", non-European front of the Second World War for *Life* magazine.

There *is* a missed opportunity here, and it relates to the subjects of these photographs. Where are they in this process? And what happens to them when the photographer hops on the plane and flies back to New York or Buenos Aires?

We are at risk, I would argue, of a terrible complacency in global discussions such as the one we are having here today. It can often seem, when you listen to how we speak about our work, as if we have accomplished the international project: *we are not narrow or insular; we are in India, Tunisia, Peru.* But this view is as Eurocentric as those early Magnum photographs. The real cultural project – and it is here where we should place our question about museums and global action – is not just to gather up the world for ourselves, but to establish a new and productive relationship to it.

Global interest among museums is nothing new. Museums have always been international. Even a city museum such as the Museum of London contains drawings of 19th-century India, not so much because they had a special connection to Britain's capital city, but because at the time they represented a key aspect of the collectors' interests. And such images matter, because one of the social histories any museum will try to honour is the history of collecting.

Yet it is the question of international *responsibility* that has changed. Once – and it is worth remembering that this question will never disappear – museums saw themselves as the preservers of the past. They were world museums keeping track of world civilization before it vanished – though this honourable intention did not prevent a fair amount of national pre-eminence at the same time. There has always been a hefty competition among nations, as European, and latterly American, museums gobbled up finds to create the best, the brightest, the biggest collection of world artifacts.

Increasingly, however, this view has been challenged, not least by those countries hitherto "preserved" and now wanting to do a bit of their own "preserving". And museums have come to see that there is a lot they can do with their collections by getting them out of the store room and onto the road. Debates over repatriation are at last generating a real acknowledgement that the symbolic power of *ownership* may require as much dismantling as overstuffed collections themselves.

But I'd like to take this debate in a slightly different direction. The museum sector is by definition international. We're thinking globally, and that's good. And yet ... there is what we might call a "cultural limit" that stops us short of our full potential as world players. This is the missed opportunity I was discussing earlier, where the actions of the powerful can be a kind of tourism: we shine a self-interested spotlight on east Africa or Latin America, and then we turn it off and walk away.

The limit is imposed, some of you may argue, by money. Museums do not have the budgets to set up elaborate programs worldwide and keep them running.

But we must acknowledge what it is we are saying when we trot out our usual complaint about underfunding in the cultural sector. Lack of funding is relative, and it is easy to forget amid the constant pressure to raise money for building projects and exhibitions that there is an enormous wealth that can be shared among the world's communities. Furthermore, the funding issue is a kind of screen that hides our own failings when it comes to increasing diversity within our institutions and working on development outside them. We are the great repositories of relics – and one of those relics may be the way we run our institutions, regardless of how much money we receive.

Nearly 190 countries have signed up to the UN's eight Millennium Development Goals. To read the list is to experience a sense of shame: eradicate extreme poverty and hunger, reduce child mortality, and so forth. Wrangling with the board of trustees over understaffing pales when you consider what it is we ought to be able to achieve as a world community.

The problems are often structural. Let's take the United Kingdom as an example. Development is a priority for the British government. Yet despite the strong links between development and culture, the main UK provider of *development* funding – the Department for International Development – makes almost no reference to cultural activity in any of its programs of education, healthcare and housing.[1]

If we shift our gaze to the UK government's *culture* department – the Department for Culture Media and Sport – where the remit of the arts is international, it is closely bound to political and economic goals.[2] Praise for the British Museum's rightly admired *First Emperor* exhibition of China's terracotta warriors cannot escape a certain sense that it is doing Britain's work on the world stage. A good thing for Britain to be doing, but not the only thing.

Even Britain's Arts Council, with its activities across the globe, is as much drawn to the language of the "creative economy" as the core practice of cultural development.

My purpose is not to criticize, but to point to a structure endemic to most countries represented here today. We separate our thinking about

1. Chapter 3 of the 2005 Commission for Africa Report, *Our Common Interest*, does raise the importance of culture, citing precedents such as the 1980 Brandt Commission (which argued that "cultural identity gives people dignity") and the 1996 World Commission on Culture and Development (which noted that "economic criteria alone could not provide a program for human dignity and well-being").

2. See, for example, Work Foundation 2007.

development from our cultural work. But we shouldn't. If museums want to act globally and be truly international, they need to rescue the importance of global involvement. It's not just about handing over objects: it's about lending a hand.

I mention the Millennium Development Goals because in the end they are not something for the United Nations, or for government, or for charities. They should be at the heart of any work we do as individuals and as members of a global community. And surely it is an obvious step for museums, already so connected internationally, to take up this responsibility.

There are signs that this is happening. More exhibitions are touring around the world, taking collections out of museum buildings and making them accessible to new audiences who might otherwise never see them. Curators and conservators in Britain are building ties with their colleagues in Latin America and the Pacific. A traditional dig in Sudan has been expanded by the British Museum into a hands-on program of archaeological training and curation. The large site between Berber and Abidiya is under threat from redevelopment and new irrigation projects. These are important signs of change, but the British Museum has recognized the equal importance of providing *cultural* development to the country. Rather than its staff stepping in from on high to rescue what they can, they are training colleagues in Khartoum to excavate, analyse and conserve finds from within Sudan itself and present them in ways that make sense for local people.

The Museum of London is sharing its expertise with partners such as the City Museum of Addis Ababa. The legacy here is not so focused on objects and self-interest. It's about transferring skills and empowerment, so that the results are ongoing and long term. True cultural development fosters a creative economy (if this is the language we need to use) that is not about quick profits and fast turnarounds, but about sustainability.

I began this essay with a reference to the ambiguous international role played by Magnum's photographers, who are both on-site but outside the cultures they represent to the world. I'd like to end with a very different project, one that responds directly to the opportunity provided by our international work.

Aïna is a non-governmental organization set up by the photographer Reza, a former sergeant in the Afghan National Army. Its role is to support the development of media and cultural expression in Afghanistan.[3] Its projects have ranged from encouraging the use of visual media in promoting voting in the country's elections to holding film screenings in Bamiyan to training women in Kabul to work as video journalists.[4]

This is culture in action: it is given international support (for there is a growing audience for Aïna's photography), but handed over to those who should be in charge of shaping it, making it work and reaping the rewards.

If the International Council of Museums (ICOM) wants to act globally, this is the model it must follow. It is time to reject an easy Eurocentric internationalism, where the world becomes a cultural playground. Museums worldwide should involve themselves in what Nelson Mandela has called the "fight to free the whole of humanity and to build a more just world for all".[5]

---

3. In the summer of 2001, Reza helped found Aïna ("mirror" in Farsi) as a nonprofit media organization dedicated not to repairing "the physical destruction from war" (rebuilding hospitals, schools and roads) but the "mental and cultural destruction".

4. See Ramsey 2004, Beck 2005 and the digital exhibition of Aïna photographs at www.digitaljournalist.org/issue0502/aina01.html

5. From a speech he gave in London on March 25, 2007.

Cultural Diplomacy

To mark the inauguration of the Polish presidency of the European Union, H.E. Basia Tuge-Erecinska, the Polish Ambassador to the United Kingdom, asked me to address London's diplomatic corps at the European Union National Institutes for Culture on June 30, 2011.

Sitting on the bus the other day, I spotted a very simple ad in a newspaper. Apart from the words, all it showed was a silhouette of a man. It would not have been very remarkable if it weren't for the single feature that stood out: a happy profusion of dreadlocks springing from the man's head. The hair alone immediately announced the connection the ad wanted you to make: with Jamaica and Afro-Caribbean life.

It is a strange thing, "picturing" a culture. How many cultures can you represent in silhouette? Would a woman in a *hijaab* evoke Arab life? Does a sombrero transport you instantly to Mexico? My own family is Polish, and I'm really not sure I could capture them in two dimensions!

The ad raises a variety of issues – about stereotypes certainly (and I wouldn't want to minimize the effects of such stereotypes), but also about the images we use less as stigma or cliché and more as a kind of insider's shorthand. As director of the Museum of London, one of the things I love most about the city is its parade of cultures. Londoners are always encountering difference: different clothes, different music, different behaviours, different languages. Such images become the markers we use to make sense of our society and to map the city around us.

Like almost every person you meet in the capital, I am – and am not – a Londoner. I proudly carry a double identity. As a long-time British resident, I belong. And as a Polish Londoner, someone with a mixed identity, I also belong in this teeming city of immigrants and voyagers from all corners of the globe. London has been like this for centuries – and that is one of the important stories that the Museum of London tells.

But the part of me that's mixed stands slightly to one side. Something in me belongs elsewhere. I have another language inside me, another culture. When I think about cultural diplomacy or about London's cultural mix, I need to remind myself that cultural identities are rarely straightforward: this category over here, that one neatly over there. They are, like so many of the most interesting things in life, hard to predict.

This doubleness also gives me an opportunity to view things across Europe with a different eye. My cultural work both in London and as a chairman of the National Museum of Warsaw gives me a unique perspective. It is a view that suggests, I would argue, the wider forms of cultural interaction that are sometimes overlooked.

Tomorrow's start of Poland's Presidency of the Council of the European Union is a great delight to me and has, amid my feeling of pride, given me much to think about. Debates about cultural depiction – from stereotypes in advertising to the problem of invisibility – are at the heart of the Museum of London's attempt to track the ever-shifting patterns and people of London, and how they affect our understanding of the wider world.

In the case of Poland, the view from outside might surprise my fellow Poles. I know it does. The films of Krzysztof Kieslowski – his *Dekalog*, the *Three Colours* trilogy – are highly admired internationally. He is one of Poland's cultural hits. But his success abroad is distinct in people's minds from the Poland they see through his cinematic eye – the dreary blocks of Soviet-style flats, the sense of doom that inhabits the urban streets. The music alone in his films can, if it strikes you the wrong way, send you running from the cinema.

There are other examples. The celebrated *War Trilogy* of the great Andrzej Wajda, or his *Man of Iron*. Roman Polanski's Polish debut, *Knife in the Water*, often makes lists of the top 100 films, but it is hardly light fare, however much we envy the yacht and the sunlight streaming across the water.

Even more recent works of art that carry Polish culture out into the world can reinforce a sense of entrapment. A great favourite of mine is the novelist Pawel Huelle. Huelle's novels are very funny, but his Gdansk (where they are set) is a place of disconnection, terrorist attacks, fatalities or, at the very least, extremely bad town planning. The hero of the novel *Mercedes-Benz*, trapped in an endless driving lesson with the taut Miss Ciwle, complains from behind the car's windscreen that everything is impossible: "It was too late in life," he says, "and I'd already missed the moment."[1] Is this how non-Poles also view the country – as belated, as having missed its moment? Huelle may be playing games with melancholic cultural clichés, but non-Poles can take the cliché without getting the game. So stereotypes, perhaps challenged in Huelle's text, end up being reinforced.

Culture abroad is not necessarily doing the work of cultural diplomacy. I am thrilled that Pawel Huelle has been translated into English (unlike so many of his contemporaries), but I sometimes worry that despite the comedy, the effect of all this is to reinforce some very old ideas about Poland, ideas with a long pedigree. In *The Comedy of Errors*, the servant Dromio speaks to his master Antipholus of – in Shakespeare's words – "a Poland winter". Most modern editors don't even gloss the phrase. What Shakespeare's audience knew, and what we all know, is that a Poland winter is a very bad winter indeed.

So how do we change that? (And I use Poland, of course, as an example with a much wider application.) The EU presidency is a marvellous opportunity to say farewell to grisly flats and blocked traffic, or at least the perception of them as cultural "silhouettes" for Poland. It's a new spotlight in a new environment. This is what the European Union has given us. So we have to make the most of it.

Let's consider the sort of cultural iterations that make the new Poland visible abroad and bring its strengths into focus. On the ground, Polish

---

1. Huelle 2005, p. 1.

immigrants have had an astonishing impact in cities like London in recent years. In Britain, magazines such as *Cooltura* have sprung up in response to this movement of the work force across the EU. The magazine's content has a very youthful sense of a culture without borders. *Cooltura* easily straddles the UK and Poland. It has a healthy circulation of nearly 50,000 – this for a magazine, in Polish, distributed in the middle of London. It's astonishing.

Such community forums (sometimes overlooked by those who define culture more conservatively) do map onto more traditional forms of cultural dissemination. At the other end of the spectrum we might take the global celebrations that honoured the bicentenary of Frederick Chopin's birth. Festivals, piano competitions and exhibitions proved popular from Tokyo to Texas in 2010. London's own *Chopin 2010* events received high-profile coverage on Classic FM and elsewhere. Are these such dissimilar things? Both magazine and music festival are marked by cultural pride and a sense of vitality. They are instances of living culture: shared, celebrated, vigorously pursued at all levels of society.

Two more examples. The Polish Film Festival in Britain, *Kinoteka*, just celebrated its ninth season. Its program included guest directors and artists, new films and old, the incidental and the mainstream. *Kinoteka* showed films in Belfast, Glasgow, Exeter and Edinburgh. In London, Polish cinema popped up everywhere from the Renoir to the Roxy, the Barbican to Tate Modern, even at Baden Powell House and the West London Synagogue. The festival was pervasive – impressively so.

And a painting from Krakow is also making its mark. With the EU focus on Poland for the next six months, the National Gallery's blockbuster *Da Vinci* exhibition (not so far as I know sponsored by Dan Brown) has chosen the *Portrait of Cecilia Gallerani* (or *The Lady with an Ermine*) as its keynote image. Press coverage has already generated the story: Will this unique loan from the National Museum in Krakow oust the *Mona Lisa* as Leonardo da Vinci's iconic painting? The portrait carries various types of cultural freight, and one of the things it does is signal an important art collection abroad many Londoners will not have seen. The Krakow painting is a reminder that there is more to Europe than the big bad triad of Paris, London, Berlin.

Whether it's a high-profile loan to a major gallery or a session of electro jazz as part of *Kinoteka*, nationally derived books, magazines, films, paintings or music raise the profile of their original cultures. But they do much more than this. Poland in London becomes London itself, and audiences brought together by difference begin to see themselves as one and the same. All heritage has the potential to do this. And this is perhaps the most important lesson any national diaspora can teach. By giving up the fixity of one's identity, one opens that identity up to others. Do I become less Polish for being in London? Of course not. Am I creating a new Polish culture in the UK or wherever I happen to be? Maybe. But it's the distance that sometimes renders the culture more vivid and makes the image snap into focus – not as longing, but as something in the age of the internet and telecommunications I want now, this instant. I don't have to remake Polish culture: I can have it, and have it in a way that Poles (or anyone in their own country) might not. Best of all, here in London or wherever I am, I can share it with you, whether you are from Mumbai or Madagascar or Milton Keynes.

The insights of this double identity I spoke of earlier could be portable. I have been speaking of cultural formations abroad and the positive impact they can have. But what is to stop us taking such values and returning them to the homeland? For there are important implications to all of this, political and commercial. The economics of success might be one way of thinking about it. "A Poland winter" (to return to Shakespeare's phrase) could be an economic one, and one we might want to change.

It is a hard truth that culture valued abroad can awaken interest in the place it was first produced. What Australians call "cultural cringe" is appeased by the so-called real plaudits of Europe and America. The overseas gong generates a new-found enthusiasm at home. It can also generate cash – no small benefit in countries that are marginalized, conflict-ridden or financially deprived. We mustn't shy away from culture's genuine connection to the marketplace, however much we need to insist that is also something else, and that not all cultural benefits are quantifiable in terms of percentage outputs and monetary targets. As a museum director who must fill in a lot of forms to this end, I can assure you, not everything will fit.

Poland proves an interesting case. Like many European countries, it has witnessed with the opening up of EU trade a successful burst of middle-class entrepreneurs. They have bought themselves sleek cars and fashionable clothes. They have built villas for themselves and acquired second homes. But many – particularly those whose income is not derived locally – feel little connection to their national culture, whether it be museums, concert halls or the theatre. How can we persuade this newly affluent middle class to participate? How do we educate them to collect works of art, say, and become involved? And how do we extend that participation into wider support and philanthropy?

One way, I would argue, is by importing the very cultural attentions I've tried briefly to sketch. If international audiences are interested in the next Kieslowski or this week's Huelle, why aren't you? If diaspora communities can plug into the music and magazines of contemporary Krakow or what's happening in Warsaw, why can't you? If the lead painting in a sellout show in London is usually in a museum round the corner, why not go?

Economic Crisis or Cultural Opportunity?

There is no exact definition of what constitutes an economic crisis, but in 2009 the arts policy platform of the Council of Europe recognized the symptoms of a dynamically changing financial landscape for museums as significant and serious. This is a speech I gave on the subject at the International Council of Museums (ICOM) Triennial meeting in Shanghai in August 2010.

There's something troubling about approaching a museum – and finding the doors are closed.

Museums, like churches or even shops in our 24/7 society, only make sense as places of welcome. Their doors should be thrown open for the world to enter. A closed museum seems to say: my raison d'être is to lock up the objects inside and keep them safe from the likes of you (a view that has sometimes been shared by the lofty guardians who determined the fate of museum collections). But we sense, confronted with the doors firmly shut against us, that this is wrong. The whole point of a museum is to bring people in, and in an ideal world, we could enter at any time. Without visitors, the unseen artifact is a poor thing, deprived of its power, lost to its rightful place in the living active world.

I have been thinking about closed doors because we are seeing a lot more of them. High-street shops are sitting empty, businesses shutting down. And museums too, in these times of economic setback, are going to feel the pinch: some will close, some will reduce their opening hours, some will show fewer of their rooms because they won't have the staff numbers to monitor them. Having witnessed a marvellous efflorescence of museums in the past two decades, we are about to experience what looks like a sudden reversal.

When funds are limited, cultural bodies risk being treated as soft targets. Are they not the luxuries one can dispense with until fatter times return? Even the proponents of culture sometimes fall prey to this truism in their agitated defence of the arts. But is it true? Perhaps it was when museums were static institutions, places of Sunday walks or an afternoon with your aunt, where little happened and so little support was needed. As long as the padlocks were in place and a bit of dusting went on, everything was fine.

The old public model of museum management saw a single provider – the government – determine an annual grant, and from this the museum did what it could with the budget it was given: maintained its collections, pursued its research and offered whatever visitor access it could. It is a model that is still widely used in parts of the world and is not to be unduly scorned: well-supported state museums may be vulnerable, but they get on with what most interests them and are gloriously free to leave other worries behind them.

But to assume that this is still a universal model and that government cutbacks are the sole determinant of museum success or failure is out of date. Museum life has changed beyond recognition in recent years. More museums, more programs, more visitors have raised the profile of the sector hugely. And they have radically altered the culture in which we operate. Recent calls for museums to be entrepreneurial, or to leap from the starting line in hot pursuit of a fast-moving philanthropist, fail to understand that we who lead the creative economy have been doing this for some time. Museums are now at the centre of societal growth, not at the margin. They have been at the heart of programs of urban regeneration – the glamorous Guggenheim at Bilbao being the most notable example in recent years, though only one of many worldwide. They have allied themselves with tourist initiatives, corporate participation, community development and a variety of other complex operational models.

And it is here, I would argue, that our situation is unlike any we have encountered before. We *are* at risk – I don't underestimate the potential effects of the global economic crisis. But we are different entities from what we were before: more developed, more embedded in our cities and states, more progressive in our methods. We are better understood as essential contributors to our countries' economic and social goals. Museums are, more so than at any point in our professional history, flexible and responsive to change. And given that responsiveness, economic recession may be, with our new position in society, an opportunity not to retrench but to rethink and cast ourselves in a new direction.

Before considering new ways of working, we need to ensure that we are asking the right questions. As museum practice has evolved in recent years, there is an inevitable assumption of progress: that what we do now is better than what we did then. Perhaps this is a good moment to examine that. Take the advocacy documents that stack ever higher on the corner of my desk. I do wonder whether all this high-minded policy and statement of obvious outcomes is really what I need as a museum director. Who reads these documents? How effective are they? Does anyone approach digesting them with hunger and excitement? *Museums of the Future: Version 20* – fantastic! It is one area where how we promote what we do could, I suspect, do with a cull.

But professional navel-gazing is not my real concern. Indeed I would warn against just such a discussion at a time like this, when the relevance of cultural life to wider social currents needs to be made clear.

So what are the big questions we need to pose and how might they lead to new courses of action? We have a duty to start, of course, with our collections, since a museum's fundamental obligation is to care for its artifacts. There is equally a body of expertise in museums that needs to grow, for knowledge of the collection is what animates it, and it is people who discover new stories in old things. Objects can only speak meaningfully to the public through the voices of experts and enthusiasts. And it is the vital interaction of the two that charges a museum, energizes it, thrusts it forward not as a passenger but as the engine of cultural (and by extension economic) life.

So our core provision needs to be kept alive. But there are new aspects to this that, rather than throw us back into the "us vs them" mentality of old where we are competing for a shrinking pool of funds, unite museums with a wide range of contemporary concerns. Environmental issues will increasingly determine many of our decisions, from energy provision to the conservation of resources. When a museum as lofty as the Thyssen-Bornemisza in Madrid sports a grass roof alongside a 19th-century palace, it is not only being innovative, but announcing its affiliation with society's interest in the greening of our public buildings and spaces. In London, a range of practices are evolving that make museums comparable to other institutions, from banking towers to government offices, as leaders in environmental progress. The Wandsworth Museum has been redesigned entirely by using LED lights that give off no heat, announcing that a new museum in 2010 can, like other buildings, have a radically reduced carbon footprint. Renovations at the Museum of London in 2010 have introduced not just an impressive new suite of *Galleries of Modern London*, but behind-the-scenes measures that focus on sustainability. The building now incorporates a rainwater processing plant that recycles and supplies all of the museum's water.

Social responsibility extends beyond environmentalism. If we ask questions about the social role of museums, we begin to see how close the contact is between the museum and society. My particular interest, as director of the Museum of London, is in city museums – how they function across the world and as part of a range of cultural opportunities in an urban context. Instead of asking "Do people go to museums?", our questioning will be more fruitful if we wonder "Where do people go in cities?", where the question subsumes museum life within a much wider context of urban activity and social movement.

And this is one way in which museums in 2010 feel new: by the way they combine an experience that is distinct (as they always did), with a much closer participation in the ways of city life and the needs of society (a change that has seen a revolution in museums in the past 20 years). If social harmony is, as it surely must be, an essential goal for the planet's survival and prosperity, we can see the value of museums as part of that multicultural discourse.[1]

The impact is real. It's not a notional attainment. The work of the National Museum of the American Indian in Washington and New York has brilliantly combined real community involvement with displays and events that have introduced compelling metaphors for us to think differently about American Indians and, by analogy, other indigenous populations. Voices unheard are not just brought into the dialogue of cultures, but generate new ways of having that conversation – a museum skill, par excellence.

The kick that a major museum can give to a city is now indisputable. Think of the impact of the Jewish Museum in Berlin, an enterprise that made its mark despite enormous competition from some of the world's great museums all lined up in one German city. Consider the effect the Saadiyat Island museums will have in Abu Dhabi, rising as architectural wonders from reclaimed land.

If you are going to shift a city's cultural paradigm, you need a big statement. Toronto's cultural renaissance (as it's been called) has been marked by impressive new architecture and design: Frank Gehry's Art Gallery of Ontario; Daniel Libeskind's crystal at the Royal Ontario Museum; Will Alsop's Ontario College of Art and Design.[2] A new Aga Khan Museum

---

1. The theme of ICOM's 22nd General Conference and 25th General Assembly, to be held in Shanghai in November 2010, was "Museums for Social Harmony".

2. See Jenkins 2005, who notes that the effect museums are having in regenerating cities is happening worldwide: "Toronto's Cultural Renaissance must be understood as a complex, global phenomenon that is being replicated around the world. The attempts by all three levels of government to 'brand' the city/province/country through cultural icons are being matched in Europe, the United States and Japan, for both economic and political reasons. Economically, cultural institutions are seen as a way to revitalize flagging depressed industrial-based economies through cultural tourism and increased spending on leisure and entertainment. Culture and cultural diversity are also seen as attractions that will draw "Creative Class" workers to a city, accompanied by the kinds of high value-added industries that employ such workers. Politically, flashy cultural icons symbolize a dynamic, modern polity, and reflect the city's and the country's global status."

and Ismaili Centre is underway. They are new buildings, but more than that, they have shifted the city's perception of itself, "freeing Toronto the Timid", as one popular paper put it, and setting culture at the heart of tourism, economic development and civic ideology.[3] Change the skyline and you change not just what people see, but how they see themselves.

For many of us here, the question we keep being asked is: times are tough, so how will we achieve cutbacks? How can we keep doing exactly what we do, but just do less of it?

But I want to dismiss this model. I'd like to propose that instead of cutting *back*, we cut *forward*. Just as the cinema I grew up with is now influenced by the speed of digital games, I want a new kind of museum edit – fast, forward-thinking, up-to-the-minute. The new *Galleries of Modern London* at the Museum of London include a vast digital screen fed by live datalinks and constantly updated streams of information. It's a perfect portrait of 21st-century London in all its complexity. And every time I see it, it reminds me that I need to keep the museum moving forward, that I have to keep pace with the world.

What will do this, I think, is a renewed focus on the relationships we've built in recent years. Whatever the constraints, financial or otherwise, it would be a mistake to fix those relationships in place, particularly in a hobbled and diminished state. We have to move them on. We no longer lock up the objects away from risk and change, we no longer avoid histories that might make visitors uncomfortable, so we mustn't lock up our operations or our thinking in a similar way.

I'd like to raise a few examples of how we might do this: with the public, across the museum sector and as cultural leaders. The relationship between museums and the public is an astonishing success story, and we should all be proud of what we have achieved. More people than ever before visit museums, and the range of visitors, from preschoolers to care-givers, is a testament to inventive programming and marketing that has worked hard to move the sector from elitist pursuit to communal resource.

---

3. Hume 2009 and Rochon 2010.

We threw open our doors! But perhaps we can now fine-tune some of that work. In the UK there is an increasing debate about active citizen participation – not just to economic advantage through the use of volunteers, but as a program for involving citizens in the state.[4] One of the many birds that nest in the Museum of London is the LAARC – the London Archaeological Archive and Research Centre. Its pioneering use of trained volunteers has produced not just efficiency, but an important blurring of the boundaries between staff and the public. Where such a division is not so fixed, where visitors are nearer to those who welcome them (members of the public like themselves), the sense of belonging to the organisation is increased. It feels risky, but it works, because we can make more of the collection available and those who visit connect to the institution in a new and powerful way. The museum becomes less a site of consumption than of participation, less "your museum" than "our museum".

Across the sector, the relationships among cultural bodies could also be taken forward. Instead of seeing partnerships as something we might have to lose as we batten down the hatches, we need to stay outward looking. In 2010 the Museum of London signed a memorandum of understanding with the Moscow City Museum. It's one of many strategic partnerships that address the museum in an international context. The nature of such alliances is fluid – from traditional means of exchanging artifacts and exhibitions to programs of training and staff development. If our needs are about to increase, then identifying solutions with others is a model worth pursuing. Culture in the 21st century is global, and so museums, however planted in their cities and states, have to stay connected. A tourist whose expectations are formed in Moscow, or Manchester for that matter, will anticipate those expectations being met in London – so we all have to stay ahead of the game. At a local level, partner museums could run joint community or education projects, where the need to have one's own programming is abandoned in favour of something broader-based, more efficient and possibly more effective.

---

4. Ongoing research by the Paul Hamlyn Foundation supports this.

The partnership idea is hardly new, but drilling down to make it more precise may be. The key is strategic "best-friend" partnerships where, like collecting baseball cards, it's not how many you have but who they are that will matter. Fewer may be better and we have to be willing to let unproductive affiliations go – not because we don't believe in joint work, but because we need that work to be effective.

Large museums must also be willing to show leadership. Transmitting skills and building capacity has been a tenet of recent thinking on shared museum practice, and that's been an important development for many small museums – not only for their capability but for their confidence. Over a quarter of the 2500 museums in Britain are unaccredited to the UK's national standard, and their work requires support and encouragement. The Museum of London established a hub of London museums to facilitate such work. But it may be – and we have to be willing to ask this – that we have built up an excess of capacity beyond what was needed. A surfeit of skilled people when there is less work is unhelpful, and we are looking again not to reduce the model but to refine it based on what we've learned. If core skills in conservation or specialist research were centralized, other museums could draw on them as necessary – by subscription, perhaps, or on the Accident-and-Emergency model of hospitals, where the approach is made when required. Services might range from digitizing collections to advising on deaccessioning unwieldy holdings to writing security policy. They could be provided by leaders with the experience and expertise, freeing smaller museums to concentrate on what they do best: knowing their communities and engaging them – the very expertise no larger body could ever match to the same degree.

I am not afraid to do a bit of rethinking and I'd like to encourage all my colleagues to do so – not in state of shock but as a way of getting better at what we do. I'm honest enough to admit that a pause is no bad thing. No, I don't want to see my museum set back 20 years. I don't want to lose my education programs or wider commitments. But I do want to sift what works from what doesn't, and to know that when I am committing to a project, it's because it is excellent – ambitiously conceived, well-managed, and directed toward a significant achievement.

What I'm saying, in some ways, is that with all this talk of recession and economic turmoil, we must not turn our museum model into a business plan. There is a pressure to do so, to think solely in terms of the budget and what it can, or cannot, purchase. Of course we're intelligent and financially responsible and we're not going to forego that. But the *vision* for a museum is what will turn crisis into opportunity. Fight for the money you can, but know that the present-day resources of museums are much richer than they ever were. Less available money doesn't turn us into lesser museums. We are all working with more value than perhaps we realize, including the capacity to reinvent ourselves – a talent we have shown ourselves more than capable of in recent years.

I see the importance to Londoners of culture and what it represents. And I see, as director of a city museum, how cities are blending culture into the very mix of urban life, not by accident but by design. If you look at the MAXXI in Rome – Zaha Hadid's splendid new museum of 21st-century arts – if you look at the Mori Tower or Tokyo Midtown in Japan (both of which include museums), you see big statements about culture's essential belonging to the world – to tourism and entertainment, to business and shopping, to architecture and what town planners now call "mixed-use activity". Some dislike this loss of an older reverential hush. But if museums want to be part of where we're heading as a society, we have to follow the noise.

Museums and Memory

Early in 2009 I was appointed adviser to four new history museums in Doha, Qatar, a relationship that continues today. This lecture, given in 2010, marked the opening of a round table for the museum profession in Doha, at which I was keen to flag up certain thoughts on museums that might help guide development.

In the bustling streets of São Paulo, museums can seem a far-off concern. The sun is shining, cars roar past, all sorts of people are shouting and hurrying by. It feels as if the entire southern hemisphere has descended on this one Brazilian city.

What you experience – as you stand there trying not to get run over by the traffic – is both a vibrant urban centre today, and what turned it into such an astonishing place. All this commotion reflects, if you look hard enough, a history of movements, a longstanding legacy of arrivals and departures, of population and trade.

There is material evidence all over São Paulo to remind you of such things: the implements of export in coffee and sugar can be found; church statues and personal belongings inscribe the less innocent histories of missionaries and slaves. Colonial architecture etches its monumental testament across the sky.

But if you were to cast your hook further into the past, to look for not just what was left but what you could find, what you might fetch up are the stories not enshrined in artifacts and archaeology. And the civic authorities in São Paulo brilliantly did just that. When one of the two large railway stations in the city was being rebuilt, they decided to convert part of this busy public space into a museum. And not just any museum. A railway station was hardly the place to be encumbered with objects. Instead, they built what is now a celebrated museum of the Portuguese language.

Language is not an obvious subject for a museum. A specialist library, perhaps, or an archive. What is there to show for language? But in São Paulo, they realized two important things. One was that the symbolic resonance of where you put your museum can be as important as what's inside. The Estação da Luz has always been a gateway. The tens of thousands who arrived from Africa and Asia, from Portugal itself, were transported here, and it was here that they first came face to face with a new continent. If both the station and language itself constitute a kind of encounter, what better place to commemorate those many past encounters, and in a spot where 300,000 passengers still, every day, move in and out of the city.

The second thing they understood in São Paulo was that museums are not necessarily about standing still and just looking. Visitors emerging from a train station, busy and bustling as that environment is, might be better prepared in fact to enjoy a museum that is about activity. For this is what language is: a living, changing, moving thing. It can't be trapped in a display case and fixed in time with a label. The exhibits in the Museum of the Portuguese Language reflect this. There are entire walls of visualization, screen layered upon screen; there are computer terminals and light displays that cast poetry in shapes across the floor; there are a host of what we might call graphic events, inspiring connection in the viewer – for this is about language now and our relationship to it – but also commemoration, for it was those past encounters that made this city of immigrants the linguistically complex place it is today.

I open with this example of a museum of language to ensure that any discussion of museums and memory frees itself of its traditional focus on the object and what we might say about. If we are going to create a potent showcase for communal memory, to give voice to the past in all its forms, we are going to have to be bolder. What we have to do is grab hold of the intangible and wrestle it into the building.

Memory in museums has often been confused with history. To recall through galleries and exhibits what happened before – as so many of our museums continue to do – constituted an exciting remembrance of things past, uniting as it did historical ideas with the material proof of their veracity.

But two problems gradually emerged from such an approach. One has been our increasing distrust of the monolithic voice of the museum. It can feel, in its authoritative anonymity, like the voice of the victors, telling visitors what they ought to think and, in its inevitable selection, what really matters. The second problem is that it excludes participation. As our understanding of what people do in museums grows ever more precise, there has been a useful shift from models of learning, where the museum provides facts and information to be digested, to those of engagement, where the past is a prompt to thought and emotion, and where the relevance of a display, while no less informative, draws a richer response from the visitor.

And it is here that we can begin to define "memory" in the museum context. While any of us might argue for the importance of history, we ought to draw on every means at our disposal to communicate that history. Memory becomes a tool we can use because it personalizes history such that any single visitor can feel that they have a connection to the matters discussed. Memory is both on display and a response that draws on the individual history of the spectator.

Of the important ways in which memory becomes subject matter, we might take, for instance, the idea of witness. The Gulag Museum at Perm commemorates 70 years of oppression and punishment in Soviet Russia. It does not do this through objects. Visitors to the Maximum Security Camp are informed through the shocking testimony of former prisoners, but just as significantly they encounter the physical environment themselves. Visitors bear witness to the prison experience: they walk along the same paths taken by the prisoners; they endure the atmosphere of surveillance, vulnerability and isolation.[1]

---

1. This example and the next are represented on www.sitesofconscience.org, an informal coalition of museums strongly committed to the politics of memory.

A similar experience is on offer at the Workhouse Museum in Nottinghamshire, where the English poor were incarcerated in the 19th and early 20th centuries and made to work for their moral improvement. Like the Gulag, the workhouse was a place designed to alienate. Groups were segregated, families broken up, husbands kept separate from wives. To visit is to encounter not the belongings of the poor – for by definition those who ended up there had lost everything – so much as the strict regime they underwent.

But what encounters these are for the visitor. There is the potency of those who bore witness in the past. There is the accumulation of their experiences – not just one voice, but a plethora of testimonies. There is our own charged response to such environments.[2]

And what is more – and it is here where memory becomes particularly powerful in a museum context – there is the magnetizing effect of gathering stories into a public display. A memory unshared is a private event. But once it is told, memory becomes story. Passed from person to person, it takes on a social vitality no book-bound history could ever hope to compete with. The writer Jamal Mahjoub has said, describing the problem of indigenous identity in colonized Sudan: "We had stories, but we didn't really have museums or books to put them in. How we came to be assembled here at this confluence of streams seemed to be a question no one was particularly interested in asking."[3]

This is what museums do. We ask the questions. We ensure that those stories – those memories made public – are given value, and we reassure all groups, however disenfranchised, that the questions they pose are worth asking.

The gathering of these stories does not require objects. As the Gulag and Workhouse museums illustrate, places can be sites of memory, and

2. The potency of such witness for the visitor is to some extent a measure of its proximity to suffering. See, for instance, Avishai Margalit's distinction between the "moral witness" who endured what went on from other forms of testimony (Margalit 2002, chapter 5).
3. Mahjoub 2004, p. 62.

those memorialized sites become powerful museums. They are particularly important because they retrieve lost histories. The absence of artifacts does not mean certain stories ought not or cannot be told, but that we must find a way, as these museums have, of capturing the intangible. The very absence of objects can itself be the starting point of the story, for such emptiness is an unsettling, often moving proof of loss or annihilation – more powerful than any display of things.

My intention is not to create a new taxonomy of museums: traditional object-led institutions versus museums of place or absence or memory. If new types of museum experiences are possible, using new technologies in particular to convey and elicit memory, then they should be used effectively across the museum sector.

The *London, Sugar and Slavery* gallery at the Museum of London Docklands is a case in point. The gallery tells the history of the slave trade as it connects to London and to the British and other empires. It is a story that crosses the globe, and the gallery contains objects that can tell some of those stories: the shackles used to imprison slaves in Africa, the tools of sugar refinery in the West Indies, the published appeals of former slaves in London. The movement to stop the slave trade is represented on everything from abolitionist sugar bowls to parade banners.

But was our collection enough? How were we to represent all the lost stories? How could we capture the history not only of commercial leaders, ship owners and politicians, but of the slaves themselves. Most had nothing and left nothing behind. Was our museum to describe them en masse, as a faceless commodity, treat them in effect as impersonal cargo, just as they were treated by the slave traders themselves?

To address this, we looked to the methods of memory. The gallery opens in a state of loss: with an empty room instilling not just a sense of absence, but of uncertainty – for a room without objects in a museum is a very disconcerting space. An enlarged register of slave ships lines one wall, a tally of all those lives torn from their country and taken away. A film splices dozens of speakers – black, white, old, young – uttering the same text to render the appeal against the indignity of the slave trade, a history in which every one of us is implicated.

"Consider slavery," wrote the Laurence Sterne in his novel *The Life and Opinions of Tristram Shandy, Gentleman*, "How bitter a draught and how many are made to drink it." And the gallery does – or rather, it encourages visitors to do so. When the lights dim, and a *son et lumière* show stops the gallery every 20 minutes, we are slaves ourselves – pinioned where we stand, hearing a toll of amplified and terrible announcements: "You will have no voice, you will have no name." Standing there, we extend our sympathy into the past, and we bring forward the missing voices of those who could not speak.

The *London, Sugar and Slavery* gallery did not adopt this set-up lightly, where imagination stands in for objects. If museums are to create a space for memory – both as content and as something visitors bring to their viewing – they have to communicate sincerely with those implicated in the narrative. From its advisory board to participating community and school groups, the Museum of London gallery has been shaped by a complex sense of the importance of remembering – for individuals; for communities still marginalized through centuries of ethnic division and misunderstanding; for society and national identity as a whole. This is not a new way of speaking on behalf of communities: it is a platform that allows them to speak.

Community involvement enriches the displays and teaches us what works. If we consider a museum like the District Six Museum in Cape Town, the very essence of it is its meaningfulness for those displaced by the policies of Apartheid. Commemorating a former South African neighbourhood that was flattened and "cleansed" – as black residents were forced out to make way for an all-white gentrification – the District 6 Museum ensures that physical destruction is not matched by a failure to remember. What is there is less important than *that it* is there – and former residents continue to bring their children and grandchildren to pay witness to the past and understand what preceded reconciliation.

These spaces free us from the tyranny of objects and widen our remit – and our resources. We find a similar direction in the cultural sector through UNESCO's Memory of the World program. Established in 1992, the program encourages us to preserve the world's documentary heritage. This too is a struggle against what UNESCO rightly calls "collective amnesia" and is a persuasive attempt to move beyond the object to highlight other forms of archival information that are often underused or at peril from looting, dispersal or destruction. Some histories are only possible to tell through such materials. The Memory of the World Register includes, for example, archives relating to human rights abuses in Argentina, Chile, Dominican Republic, Paraguay, Cambodia and the Baltic States. If we are to record the past fully, raise awareness and build reconciliation, we have to ensure such documents of memory are rescued, conserved and disseminated. The program is admirably capacious, ranging from centuries-old maps, charters and account books to recent film, photographs and electronic communication.

Our experience at the Museum of London is that archives fascinate the public. When the museum acquired the papers of Thomas and John Mills, two 18th-century plantation owners on St Kitts, they drew immediate attention from our visitors. They were especially moved by a list that named the plantation slaves – Celia, Dorinda, Dinah, Doll, Pompey, Polydore, Patrick. The men and women, boys and girls, carry no surnames. Some are succinctly memorialized as "dead". The archival documents pick up exactly the missing voices the gallery design seeks to retrieve. It is hard not to be moved by these brief lives. One is proud to put them on display and commemorate them.

Access to such material raises awareness. It creates, as do all memory-related projects, a pathway of emotion, as we re-experience the past and carry that sympathy out into the world. It helps to build a sense of community.[4] The London Archaeological Archive and Research Centre (LAARC) holds the archives for over 3000 site excavations in Greater London over the past 100 years. It is a vast resource and attracts significant public participation through its Volunteer/Visitor Inclusion Program. Volunteers

4. The creation of community is a longstanding museum practice, where collections defined a certain collectorship, represented group or visitorship. Writing on Renaissance portrait collections, Paula Findlen (2000, p. 170) states: "Collecting and displaying portraits made it possible to tell a history of a community, a discipline or even a society through the selection and arrangement of this one type of object." She notes that such displays often included a portrait of the collector himself, who became an object in his own collection.

describe the power of handling historical materials and encountering the untouched past. Many testify that traditional museum displays have now come to life for them in a new way, through their direct behind-the-scenes work with archives and archaeological material. They feel more strongly that it is their history on display.

Such an approach can be drawn in to all museums. All those objects I have so lightly shunted to the side are, of course, a part of this. In the new *Galleries of Modern London* at the Museum of London, the approach has merged traditional gallery display with the wealth of innovative methodologies that have emerged from new forms of archival access, sites of conscience and museums of memory. Community groups contributed to several displays, creating in one instance a cabinet of curiosities relating to the Great Fire of London and the rebuilding of the city. They selected objects from the museum's collection that they thought audiences today would find interesting and informative – copper coins and gold rings, inkwells and animal bones, wig curlers and chamber pots. Most importantly, they chose objects they thought were relevant both to the museum and to audiences, for if no one looks inside, the best produced display case in the world is a waste of time. The very fact of their participation has appealed to many of our visitors, for it breaks down the divide – as has happened with the LAARC volunteers – between curator and public. Visitors feel they are more a part of the museum.

Technology proves an increasingly useful tool for this blend of the material and the memorial. Oral histories tell the stories of individual Londoners during the Blitz with a personal appeal no object or photograph could muster. Displays on civic life encourage public interaction, as visitors add their views on political issues and civic concerns. The results of these living debates are in a perpetual state of change, updated on computer screens for all to see. By interacting, the visitor presence becomes a part of the display and their own voice one of a series of commemorated voices – a powerful moment in terms of making the museum a significant element in defining who they are. Their lives are recorded, just as the historical displays are records of past lives. The inherent value they find in themselves accords an analogous value to those who went before them. The museum becomes a memory bank.

In 2010, Seamus Heaney, the poet and Nobel Prize winner, published a collection of poems entitled *Human Chain*. For Heaney, it is this human chain that links us to those who went before us, and those who will inherit what we leave. His book is a series of poetic testaments. He attempts to catch hold of every life, however inconsequential, before (as he puts it) "the memorable bottoms out / Into the irretrievable".[5] For Heaney, memory is at the heart of who we are. And so he has defined our task for us: to ensure that we collect not just things, but all that is memorable too and join ourselves in the great human chain.

---

5. Heaney 2010, p. 84 ("In the Attic"). Heaney's strong sense that we carry the remembered forward into the future can be found in the poem "A Herbal (after Guillevic's 'Herbier de Bretagne')", where it is not the hearse itself, but memories of the hearse that endure: "On sunlit tarmac, / On memories of the hearse // At walking pace / Between overgrown verges, // The dead here are borne / Toward the future."

Building Time:
Experiencing Architecture as History

I was appointed professor at the Bergen National Academy of Art, Norway, in 1997. The position gave me the opportunity to articulate my thoughts on museum architecture and test these out on students. This lecture marked the introduction to my seventh year as professor.

If you order a Diet Coke at the Black Country Living Museum in Dudley, the buxom barmaid in her floor-length skirt is likely to put her hand on her hip and expostulate: "Diet what?! Never 'eard of it! We've shandy. Or a nice dandelion burdock."

If you grew up near Birmingham, the experience offers a frisson of familiarity, for the Black Country Living Museum is that sometimes embarrassing artistic phenomenon: a historical reenactment. English pubs and churches, bakeries and shops have been preserved from a multitude of sites and brought together to capture an image, a photograph almost, of a certain place during a certain, significant period of its history: here, the West Midlands in its industrial heyday from the late 18th to early 20th centuries.

Such cultural manoeuvres have their fashion, and people generally have strong views for or against them. But the popularity of the Black Country Living Museum is a testament to something perennially important, and that is: *that one has a physical relationship with the past.* Photographs are one thing, and actors strutting their stuff as saucy Edwardian barmaids are another. But to stand where real miners and metalworkers stood – beneath a smoke-darkened ceiling of pressed tin, caught in the polished gleam of solid oak and centuries-old cut-glass – is to be swept up in the history that lives on through architecture.

It may strike one as a cliché – of course old buildings carry histories – but there is a larger matter to acknowledge about the relationship between architecture and the past: each time we enter a building, however modern, however shining, we are already moving through a determined space, caught in the moment of its concept, of its making, of its use. A completed building is, as its foundation stone wants it to be, fixed – anchored not just physically, but temporally.

One argument that the barmaid with her old-fashioned burdock drink is making is that whenever we enter a building, we are *always* stepping back in time.

The relationship between time and architecture is a complex one. Can we, for example, relate speed to our experience to structure? Are there fast buildings? Slow buildings? Any of us might suggest a few examples for either category – and not always happily!

Anyone who has worked on a project that requires accommodating the pressure of crowds in public spaces knows that there are definite mechanisms for hurrying people along, or slowing them down. Colin St John Wilson's sunken piazza in front of the new British Library takes its visitors from the roaring traffic of London's busy Euston Road and deliberately delays them with its wide steps and irregular plateaus. The architecture makes you pause. It makes you reduce your speed even before you enter the building proper. What the piazza does is prepare you for the sensibility of the library space. Or, we might say, library pace. It is architecture that slows you down.

It is these ways in which buildings permit the experience of time that I want to examine, both actual and, more suggestively, metaphorical time. And I want to begin to ask: if buildings do permit an experience of time, to what purposes might such an experience be put? How can we harness the power of what we might term "architectural narrative"?

Let's begin in Osnabrück in Lower Saxony. The Felix Nussbaum Haus was the first of Daniel Libeskind's buildings to be fully constructed, designed in 1991 to house the collection of the 20th-century German painter Felix Nussbaum. It is a compelling building, and its three intersecting volumes carry a variety of narrative determinations, from its larger symbolic triptych of house, path and bridge to its deliberately metaphorical interiors of blind corridors, slashed windows and fragmented space.

As in many of Libeskind's buildings, the architecture represents a kind of journey. But what first strikes one, even before one has begun to engage with the intricacies of the building proper, is the bold delineation of materials. For the three parts of the Felix Nussbaum Haus are made of strikingly different materials: the first part panelled in long strips of oak, the second a path of concrete, and the third a bridge covered in sheets of zinc. The best laid plans of architects can, experientially, be lost on visitors, who may be distracted by the myriad competing elements of function and form. But Libeskind uses a straightforward – and unmissable – inaugural gesture to dramatize the three parts of his building's story. To move through his museum is to remember one's initial sighting of it, and as such, the materials constitute a kind of narrative.

Frank Gehry once said, in a characteristically unfussed manner: "It seems to me that when you're doing architecture, you're building something out of something." He went on to explain that what exists prior to the building – whether it's materials or the city itself – is already rich with meaning: "There are social issues, there's context".[1]

Describing the plethora of new buildings near the Brandenburg Gate in Berlin in the 1990s, he was critical of an overly conservative approach: "The other new projects on the square, which are trying to be copies of the 19th-century buildings that used to be there, look pastichey and miss the point. They didn't learn."

Gehry's language to describe the bank he'd been asked to design (and describing what any of us can *learn* from other buildings) is exciting.[2] He

---

1. Gehry 1999, p. 44.
2. In the late 1990s Gehry designed the DZ Bank in Pariser Platz, which

talks about how "the scale of the moves I made on the facade of this building relates to Pariser Platz". He also focuses on material. "The stone is four inches thick because the [Brandenburg] Gate's stone is also very gutsy."[3] For his building to make sense, he needed to understand the way it would be shaped by the architecture of the past, not just as imitation, but as a set of historic principles – gutsy, large-scale – which could be adopted to make something new.

The material build of a structure is one way in which architecture can alter the nature of our experience, an experience we cannot help but understand in chronological terms, whether it is by association with materials of the past or by establishing a deliberate sequence of fabrics that tells a story.

Yet what is enclosed by all that material? There are equally in many buildings what we might call narratives of space. Indeed one of the most long-established aspects of public architecture is its connection to *ceremony*. Buildings do not offer a random sequence of possible movements, but instead cultivate a consciously hierarchical approach to them. Buildings have their own story to tell, and physical progress through them (as well as waiting and delay, to say nothing of restricted access) are ritualized events in which time and motion are made to carry symbolic meaning. Indeed, they are buildings that insist on a sensibility of time.

Let's look to India for an example. Traditional principles of kingship in India were set down in a wide-ranging literature of princely education. Among the many theories that explain royal authority was the idea that

> sovereigns were exalted above ordinary mortals because of the magic power of royal ceremonies. The consecration was the most important of these since it infused the king with cosmic force. In the central rite, the *abhisheka*, or ceremonial bath, the sovereign was identified with a divinity such as Indra, the king of the gods.[4]

---

sits between the American Embassy and what had formerly been Albert Speer's studio. Among the building's notable features is a giant chamber in the shape of a horse's head, which serves as the main conference room.

3. Gehry, pp. 203 and 205.
4. Michell 1994, pp. 10–11.

As the ritual, so the building in which it takes place, which itself becomes structured and designed to accord with proximity to the king, and by extension, to the divine. As George Michell writes:

> Sun motifs appeared on the walls and ceilings of palaces, suggesting the beneficial influence of the heavens.... Gem-encrusted *chhatries*, or umbrellas, were held over the king as he sat on his throne.... [Their] multiple tiers indicated the ascending realms of the heavens.
>
> That the king's throne was intended as an *axis mundi*, or cosmic pillar, is demonstrated in the late 16th century at Fatephur Sikri, where a massive monolithic column inside one of the royal pavilions supports a seat used by the Mughal emperor Akbar for private acts of meditation. The importance of free-standing columns dates back to the early Indian kings, who used them as emblems of power and as appropriate vehicles for royal proclamations.[5]

The monolithic column – as fundamental an architectural feature as we could wish for – becomes the very heart of the princely story. It is not just the place where power is wielded but the architectural endpoint toward which visitors of state and envoys from other countries hoped to journey, moving nervously through outer precincts, through audience halls and private chambers, as they were gradually led through the royal palace to meet the king.

Palaces are not unique in this, though their formal scale lends itself to such complex paths. Indeed the papal palaces of Rome have a particular language to describe the size and sequence of rooms through which visitors had to pass. The more important such ambassadors were, the further they were allowed to advance and the larger the rooms became.[6]

---

5. Michell, p. 11.

6. See Hyde 1999, pp. 307–08: "Apartments within the Roman palaces were arranged according to strict matters of protocol. Their typical layout suggests by the number, size and shape of the rooms, the stages of protocol necessary for daily life and social commerce.... Depending upon the ranks of the visitor and the occupant, after ascending the main stairway, the visitor would pass through several rooms, moving from the sparsely to the more elaborately furnished, before entering the *camera d'udienza*, or meeting room. The occupant (often a cardinal) would have his own room further away, to which only the most esteemed visitor

Temples and churches carry similar narrative potency, as do buildings of government and judiciary. In the 18th century, proponents of the baroque encouraged a new ideal of movement through space. Architects and town planners laid public squares in Paris and Turin, improved street layouts in cities as convoluted as Rome and designed buildings marked by what one critic has identified as "an interest in movement above all, movement which is a frank exhibition of energy and escape from classical restraint".[7]

Buildings became a kind of theatre, where the performance of the liturgy, for instance, became much more open, rood screens and chancels withdrawn and the venture from noisy street to high altar unimpeded, and all the more dramatic for being so.[8] Open spaces might seem less narrative, less determined. But what baroque artists strove for was an immediacy of emotional impact that reinforced the prevailing ideology, whether religious or political, as natural and inevitable. The story in a baroque church or *palazzo* becomes an unequivocal one, not so much free as singularly, perhaps ruthlessly, effective.[9]

---

would be admitted. The etiquette manual specified who was to meet whom in which room and what pleasantries were to be exchanged, who was to speak first, who was to bow, who was to be seated, how chairs were to be positioned, what were the appropriate sizes of chair and so on. Naturally the appearance of the palace itself as well as the size and decorations of these formal apartments were crucial to the overall meaning of ambassadorial receptions. Social, diplomatic, and ecclesiastical life was a matter of negotiation; art and architecture were crucial mediating terms in these encounters."

7. Harbison 2000, p. 1. See also Norberg-Schulz 1980, pp. 24–28, on architecture's extension through the capital city.

8. See Hyde, p. 119: "The church building is a setting for mystery and ideology.... Most Baroque churches pull the worshipper right off the street, transporting him or her from the brightness and noise of city life to a region of half light and incense. Although temporary benches would be set up toward the high altar for Mass, baroque churches were generally open spaces. Because the services were now, as a result of the decisions of the Council of Trent, orientated toward the laity or congregation, all those devices such as rood screens and chancels that gave priests their privacy when performing their duties were taken down so as to make the interior more like a huge theatre."

9. Hyde, pp. 119–20.

My point is that in all such spaces, a story is told. There is no escaping the ascent of the stairs, the movement along the nave, the gaze drawn upward toward the dome, the apse, the pillar, the monumental edifice. One moves toward these things in a series of ever more powerful approaches, stopping at thresholds, identifying transitions from one defined area to another. Walking through architectural space is not like swimming across a lake or crossing a field. It remains, as it has so often been in the past, a highly ritualized movement through time.

There is a third principle I'd like to mention briefly in this examination of how buildings make us experience time. We have materials; we have the construction of space itself. There is also a sense of outlook that architecture provides. Buildings have, of course, in a variety of ways always had an understanding of prospect: from the pleasing room with a view to the highly symbolic importance of directing the human gaze religiously or politically in a particular direction.

But contemporary architects such as I.M. Pei have found brilliant solutions to the problem of competing with the past by taking the "view" as an integral part of their new buildings' design. When you are asked to build near the *grand palais* that is the Louvre in Paris, how on earth do you respond? Pei's solution was neither to compete nor capitulate, but to take it as a given that any new building has an inevitable relationship with those that have preceded it. With this idea as his starting point, his new entrance to the Louvre brilliantly draws visitors to its noticeable modernity, then surprises them inside by its self-effacing transparency. To descend the escalators of Pei's glass pyramid is to be forced to cast your gaze upward toward the old palace itself. His showpiece allows the former showpiece its own importance and gathers up history as part of its modernity.

The Acropolis Museum in Athens does a similar thing, setting out its own expressive interest, while at the same time, subduing its importance to that of its unparalleled site, with glass floors and open spaces that provide constant views of the Acropolis above and ongoing archaeological excavation below. The addition of I.M. Pei's exhibitions building to the German Historical Museum in Berlin has been similarly evocative of itself and of its neighbouring buildings. As Hans Ottomeyer, the director of the Deutsches Historisches Museum, has enthused:

The profound scepticism predominant among architectural critics and architectural professionals that architecture of quality may
represent a disruption because it does not adapt to and fit in with
the surrounding built environment, can be perceived as absurd in
the context of Pei's architecture. The facades respond to, reflect and
resist the urban buildings and streets around them in a kind of dialogue. They open up new vistas and meticulously composed perspectives and images that have already become subject matter for
postcards and souvenirs of Berlin.[10]

Postcards may not be our ultimate goal, but what a thriving testament
to a building's impact: a building that says not just "look at me" but "look
around you".

We can agree then, I hope, that buildings offer a particular experience
of time. I'd like to move on to consider to what uses such an experience
might be put. If time matters, as it seems to in our hurrying world, and if a
sense of history is thus an inescapable aspect of the human condition as we
perceive time passing, how can architecture be used to help us understand
that condition or improve it?

My interest is, as you might expect, cultural, for I've learned over the
years how important it is for people to have a sense of time, to appreciate
their own history and to connect that history to the many other stories to
which it relates. You could say that, as the director of a museum, I work
with time.

And it is not an accidental content. To understand the cultural weight
of museums as a few rooms of ancient objects set out to be admired is to
miss their impact. People are moved by history. It is as if their place in the
world demands that they make sense of what has gone before them. What
museums permit – rather like the buildings of I.M. Pei – are perspectives
on the past: they provide windows into the actuality of lives in other times
and other places, and they encourage a sense of connection to those lives.
When museums communicate well – and it is here where architecture and
design feature so strongly – they create sympathetic spaces, where what

---

10. Ottomeyer 2003, p. 7.

one gains is not just knowledge of past lives and other cultures, but an appreciation of their connectedness to our own.

Let's retrieve some of the principles of architectural narrative I've examined and see what their potential might be for cultural communication. We know that materials carry cultural value. A bronze statue is different from a terracotta figurine, just as a marble column conveys a notably different message than a thatched roof. But the relative importance of materials is not an abstract or universal hierarchy. A building made of the local limestone or a particular shade of brick may be far more meaningful than the wished-for importance (one might say self-importance, at times) of imposed materials, however valuable they might be in worldly terms.

By extension, cultural architecture often benefits from being site-specific. One can think of any number of museums founded in a historic building, from the Fortress Museum of Vladivostok to the many civil war museums that dot the southern United States. Here, materiality becomes a larger principle: not just the building itself – bullet-scarred and embattled as it might be – but the very terrain is suffused with *memory*. We can remind ourselves that classical models from Plato to Quintilian for training the mind, especially for making public speeches, drew on architectural images as sites of memory: one placed the various "topics" in different rooms and so imagined moving through an intellectual argument as one moved through a building. What the rhetoricians understood was how deeply rooted, how unshakable, our sense of association with place is. You might forget any number of things – from your car keys to the plethora of passwords and PINs we all apparently need to survive. But one is never likely to lose the potency of a remembered space, the texture of wallpaper, the colour of a door, the slope of a roof.

In the largest sense, a cultural building can absorb an entire city, as the Museum of the Warsaw Uprising does. Here, a former tram power plant houses a busy array of interactive and historical exhibits about the terrible events of 1944. The material power of the building is its symbolic connection to the entire city of Warsaw: it both survives as a pre-war building and only exists (like so many others in the city) as a structure punitively bombed and extensively rebuilt.

Traditionally, museums see themselves horizontally: their self-concept is one of spaces arranged for display. When one wants to grow as a museum, one wants an extra wing, a new building, more room. But a focus on the material reminds us that, like the layers of geology on which any building sits, museums can convey meaning vertically. Whether it's a local stone, part of a surviving wall, or a larger context of land and cityscape, cultural architecture builds up from the layers of the past on which it stands and its meaning speaks from the historic material out of which it is made.

Spatial narrative poses different problems and unleashes different strengths in cultural buildings. It will come as no surprise that the familiar narrative of palace and church has to some extent been co-opted by museums. As one writer has said, museums are increasingly "places where society likes to come together and seek its own heart. Museums have inherited or secularised the religious or political ceremonials of the community."[11] And museum buildings, naturally, follow suit.

Indeed, one might argue that museums are buildings where architectural narrative finds its most suitable content. The traditional museum has to a large extent been chronological. Its subject is, at one level, the passage of time. You start at the beginning, whether it's prehistoric tools or the first postage stamp, and you proceed to tell a story over time as you advance through the building.

Such chronologies are not, of course, inevitable, any more than is the architecture itself, which can offer more or less in the number of chosen pathways through the space. Other ways of organizing – or not organizing – museums have always been possible. When the German art critic and curator Wilhelm von Bode pioneered period-room displays in museums in the late 19th century, he wanted to get away from crowded cabinets where all sorts of objects were jammed together, as he said it, "like herrings, one above the other".[12]

It is not just the spatial arrangement of the objects that defines a museum's temporal argument. The building itself can constitute its own

---

11. Sewing 2003, p. 44.
12. Baker 1996, p. 143.

chronology. A mesmerizing example of a powerful building that does so is the museum of the Hagia Sophia in Istanbul. Here is architecture that quite literally spans, with or without objects, 15 centuries of history, from its celebrated dome – seemingly "suspended by a chain of a gold from the height of the sky", according to the Byzantine historian Procopius – to the solid buttresses of its many precincts. Even the most casual observer cannot fail to notice the contrasts of period, where Islamic calligraphic roundels are suspended next to Christian mosaics, and mosque and church co-exist simultaneously.[13]

Architecture in such a building is as powerful an expression of time as any rare artifacts a museum might choose to display. But we cannot build the Hagia Sophia! It is what it is by virtue of its history, not because we can imitate it. But architects have found various means to connect their modern buildings with the past, so that what is expressed architecturally conveys historical meaning without being itself historical. It is not the easiest of tasks, as Paul Cattermole has noted:

> The conundrum that faces architects, artists and film-production designers alike when set the challenge of physically realizing our future, is how much to borrow from the past. For many this is a straightforward "cut and paste" exercise, taking existing historic or contemporary elements and combining or exaggerating them to create a distortion of both past and present. But this method does little justice to the essence of a culture's architecture, its underlying ethos or the spiritual significance of its component parts.[14]

To recall Frank Gehry's terms, they produce "pastiche" because "they don't learn". But there are wonderfully modern buildings that have a clear sense of historic time and place. Renzo Piano's Tjibaou Cultural Centre in Noumea, Melanesia, designed and built in the 1990s, presents a cluster of towers strung out along the line of the main complex. The towers are a reference to the Great Houses typical of Kanak culture, for which Jean-Marie Tjibaou had done so much to get international recognition. Piano took

---

13. See Mainstone 1988 for a detailed reading of the building's development, as well as an examination of the architectural narrative in relation to ceremony.
14. Cattermole 2006, p. 45.

inspiration from many Kanak sources while avoiding any direct replication or objectifying closure, as if the Kanak people were somehow finished and his to exploit architecturally. His cultural sensitivity is vivid enough that he has left the ends of the towers open to "signify that the culture whose artifacts they exhibit is still expanding and evolving, rather than being a remnant of history".[15]

That such historic reference is a living relationship is what preserves it from parody. A similarly nuanced approach can be found in the First Nations Garden Pavilion in the Montreal Botanical Garden, designed by Saucier and Perrotte in 2001. The pavilion stands as a modest intervention between a spruce and a maple forest, sunk unobtrusively into the ground, its undulating roof recalling a wisp of smoke through the trees. Much of the building projects its space outdoors, where even its exhibitions are often held.[16] What begins as cultural reference modulates in successful buildings like these into a true connection to the history and the beliefs of the peoples they are striving to represent.

There are, inevitably, risks to such historicizing procedures. In trying to make sense of time, contemporary buildings can end up as pastiche, as we've noted, or even competing with the past. The Caen Mémorial in France aims to animate the history of the Second World War through a bravura *mise en scène*. Its austerely modernist facade is split in two by its dramatic entrance, a jagged crack symbolizing the terrible destruction visited upon Caen by the war. The galleries include a theatrically bare room containing a single, large projected photograph of Hitler, around which the electronically distorted sound of one his speeches is broadcast. The museum has had a great success for its innovation – war memorials are certainly not known for being lively. But its critics argue that it forecloses true memory, by reducing experience to spectacle. Instead of sympathetic paths for viewing and contemplation, the visitor is left unengaged, a voyeur rather than a participant in the historical exercise.[17]

It is not just the representation of time – architecturally, or in terms of

---

15. Cattermole, pp. 45–46.
16. Slessor 2004, p. 147.
17. Sherman 1995, pp. 60–65.

design and display – that poses a risk. The power of authenticity I noted earlier, where the museum exists on the site of a historical event, can be troubled by the passage of time itself. Writing of Holocaust memorials, James Young notes that remnants can be "mistaken for the events from which they have been torn; in coming to stand for the whole, a fragment is confused with it".[18] It is here that the perceptual nuance of architecture is required, finding a balance between displaying temporality and acknowledging – as Renzo Piano's unfinished towers do – the world moving on around it. The point may be to enter time rather than try to fix it – the very place where pastiche gets it wrong.

Indeed, one needs to acknowledge that buildings are not merely responsive to context. They alter the environments into which they are put. Arata Isozaki writes in an essay on architectural narrative that "new buildings should stimulate the creation of new contexts in their surroundings". Whether defensive or aggressive, he argues, "once the struggle with the location is over, direct confrontation with the broader culture behind it becomes possible".[19] His understanding seems to me profound: the building exists as both initial intervention and an ongoing process through time, connecting it to people and place, "the broader culture", as Isozaki puts it, that changes and is changed by it.

Related to this is the third way in which we see that architecture can present time. The buildings of I.M. Pei, or the new Acropolis Museum, take up the architectural gaze as a powerful means of gathering up time. They allow themselves to be excitingly modern, while benefitting from the beauty of the past, not through imitation, but through recapitulation.

We might imagine such procedures, where the visual is absorbed as a series of snapshots and moving pictures (for one is always moving past such perspectives in these buildings), as troublingly modern. Is it not emblematic of contemporary culture, this superficial insistence on the visual, the transient image, time as disappearance? Might it not be history as consumable heritage, rather than a meaningful communication of the past?

---

18. Young 2005, pp. 62–63.
19. Isozaki 1998, pp. 113–14.

It seems to me that we must disagree on two counts. One is that myriad visual games on an architectural scale have been enjoyed by cultures across the ages. The very pyramids of Egypt are a kind of delight with shape and perspective, thinking on the largest scale about the eternal gaze. The 18th and 19th centuries – hardly "fast" cultures of the sort we are now nervous of – saw the rise of the panorama, a perspectival game in which cities, battles and seascapes were captured in the round, often housed in top-lit, purpose-built buildings specifically designed to transport visitors to another place and time.[20]

The second objection we must make is that people are who they are, whether they are visiting a school or a shopping mall, a bank or a leisure centre. When young people visit a museum, they are the children of Xboxes and websites, computer games and mobile phones. To refuse to speak their visual language would be patronize them in the worst sort of fashion. Even worse, it would be to lose their interest, to refuse to engage them. If architecture is to convey a sense of time and history to them, it must allow a measure of familiarity with all ways of looking. Indeed, in their strongest moment, the most successful buildings we encounter appeal to the widest possible experience of them.

All buildings are the playthings of time. On the one hand, as the Black Country Living Museum celebrates, they belong to the past. They have made their statement, chosen their materials, configured their space, established their views. They are complete and have entered history, evoking myriad associations from the very moment they first open their doors.

Nevertheless, buildings continue. They exist within cultures and environments, and as such, evolve over time. Buildings live, just as the people who use them live. They change, they age – and in this way, they belong to the future as much as the past. For an architect like Frank Gehry, there is no boundary between a building and life itself. Speaking of his love of the novels of Trollope and Proust, he confesses: "I hear the descriptions of the parties, and they're architectural for me."[21]

---

20. For a detailed history of the panorama, see Bernard Comment 1999.
21. Gehry, pp. 42–43.

If life is architecture, then we can safely assume that the experience of time in buildings is as fundamental as any temporal awareness. But the particulars matter. Any sense of foreclosure – of history as pastiche or empty spectacle – deadens time rather than enlivens it. It may be a question of a relationship as much as representation. Buildings may be oppositional and striking or modestly accommodating to their contexts, but ultimately it is those that make sense of an ongoing relation with the broader culture that thrive. Cairo's eagerly awaited Grand Egyptian Museum looks to do just that, as much a vision of the past one can experience as a repository of it.

It is this feature of the living building that makes architecture such an exciting and important part of our lives. As Winston Churchill once said, "We shape our dwellings, and afterwards our dwellings shape us."[22]

---

22. Speech in the House of Commons, October 28, 1943, cited in Fowler 1989, p. 11.

Museum Architecture:
New Glories, Old Concerns

In 2004 I spent the summer as visiting professor at the School of Architecture at Ain Shams University in Cairo. This lecture was a contribution to a symposium the faculty organized to examine aspects of the then developing Grand Egyptian Museum.

The writer Naguib Mahfouz once said: "I defend both freedom of expression and society's right to counter it."[1] He was speaking from within a culture he understood, where the just man must speak out against injustice, where a social norm must assert itself if society is to remain a coherent whole. When Mahfouz was awarded the Nobel Prize in 1988, he saw the achievement as an acknowledgement of the culture of the East, less about him as an individual, modest as he was, than about a tradition of literature finding an international platform for new readers.

Prizes can have such an effect, pointing a spotlight, drawing people toward a person or place, a book or a building. The Pritzker Prize can cast new light on buildings across the world by singling out a talented architect. More specifically, in the museum world, the culture in which I work,

---

1. El Shabrawy 1992.

there is now something called the Bilbao Effect. Frank Gehry's staggeringly successful Guggenheim Museum in Spain has had not merely a cultural impact, but has altered the very fortunes of the city in which it is set. The industrial smokestacks and wharves referenced in Gehry's architecture have become, in the building itself, a metaphor for new economic power: the prize has become the flourishing tourist industry that the Guggenheim Museum has created.

Since Gehry's building opened in 1997, we have seen dozens of first-class museums march confidently onto the world stage, from the colossal Tate Modern in London to the colourful National Museum of Australia in Canberra, from the supreme statement of the Capital Museum in Beijing to the organic filter of the De Young Museum in San Francisco. Cairo itself, of course, will soon see its own cultural presence wonderfully asserted in the Grand Egyptian Museum.

It all sounds delightful, and easy. Beautiful collections. A grand building. Some public fanfare – and you're away. The world is increasingly at your doorstep. They want your museum as much as you do.

But as we've seen most recently in France, the risks with a building as publicly sensitive as a museum are huge. Museums are not entertainment or decoration. They are central to a community's idea of itself. How we present our national collections announces to the world our understanding of ourselves and of our neighbours, of the world we live in. President Chirac's Musée du Quai Branly should have been a straightforward success. It had a renowned French architect, Jean Nouvel, design it. A strong political will behind it. An amazing collection of African, Oceanic and Asian art.

And yet, perhaps because of the very political nature of Chirac's gesture, it is mired in politics. Has it merely recreated in modern terms the worst sort of ethnographic museum of the past, where "the other" is on display as primitive and strange? Has it run away from the tough issues to do with colonial rapacity and how the collections were formed? If it aims to honour its works as art (rather than anthropological artifact), why was Chirac not able to persuade museums such as the Louvre to display their own collections of European art alongside them?

The critics have been loud, the debate will continue and the Musée Chirac (as everyone imagines it will ultimately be called) may eventually find its cultural place. But the controversial reception of this world museum points to a key aspect of contemporary global culture I would like to address:

Statements of cultural power – big buildings, if you will – once were, but are no longer enough: what's truly meaningful to people comes from their experience of what's inside them.

The architect Charles Holden once did a terrible thing. Holden was responsible for much of the new London Underground in the 1930s. He was a big thinker with a big mandate, and the stylish modernism of his stations across London still holds its own among the city's most enduring architectural works. But in 1937, he and a small group (which included the president of the Royal Academy of Arts) mounted scaffolding outside what had been the British Medical Association's headquarters. Their target was a frieze of 19 figures carved by the celebrated sculptor Jacob Epstein. Some said that their style was too crude, their nudity offensive; others that they were falling down and posed a threat to pedestrians below.

Holden – an architect, not an artist – showed no interest in removing or repairing them. He took a hammer and chisel and tapped each figure to identify the weak portions. Those portions of the sculptures were then hacked off – heads, arms, legs – with no regard to the sculptures' integrity. And so they were left, mutilated, stuck on to a building. Holden later said, complacently, "Although some of the stones were disfigured in this process, the *general decorative* character of the band of figures was not seriously destroyed." The sculptor Henry Moore was so outraged that he refused ever to show at the Royal Academy in protest at their involvement.[2]

---

2. The story is told in Rosenberg and Cork 1992, p. 9. Their sources are: Charles Holden's memoir, March 5, 1958, in the Adams, Holden and Pearson archives, London; Epstein, 1942; and Cork's interview of Henry Moore, May 26, 1981. At the very end of his life, Moore did finally agree to a Royal Academy exhibition when he was ill; it was held posthumously. Today, moral rights in many countries protect the integrity of an artist's work from alteration, distortion or mutilation.

It's a Bad Architect story. What did Holden think he was doing? I fear his attitude encapsulates a problem we still find. He is thinking about the building: the big statement, the public face. He seems genuinely to have believed that the building's exterior existed as a form, with more or (after 1937) less decoration. What he is not thinking about is content, in this case a work of art with its own merits and purpose, something which required a closer form of attention than what he describes as a *generally decorative band of figures*.

Museums, you would think, no longer suffer from these problems. Museum interiors are now as sexy as their facades. Spaces are more open and easier to move through. Signage is clearer. Rich programs of learning are now in place to draw visitors in. New technologies have revolution-ized access to historic material, updated and animated collections, thrown obscure objects open to a wider public.

Yet so often these interiors seem out of step with their grand new buildings. It is as if the museum interior has had a lot of things thrown at it, without a real sense of how the drama of contemporary museum archi-tecture can be carried through. It's a difficult transition. Externally, new museums have been very good at engaging with the space around them. One thinks of the metaphorical connection of the Guggenheim in Bil-bao with the industrial buildings around it. Or Tadao Ando's Modern Art Museum of Fort Worth, Texas, given the nervous commission of having to be placed next to Louis Kahn's iconic Kimbell Art Museum. Or Zaha Had-id's extension to the Ordrupgaard Museum in Copenhagen. Hadid's new building creates an exciting set of relationships with both the old museum building and the garden which, as she explains, necessarily alters the build-ing's contour with its own spatial qualities.[3]

This is all very good. One doesn't want a building so prize-worthy that it forgets to join in with its setting. Indeed, it is essential for the public that the building makes sense of their approach to it.

Yet step inside and some of those meanings are no longer quite so con-genial. Who has not been overwhelmed by the vast foyer or the plethora

3. www.zaha-hadid.com

of competing directions? Who has not felt let down by the transition from grand statement to historic text as one approaches the first display case, even though the purpose of the visit was to get inside and see that Ming vase or those rare hieroglyphs? Rem Koolhaas sums up the conventional tedium of museum interiors by complaining that there are too many atriums everywhere![4]

Broadly, the problem falls into two categories: under-communication and over-communication. With under-communication, the Charles Holden principle of "building first" seems to have won the argument. Such museums are incredibly beautiful. The light drops from tall windows and glass roofs, the vistas are pure. The long lines and curves of the architecture are as much on display as the objects themselves. The overwhelming sense is of something cool, calm, orderly. And that may be appropriate to many collections. Praising the monastic sensibility that informs Barry Gasson's Burrell Collection in Glasgow, Jonathan Glancey wrote: "Despite the museum's immense solidity, the lasting impression is of Sir William Burrell's collections of precious objects, spanning 4000 years, set wherever possible against a changing natural backdrop of chestnuts and sycamores, bluebells and bracken."[5]

Where it is felt that such a spacious repository is not appropriate, the opposite approach tends to kick in, that of over-communication. Imagine any number of science museums or children's museums you have visited, and you get the point. Here nothing is allowed to be: everything must be described, enlivened, circumscribed with every support that text and technology, sound and cinema screen can do for it. One can admire the intention, but in terms of interior architecture, the result is inevitably disappointing.

In neither case, I would argue, has a proper understanding of museum experience and museum content been brought to bear. The objects are either sacrosanct or overwhelmed. The clean approach honours the collection with an appreciation that is principally (and, it must be said, narrowly)

---

4. OMA/AMO and Rem Koolhaas, 2004 (quoted in Zeiger, 2005, p. 15).
5. Glancey, 1989, p. 115.

aesthetic. The other ditches beauty for interaction, losing something of what makes museums definably different from other forms of cultural pastime.

Is there a solution? A resolution between the two? Before we can resolve these two seemingly incompatible approaches, we need to examine the causes that lie behind them. What is it that leads architects, museums, French presidents even, to push for one or the other of these styles?

Architects are interested in making statements – and not just with bricks and mortar. They often describe the architectural statements their buildings make in terms of challenge, engagement, contrast. They speak eloquently on the relationship every building has with its environment, its situation.

The results are compelling. Yet perhaps the problem with statements is that they preclude conversation. My statement is what I have to say to you. Our conversation is a dialogue between us.

When it comes to museum architecture, this division is palpable. The statements are exciting: Frank Gehry's silvery mitres in Bilbao, I.M. Pei's glass pyramid in the courtyard of the Louvre in Paris, Tadao Ando's Hyogo Prefectural Museum of Art in Kobe, Japan. These structures lay claim to their own importance. And rightly so: they are indeed grand and important statements, worthy of our attention and admiration.

But the problem with "big buildings" (if you'll forgive the category) is that they make it enormously difficult to scale down your expectations when you enter them. That's fine if the corridors of power allow for grand foyers and luxurious boardrooms, rocketing lifts to the 40th floor, offices whose whole point is a raft-like desk and a vast skyline. But in a museum, the scale of attention has to be immediately reduced, and it is at this crucial moment that museum interiors so often seem to fail. Too much space, and the contents look like ornaments to the building. Too little, and the first thing visitors experience is a sense of feeling pinched, a sense all the more exaggerated when the building itself has thrilled the visitor with the ambition of its exterior.

Robert Venturi recognized this conflict when he was designing a house in Chestnut Hill, Pennsylvania. Sensing the aesthetic determinism of his tall, A-frame front, he wrote eloquently about the ways in which one can achieve "big *and* small" – largeness of external scale but meaningful, necessarily smaller interiors. Admittedly, this does include placing a staircase on the second floor that leads nowhere.[6] Just the sort of thing museum visitors don't want – a path that leads to nothing! But Venturi is brilliantly drawing down the space to make a workable, humane interior.

I'll come later to more pragmatic solutions, but we need first to admit that large-scale buildings have two principal difficulties for any cultural institution. First, they establish an artificial size that, in reality, once people are engaged with what's inside, leaves them disappointed by grandeur. Secondly, and this too I shall return to, they make too strong a statement, not "we are talking", but "I am speaking".

Architectural statement might be described as one traditional environment that is being troubled by the demands not simply of global expression, but of the implied communities who are the audience for such cultural monuments. Yet another traditional environment lies within the very institutions who commission such buildings.

The museum mindset is hard to shift. The fundamental concern within museums is curation, quite literally the care and preservation of objects. It is almost as if what draws people to work in museums is a desire to hold on to the culture of the past, to build a bulwark against the speed and transience of modern society. It must therefore be acknowledged that before we free the museum space for compelling interior architecture, it may be that we need to free the curatorial mind.

It is often a question of expectations and expertise. Wishing to enjoy the benefits of the latter (for museums are nothing without the expert knowledge of their staff), we run into the attendant limitations that expertise can bring. Knowing an object well (better than anyone perhaps) or a subject intimately prefigures a strong sense of how it ought best to be presented to the public. Worse still, progressive curators can often be even more intransigent than their conservative counterparts, for they are equally confident not just of their subject matter, but of their currency in knowing about design, education, community access. The results here are

---

6. Venturi, 2002, pp. 118–19.

often cringing: comparisons with popular culture 20 years out of date, language that local groups no longer use, educational ideas long since trialled and binned. Such colleagues get the idea of engagement, but not the tone of it, and so insist on approaches which are no longer coldly erudite, it is true, but are instead parochial, patronizing and misguided. It's not hard to see the pendulum swing here from old-fashioned under-communication to embarrassing over-communication.

The problem, I would suggest, is not in the thinking (for the intentions here are good), but in finding real engagement with local communities. The ideas are there, but not the reality. We have rhetoric, but not result. The reasons for this are complex. They range from the narrow cultural make-up of the staff (and the assumptions they share) to the power structures within museums themselves – it is often not clear, as I'm sure many an AREP[7] consultant could tell you, who has final control over the content. For curators really to speak to new communities – and, by extension, for designers and architects to do so, too – they need to welcome local communities in. It means giving up some authority over public spaces – how they look, how they're used, what goes in them. But the result embraces the community in a way that good intentions never can. To bridge the gap between a perceived high-statement building and a low-result interior, what may be required is a dialogue with the most obvious voice usually excluded from the process: that of the visitor. If we're genuinely to listen and engage, we need to turn down the volume of the architectural and curatorial voice.

Martijn de Rijk and Gert Staal, describing the redesign of Leiden's National Museum of Ethnology in the Netherlands, wrote: "The greatest achievement of this project was probably that the individual passions and skills of all of these people contributed to the final product without it having become a patchwork of their personal ambitions."[8] It's not easy, but

---

7. Created in France in 1997, the AREP group consists of architects, planners, engineers, economists, technicians and designers – now more than 500 people in a dozen countries. It has undertaken hundreds of projects around the world, including train stations in Paris, Strasbourg and Shanghai.
8. Stall and de Rijk, 2003, p. 63.

they did it. The museum completely transformed itself for a modern audience without losing sight of its intellectual or architectural integrity. The Leiden experience is encouraging, for it draws on the strengths of tradition and innovation in different professionals to produce the best result. And the National Museum of Ethnology in Leiden, with its colourful sense of cool, is a wonderful result. It shows that we mustn't fear such a dialogue. Correctly marshalled, we end up not with decision by committee, but with vision by consensus.

I feel I'm being a bit hard on the experts. What makes museums hum is the commitment such people bring, the will to excellence, the pursuit of perfection. I would not for a moment wish to limit the curator, the architect or any of the host of designers and other professionals who make contemporary museums such exciting places. But I want museums to do even more. I want their international presence to be truly international, not just as peer review but as popular success with local communities across the globe. And it means thinking hard about the gap I described earlier between the big statements we so admire in museum buildings from the outside and the need to make their interiors match that first impression.

There are various ways of managing. Richard Rogers, for instance, flags up the need for sustainable architecture, sensitive to issues such as the environment and energy consumption. Indeed, he goes further:

> As a civil society we have to be conscious of what is needed not just
> to maximise profit, but to maximise value.... If we can fuse social
> concerns, technological and structural innovation, and environ-
> mentally responsible design, I believe we can create architecture that
> properly reflects the requirements of the 21st century.[9]

The social concerns Rogers speaks of take a variety of forms. Gehry's Bilbao museum manages to be thrillingly new, and yet honours the industrial architecture that surrounds it. He reinvests the historic meaning of the working community. The Phoenix project in Coventry aims to unify the rebuilt English city by incorporating the surviving buildings of its bomb-damaged past into its present architectural features. Such symbolic

---

9. Interviewed by Nina Rappaport in Gissen 2003, p. 173.

incorporation is not new, as Louise Campbell points out:

> The idea of preserving ruins as a token of endurance and recovery is an ancient one.... In 1948, Le Corbusier produced a design for the bombed French town of St Dié in which, by sheathing the ruins in concrete and glass, he proposed "to make the charred and ruined cathedral a living torch of architecture; to take charge of the misfortunes which have struck it, and make it a perpetual witness to the tragic event for the rest of time. The roof has fallen in, and the choir and transepts ... allow through their jagged shreds of red stone a glimpse of mountains and the waving foliage of great trees."[10]

Such a use of the past, building it into the city rather than lifting it out and displaying it as something "other" in a museum or civic forum, has enormous power for local residents, whose own experience is thus mirrored in the ongoing city. Past and present are fused. We can witness such sensitivity equally in the nuanced relationship with nature seen in Gasson's Burrell collection, Hadid's Ordrupgaard extension and many other successful buildings. Norway's Glacier Museum takes its strange planar forms from the nordic ice it explores: the building could hardly be a museum of anything else! And this is no easy metaphor, for landscape is primary to how communities understand themselves. Even the very colours new buildings use need to make sense of community feeling, for the choice of colour in vernacular architecture is often the result of long collective processes which can be easily offended or uncomfortably ignored.[11]

The point is perhaps to understand something Robert Venturi describes. Writing in the 1960s, Venturi complained that architecture was too definitive: it tended to be "either-or" (in Venturi's terminology) rather than "both-and". "Even 'flowing space'," he wrote, "has implied being outside when inside, and inside when outside, rather than both at the same time. Such manifestations of articulation and clarity are foreign to an architecture of complexity and contradiction."[12]

---

10. Campbell 2004, p. 22. Campbell quotes Le Corbusier from Collins, 1959, p. 478.

11. See Swirnoff 2000, and Lenclos and Lenclos 1999.

12. Venturi, p. 23.

Sensitivity to landscape or the built environment, willingness to address social concerns, produce, I would argue, the kind of complexity Venturi is talking about. Rather than reversing the building's meaning, they blur inside and out, so that something riskier, but more meaningful, occurs. Museums already do this, of course. Indeed, what the museum is has changed hugely, for it is no longer a chapel or a cathedral or (at its worst moments) a mausoleum. It is increasingly full of non-museum spaces more closely allied to the outside world: classrooms, cafés, cinemas, theatres. And more recently, museum design has shown a willingness to break down the old idea of fixity within the building itself. As Mimi Zeiger points out in her book *New Museum Architecture,* floorplans are out and flexible spaces are all the rage. With travelling exhibitions and alternative events, "museum gallery spaces are designed for endless possibilities", less for storage than for staging.[13] The spaces work harder these days, and if the garden blends into the building, then the street with all its community potential must be welcomed in, too.

This includes an understanding of the sheer physical process of making your way through a museum. Those very atriums Rem Koolhaas was mocking are essential, for museums are tiring places. And whether it's the Gemaldegalerie in Berlin or Tadao Ando's Kobe Museum, they require places of rest and contemplation to help visitors absorb what they see and to shape the experience at their own pace. As Kenneth Frampton has said of Ando's Modern Art Museum in Fort Worth (next to Kahn's Kimbell Museum):

> This labyrinthine megaform is a particularly compelling work, since the "museum fatigue" syndrome is dealt with by treating the galleries as self-contained volumes flanked on *all* sides by promenade space where visitors may momentarily pause before the prospect of an all-encompassing waterscape.[14]

Ando himself said of the building:

> My intent was to create an oasis.... Nature in the form of water, light and sky restores architecture from a metaphysical to an earthly plane

---

13. Zeiger, p. 11.
14. Frampton 2003, from the Introduction.

and gives life to architecture.... I want to emphasize the sense of time and to create compositions in which a feeling of transience or the passing of time is a part of the spatial experience.[15]

Ando's statement is a large one, and such ideas apply across a range of architectural experiences as they try to make sense of urban speed, noise and other distractions. They address all people and are right to do so. But can we be more specific still? Can we refine the idea, the problem perhaps, of who we are talking to?

I was recently invited to the new Capital Museum in Beijing. It's an exciting building, designed by the China Architecture Design and Research Group with the French practice, AREP. Its wide modernist eaves are inspired by traditional Chinese architecture, the rotunda bursts like a rocket from the building's glass-roofed facade.

As you enter, you see the red columns and elaborate colours of an imperial gate that stands at the back of the foyer, and behind, a huge biscuit-coloured brick wall, very modern, with a widely spaced pattern of recessed bricks. The gate made sense to me: I was in the Capital Museum of Beijing. But the wall behind looked monolithic and dull. Or such was my first impression, until Chinese colleagues explained that the pattern was familiar to every Chinese visitor. The design was resonant, even if my Western eyes needed to be taught how to see it.

Globalization sometimes runs away from such particularities. Rather than lose one pair of eyes, it reduces everything to a monoform meaninglessness. It was not hard to imagine a clean, bright wall in the striking new building, a pleasing neutrality that would create that familiar vast, cold interior we are getting used to in museum entrances. But how much more impressive to create something architectural that spoke to every Chinese visitor from the moment they walked in, bringing the scale of building and vast opening artifact together and thus working down into the museum.

There is something here of the ideals I.M. Pei articulated back in the 1940s. Discussing a student project at Harvard to design an art museum in Shanghai, Pei spoke of his search for an architectural style appropriate to

---

15. Ando 1995, p. 234.

modern China. He wrote to a friend that for some time he had "been wondering about the process of searching for a regional or 'national' expression in architecture ... to find an architectural expression that will be truly Chinese without any resort to Chinese architectural details and motives as we know them."[16] Walter Gropius, his teacher, was at first dismayed, but he later praised Pei's design, which "clearly illustrates that an able designer can very well hold on to basic traditional features – which he has found are still alive – without sacrificing a progressive conception of design".[17]

This is what the Capital Museum in Beijing does. It is absolutely modern and makes its big, 21st-century architectural statement on its own terms. But it has found a way to refer to meanings that make sense locally. Within its larger global remit, it has defined a traditional community that it can and wants to speak to.

Other communities have learned that one needs to risk difference in order to succeed. The glorious diversities of the National Museum of Australia in Canberra celebrate diversity. The team started from "the proposition that identity comes from facing difference, from finding it enjoyable as well as distressing".[18] The very suite of buildings – this one a progressive zigzag, that the pure curve of a sectional amphitheatre – rejects any notion of totality. They look instead for differences that co-exist alongside one another, much like the mixed Australian society they represent.

It may be fear of difference that leads to both under-communicating neutral spaces and over-communicating nervous ones. Yet where difference is celebrated, it succeeds. The Smithsonian's National Museum of the American Indian mixes various "native sensibilities" (as it terms them) in its attempt to represent the sheer multitude of native voices, from the palette of colours to the choice of materials. The desire is best assumed by the welcome wall, which is impressed with words of greeting in hundreds of native languages from across the Americas. Indecipherable, perhaps, but how important if one of those ciphers was your own submerged community, at last represented in a state building of international importance.

---

16. Wiseman 1990, p. 44.
17. Quoted in Wiseman, pp. 44–45.
18. Reed 2002, p. 64.

These new museums go further. They do not merely represent difference: they welcome in the voices of the people. The success stories are beginning to reshape both museum design and museum practice, making traditional approaches (architectural or curatorial) question how authoritative they need to be and what can be gained by letting some of that authority go. Examples range from the rich community-centred sensibility of the District Six Museum in Cape Town to the meeting place that has been built into Te Papa in New Zealand. Passing through the traditional gateway into the *marae*, the traditional Maori meeting place, visitors to Te Papa both witness indigenous culture and are welcomed into it. The traditional environment has found its new global aspect: explanation has become experience.

Naguib Mahfouz's statement about the will of the individual and the needs of the community stresses the importance of a balance that finds an analogy in the presentation of public collections. Global environments don't dissolve difference. They incorporate the specific not by overriding it but by speaking to it.

The Art of Redesigning our World

I gave this speech to mark the 100th anniversary of the Bergen National Academy of the Arts, Norway, in August 2009.

I feel deeply privileged to have had many opportunities to be involved in the extraordinary world of creativity and design, the world of art. These opportunities have taken me to many parts of the world – the East, Africa, the Americas, all over Europe and, not least, to Scandinavia and to Bergen, this place which has over the past 12 years been, and continues to be, such an important and meaningful part of my life.

Living and working in London, a city which is arguably the veritable mecca of design, has positioned me to take advantage of many gracious invitations to make pilgrimages to other parts of the world to share with and learn from those who, like me, have found ourselves drawn to engaging the world through the creative arts. As a result, my personal creativity has been expanded, shaped, challenged and changed by these many interactions and exchanges. Hopefully they have been deepened and broadened and, in turn, I also hope, I have added to the creativity of others. The saying that the only person who learns in the classroom is the teacher has been proven true over and over again here at the Bergen National Academy of the Arts. I am grateful to all of you today, to your many predecessors of the past 12 years and also to those I am proud to call my colleagues for allowing me to be part this dynamic and innovative community where, as we publicly state, we "encourage fearless discussion of tendencies and change in the contemporary art scene, culture and wider society". I am deeply indebted to all of you for your shaping of me professionally and personally.

We live in a world undergoing rapid transition. The scale and speed of globalization, driven by the twin engines of economics and technology, create many benefits but also leave many feeling left out. The question we should ask of this brave new world is one we could also ask at the national level: Is it art? Are we willing to leave the creation (the art) and the ordering (the design) of our changing world to those who place profit and expediency above all else, those for whom the pursuit of innovation comes at the cost of aesthetics, those for whom self-interest is the measure of all things?

The arts of any nation (and indeed of the one world we share) are the vibrant components of its soul, expressing not only the powerful mechanics of history in the making but also the spirit and vitality of its people and culture. There is much to be done about creating spirit and vitality among the people of today's world. If our "global village" is reflective of anything, it is that we have deepening divisions and inequalities between the peoples of the Earth and that the very planet is straining under the impact of our mindless and soulless continuing exploitation and plunder of her resources. David McFadden, curator of the New York Museum of Art and Design, has this to say: "If art has any kind of remedial value in the 21st century, it is going to be its ability to help us contemplate and deal with what we have created as a consumer society."

In an age of profound cultural transition, art is going through its own rite of passage. For some it is a time of crisis; for others it is a time of vibrant change. I see art as moving forward toward a diminishing of mere self-expression and an increase in social engagement, guidance in thinking, and contemplation and care of nature. In this new setting, the artistic endeavour of creativity and design can become more a spirit of the age than an institution, one element among several in establishing a global community of mutual care and respect that invites beauty and culture into a world of technological efficiency.

One of the greatest temptations into which any creative person can fall is to believe that all art is simply and uniquely about self-expression. Of course, self-expression is what makes artistic creation so variegated and unique, but we miss the mark if in all of our personal designing, inventing, developing, taking risks, challenging, rule-breaking and innovating, we fail to acknowledge the social nature of art and design. Let me attempt to explain this.

In a world having to redefine itself (financially, socially, geopolitically, etc), art will need to be more socially engaged, more connected to reality, more about ideas than about creating personal brands for artists in order to sell their work. Art is entering a new phase that is more reality-based, in which artists will have to learn to cooperate and collaborate, no longer as a one-person business or a marriage of convenience between art and money. As artists, as designers, looking inward for inspiration is something we can do fairly naturally. Looking outward at a world that is forever changing before our very eyes is a skill we will need to acquire if we are to help direct its formation. This will demand of us that our art not only reflects what we are but what we should be. In a world riddled hollow by consumerism we are challenged to say, "Enough!" Art, like morality, should dare to draw the line on the world's excesses. But art should also be fearless and daring in pushing boundaries and extending horizons. In my dealings with many students here over the past 12 years, I have realized that my work and that of my colleagues, I respectfully suggest, is not to open doors for them to enter in pursuit of future careers. Rather it is to identify and encourage those students who understand that this is their time to break down doors and reveal to those who are behind the times where they are stuck and what future awaits them.

Our age has been described as "The Age of the Death of Civilization", not least of all because all the resources upon which we have built past civilizations are close to running dry. The artist has a special task and duty, that of reminding people of their humanity and the promise of their creativity – creativity which, if shared in collaborative endeavour, has the power to breathe life into a world in which the rumours of the death of civilization may yet prove to be greatly exaggerated.

Dwight D. Eisenhower, post-war president of the USA at a time of great rebuilding and the dawn of the post-modern era, said: "The world must learn to work together or finally it will not work at all." He had seen the world come close to the brink. We are once again at such a moment. This academy is a leader because of its openness to including students and faculty from around the global village. You have instinctively understood the importance of reaching out and connecting to the world beyond Norway.

This celebration of 100 years of teaching art and design affords us a singular opportunity. It is an opportunity that will only come around once. It is one to which we have already shown our commitment and one which we need to expand: It is the art of redesigning our world consciously and intentionally.

Back Where It Belongs

Cultural restitution forms an important strand of work today for most museums working at an international level. This extract formed part of my acceptance speech for the honorary doctorate I received from the University of Westminster in June 2010.

Napoleon was so pleased with the art treasures he'd looted from across Europe that, recalling Andrea Mantegna's *Triumphs of Caesar*, he held a parade to display publicly the transport of all his continental booty into Paris. Lacking television crews, he did what any sophisticated Frenchman would to commemorate his triumph: he commissioned a two-metre-high Sèvres porcelain vase depicting the event.

Napoleon's reputation on culture was not good. He was famed for decades for having pointed his cannons and shot the nose off the Great Sphinx of Giza in Egypt. Perhaps it was too big to fit on the boat back to France. Perhaps it was too late to go on the vase. Perhaps it was the fury of a small man in front of a very tall thing.

We now know the Sphinx story is not true – the nose had gone several centuries earlier. But Napoleon's approach tells us something about cultural relations in the past: that to conquer another country is not simply to vanquish its people, but to appropriate its cultural history. What the story of the Sphinx reminds us is that what cannot be stolen is often destroyed.

My interest in this subject is not so much what has happened as what can be done to put things right. Two years ago I was approached by the

National Museum of Kosovo for help. They had heard that I championed the restitution of cultural property. Objects of art and religion, of strong communal value, are often seized along with other spoils of war. They can be forgotten when the treaties are signed and people are struggling to rebuild their houses, find clean water, put food on the table and set up schools for their children. Culture can seem a luxury. But the value of such objects must never be overlooked. In the places of conflict where I have worked – South Africa, Northern Ireland – I have seen that re-establishing cultural heritage is essential to healing the wounds of war.

On the eve of the collapse of Yugoslavia, the Kosovo Museum in Pristina made a huge mistake. It sent its entire permanent collection – 1368 archaeological objects – to the National Museum of Serbia in Belgrade for an exhibition on the treasures of Kosovo. When war broke out, this collection was impounded in Belgrade for safekeeping. As the conflict settled and a United Nations protectorate was set up in Kosovo, the Serbian authorities announced that they would not return the collection, claiming it as theirs.

My job was and is to negotiate the return of the collection back to Kosovo. I have insisted on depoliticizing the issue, explaining that collection belongs to the people of Kosovo, who have a right to see it. The objects in it can help heal a very damaged society, and are better seen in Kosovo than unseen in a basement in Belgrade.

The negotiations continue, as they must. But the result so far has been the return of the most important item, a 6000-year-old neolithic goddess on a throne, which now graces the stamps of Kosovo, so proud are they of her return. Discovered near Pristina, this beautiful and ancient terracotta figure, with her arms akimbo and her powerful head, is both a focus for national pride and something much larger, for she represents a past that is to be honoured, not impounded. By having her returned to Kosovo, I and my colleagues have tried to make the point that you cannot kidnap culture.[1]

---

1. The neolithic goddess was returned with the help of United Nations Special Envoy Michael Steiner. The other pieces remain to this day in the basement of the National Museum of Serbia.

The situation in Kosovo is not the first, nor tragically the last, in which the ravages of war have taken their toll on our common cultural heritage. Nor is the notion of cultural restitution without its precedents. The treasures of Europe amassed by Napoleon were returned to their countries of origin under the terms of the Second Treaty of Paris, following the French general's defeat at Waterloo. Restitution of art seized during the Second World War began almost immediately after the war ended. My great uncle, Professor Karol Estreicher, was the rector at the Jagiellonian University in Krakow at the time. He went to Nuremberg at the end of the war to negotiate and collect the famous Veit Stoss late gothic altar that today is the main attraction in St Mary's Church in Krakow. I would like to think my own work follows in his footsteps.

Individual or private restitution is one thing; that of entire public collections is quite another. Museums such as the Museum of London play an invaluable role in preserving culture and ensuring that it gets to the audiences it needs to reach. These days, our outlook extends even further. Sharing knowledge isn't just a question of passing over last week's lecture notes; it's a process that continues throughout one's professional life. When museum staff from Iraq visited the Museum of London, they were looking for work practices they could adapt in Iraq, yet their very questions, founded as they were in a different culture, brought a new perspective to our understanding of what it is we do.

The University of Westminster's own mission is analogous: "To provide high-quality education and research in both national and international contexts for the intellectual, professional and social development of the individual, and the economic and cultural enrichment of London and wider communities." It's a mission that the Museum of London happily shares.

But we are not the only ones looking to broaden our perspective. The Tropenmuseum in Amsterdam is devoted to the study of tropical cultures. Far from restricting its displays to single countries, its approach is global. It honours the local, with its displays on Latin America and the Caribbean, Asia and North Africa, but treats them in a world context, exploring their independent identities but also their shared relationships. As part of the Netherlands' Royal Tropical Institute, its mission sees cultural preservation and restitution in the widest sense. The concern is for "international and intercultural cooperation ... to contribute to sustainable development, poverty alleviation, and cultural preservation and exchange".

A better approach for world peace could not be imagined. Perhaps it is time we stopped thinking about the global *economy*. Perhaps it's time we started imagining a world culture – where individual identity is celebrated, not subsumed, and is to be shared as a universal human good.

Cultural restitution can seem a thing of the past. And yet we have only to open our newspapers to see its relevance to our own time. Take Afghanistan, where international outrage at the Taliban's destruction of the famous statues of the Buddha at Bamiyan has brought plans together to have them rebuilt. *Seventy per cent* of the exhibits in the Darulama Museum, 10 kilometres south of Kabul, were either destroyed or looted. (Imagine the National Gallery up the road losing 70% of its paintings!) Many of the Kabul artifacts ended up in neighbouring Pakistan. The prime minister of the time, Benazir Bhutto, pledged to set aside funds to enable the return of these precious objects. International pressure has encouraged Islamabad to honour her commitment.

Iraq remains an even more pressing concern. The director of the National Museum of Iraq in Baghdad has recently spoken in London and elsewhere of the devastation caused to Iraq's cultural legacy. Each week seems to bring new losses. Money has been committed, expertise in conservation offered, the Department for Culture, Media and Sport has pledged its support. But the circumstances are worsening.

What can *we* do? We can work toward a better understanding of other cultures and toward ensuring their autonomy and preservation. The director-general of UNESCO, Koïchiro Matsuura, makes this point strongly: "UNESCO's recent experience in war-torn and post-conflict situations has shown that culture can play a key role in consolidating the peace process, restoring national unity and building hope for the future."[2]

Michelangelo's *David* was restored earlier this year in Florence. He had his spots removed, his stains wiped. His former figleaf offered no protection

---

2. From Koïchiro Matsuura's speech responding to points 4, 5, 6 and 21 of the executive board's agenda at UNESCO's 180th session, October 9, 2008.

from restorer Cinzia Parnigoni's capable hands, and she swabbed and buffed every marble inch of him.

This may be what people think of when one speaks of "cultural restitution". Something old that the worthy see fit to clean up now and then and return to its pedestal.

And yet it's worth remembering that among those who paid for the restoration were Mel Gibson and Sting.

Culture isn't something old and dusty. It is the things we would not be without. As you walk down the streets of Westminster, it is the Charing Cross built by Edward I for his beloved Queen Eleanor and restored as part of our common past in the 19th century. It is the beautifully maintained parks of Pall Mall and St James where we've all walked in the sunshine and admired the ducks. It is what is felt by the crowd gathered from around the world who stand at the feet of lions in Trafalgar Square, feeding pigeons, photographing Nelson, listening to the toll of Big Ben. It is a thousand protestors gathering from across the country in the same place to argue their democratic rights.

Culture is not the past. It is living history that means something to us now. In London especially, it's how we live. It is our duty to cultivate and maintain it; to defend and restore it where we may; and most of all, to enjoy it.

Contested Human Remains

The Museum of London's international conference on human remains in October 2004 marked an important step in recognizing the variety of global practices to care for and manage human remains in museum collections. This paper formed my keynote address.

In the 25 years or so during which the issue of human remains in museums has been argued are we any nearer to an agreement or a consensus as to what should be done about these extreme collections?

The fact that many museums have voluntarily repatriated such holdings or that others have been forced to do so by legislation has helped to move the discussion along in practice. But in principle, the divide remains between those who argue for their return on cultural-religious grounds and those who argue for their retention on scientific grounds. Is a middle ground possible between what seem to be mutually exclusive positions? Is compromise possible, even desirable, or is this a case of all or nothing?

The case for both sides has been made many times over. Both have power to convince and convict. Indigenous arguments cite such values as living legacy, cultural identity, social meaning and living ancestry as motivation for repatriation while the scientific community values these collections for what they can tell us about our development as a species and also for the potential they may hold for future learning.

It is argued that this contestation highlights the difficulty of reconciling differing value systems, that of *natural* science and of *supernatural* belief systems; between the rationalism of the West and indigenous belief systems. The unarticulated assumption of the superiority of Western rationalism sits uncomfortably with many who are sensitive to the historic circumstances under which the remains were acquired in the first place and are concerned with the ethical implications that, up to now, have been neglected or ignored. (We are of course not talking about the massive uncontested collections but the disputed collections, which often form a small but important part of such holdings.)

I think it safe to say that few of us who curate and study human remains would totally dismiss the social and spiritual values and significance they hold for others, not just for indigenous communities but also for modern individuals and communities in the West and elsewhere. And not all indigenous communities reject the scientific value of these collections, nor do they all demand their return. The museum community has made significant progress in appreciating the relevance of the non-scientific side of the argument. The remaining gulf, I believe, is a diminishing one. It may be one that we will have to learn to live with rather than attempt to traverse at all costs. It may also be one that requires far more than the appreciation of opposing views or the careful drawing up of ethical and legal guidelines, whether by the museum community itself or by governments and global cultural institutions such as the International Council of Museums (ICOM) or UNESCO.

We are mostly familiar with the wide spectrum of opinion that has been eloquently presented over a quarter of a century, and it is not my intention to restate the many positions on this issue.

A position based purely on the higher principles of the rationality of Western science, while downplaying the broader and deeper cultural-spiritual principles at work in indigenous communities, has not served up an adequate solution as yet and probably never will. Nor is it likely that the arguments for repatriation on those now familiar grounds of cultural identity, tradition and spirituality will succeed in persuading those who are not open to such persuasion. Not only do we have opposing cosmologies at work here – we have no common language with which to communicate even our differences.

While not all extreme collections have been acquired though illegal and sometimes violent means (nor do they all come from outside of Britain), for the sake of this paper, I will focus mainly on what has been described as "bones of contention" – those collections whose return is being demanded by various claimant communities.

Of considerable concern to the issue of these contested human remains is how they were acquired and how they come to be in our museums in the first place. Suffice to say that many find it difficult to articulate the harsh truths surrounding many such acquisitions. Take for example the following statement from a draft of "Code of Practice for the Care of Human Remains in Museums" by the Department of Culture, Media and Sport:

> However, there is also recognition that, because of their origin, human remains should hold a unique status within collections and this puts responsibilities on the museum in the way they are acquired, curated and displayed. It is also the case that a number of human remains held in British museums and collections were acquired, often between 100 and 200 years ago from indigenous peoples in colonial circumstances *where there was a very uneven divide of power. There has also been recognition that some human remains were acquired in circumstances that by modern standards, and those of the time, would be considered unacceptable.*[1] [My italics.]

Contrast this with the following statement from a newspaper article on the subject written by Jane Morris:

> Items were collected in various ways. Some were taken by amateurs and trophy-hunting soldiers. Others were taken by scientists looking for evidence of evolution and racial variance in studies that speak overwhelmingly of the attitudes of empire as well as enlightenment.... No one would, or could not, collect like this today.[2]

She goes on to point out that there existed no collections of victims of, for example, the Holocaust.

---

1. DCMS 2004, p. 7.
2. Morris 2002.

For all our codes of ethics, best practice and legal guidelines, there continues to exist distrust and antagonism between the parties concerned. We have members of our profession who do not seem to be able to temper their positions, and they come across as arrogant and totally devoid of sympathy to any argument other than their own.

In an attempt to contribute to this debate, I want to explore drawing a parallel between this issue and that of a well-known example of conflict and one of the methodologies employed in bringing about a mutually acceptable solution. The example I have in mind is that of South Africa and the national program of seeking reconciliation post Apartheid.

The role and function of the South African Truth and Reconciliation Commission in helping victims and perpetrators come to terms with the atrocities committed during their divided past and to assist in building a shared future in a post-Apartheid society hold some interesting parallels. Despite the obvious injustices of the system and the existence of a mountain of evidence that would have been sufficient to convict the Apartheid leaders and their various agents and instruments of oppression and state-sanctioned criminality, the path to reconciliation did not focus upon the imposition of justice through the application of law. Rather, it emphasizes the acknowledging of guilt and the willingness of perpetrators to tell the truth.

This process of truth-telling on the part of perpetrators in many cases led to the revealing of the location of the remains of victims of torture and state-sanctioned murder. For those who told the truth, amnesty was (in most cases) granted. For the families and comrades of the victims, having heard the public acknowledgement of guilt and the facts surrounding the victims, these revelations helped them to lay to rest both the physical remains of the victims and their own powerful feelings of grief and anger. In some instances, the remains were never recovered, yet because it was believed that the truth had been told, amnesty was given.

At the heart of this process was a simple but profound realization, that while not necessarily universally true, enlightened self-interest is a powerful incentive for many to do what is right and thereby achieve the best (not necessarily the perfect) possible result under difficult circumstances.

Enlightened self-interest is usually defined as a philosophical stance from which one acts to serve the interests of another or others, the consequence of which is ultimately to achieve or serve one's own ends. In the case of the South African example, telling the truth served to help the victims' families know the truth about their loved ones' deaths and the location of their remains while at the same time availing amnesty from prosecution for the perpetrators (who also had to prove that they were acting under orders). It is now part of the historic record that, in many cases, victims' families and perpetrators were often publicly reconciled during and after the Truth and Reconciliation hearings.

In contrast, *unenlightened self-interest* places the interests/ends of the individual or group above that of others in order to protect those interests at all costs. This results, more often than not, in ongoing conflict, decreased efficiency and increased costs as a result of having to concentrate energy and resources on protecting one's interests.

Rather than arguing that we are dealing with conflicting sets of beliefs, is it possible that we could commit to exploring the potential acting in the interests of others in order to achieve our own? This would of course require that the other side similarly commits. But the all or nothing option is clearly not working for either party involved. Both sides are in danger of being so right as to be dead right, and there is no merit in being so right that the potential for cooperation dies in the process. Tristram Besterman, director of the Manchester Museum, makes an important point that is often overlooked:

> Good science rests on humane, moral and ethical standards underpinned by the principle of informed consent. But this is not just about the legitimacy of science; it is also about having the generosity of spirit to recognize the moral legitimacy of indigenous claims on such human remains. The contested human remains in Western museums were collected at a time of gross inequality of power.... We now have the opportunity to redress that historic imbalance acknowledging that this may well entail a loss to science that will in its turn heal open festering wounds. And it won't all be a loss for the Western museum or the anthropologist; there is plenty of evidence that dialogue and transfer of authority back to where it rightfully

belongs leads to a healthy relationship in which cultural exchange and understanding can flourish between the museum or the scientist and the indigenous community. That seems to me at least a pretty good dividend for addressing past injustice and working with the willing consent of indigenous peoples.[3]

The past is not the only consideration with which we should be concerned. Our relationship with communities around the globe with regard to the sharing of knowledge cannot be sacrificed upon the altar of either myopic self-righteousness or misguided altruism.

As we begin the 21st century, it is clear that neither the natural sciences nor the supernatural belief systems have sole claim to the minds and hearts of humankind. This will probably be the case for a long time to come if not for all time, and there is, therefore, a need to find a language that is able to help both sides communicate across this cosmological divide. Such a language will need to speak to some common interest. I would argue from pure pragmatism that the most common of all interests is that of the enlightened self.

But this requires a commitment to understanding, if not totally accepting, the concerns and interests of the other side and the willingness to consider making concessions. By way of example, the availing of dedicated "sacred spaces" within the museum environment for the displaying of human remains is one way of acknowledging the particular significance of such a display.

Enlightened self-interest draws on the appreciation that we already share common ground as a species that has a shared humanity. Such a shared humanity is not only that of a shared past but of a shared present and future. Anthropology has shown us that race and ethnicity are false categories and that there is universality to humanity. Such humanity, it seems to me, cannot easily divorce its soul from its mind. When we attempt to do so, we do not cause the other side injury but rather inflict a universal pain on the single species that we are.

---

3. Personal correspondence with the author in 2003.

Just as in South Africa, the people of that formerly artificially divided nation have had to strive toward reconciliation based upon more than the mechanics of justice, so it is likely that we will only move forward if and when we acknowledge the artificiality of a world view based purely on science that excludes the persistence of the existence of a wide range of unscientific values and authorities.

Critics of the Truth and Reconciliation Commission have argued that the absence of any reference to justice has severely weakened the prospects of reconciliation in South Africa. With the benefit of hindsight, it is arguable that such an emphasis would have severely impeded what reconciliation and nation building has been achieved thus far.

Restoring the legitimacy of more than a single world view and acknowledging that there exists the possibility of understanding ourselves and our world by way of different truths may open up for us all new paths of exploration and lead us to deeper discoveries.

Debating the issue among ourselves and developing solutions that largely serve our own interests will not work. We may not be able or indeed willing to restore or repatriate these bones of contention. But as South Africa has shown the world, restorative justice is not demanded when there is the willingness to take the path of truth-telling and enlightened self-interest.

Repatriation in the Service of Society and its Development

In February 2007 UNESCO held an expert meeting in Nuuk, Greenland, on the repatriation of cultural heritage. This paper formed my address at the conference.

The *Codex Siniaticus* in the British Library is the oldest complete New Testament in the world.[1] In terms of surviving manuscripts it ranks among the most valuable. In the 19th century it left Mount Sinai, where it had happily survived over a thousand years, and arrived in London via Leipzig and St Petersburg. As it travelled, pages went missing, and today there are fragments in three locations. This year the *Codex* is being reconstructed and repatriated digitally in a three-year project involving stakeholders in four countries. New narratives of its provenance are being researched and written, and a joint effort is being put into applying the latest techniques to its interpretation rather than separate efforts directed at securing title against each other. This project shows the creative and innovative approaches to different forms of repatriation where an actual claim to title does not exist but where the cultural value of the work underlines the importance of the

---

1. I am grateful to Oliver Urquhart Irvine at the British Library for bringing this project to my attention.

object to both source countries and more recent owners. It's a positive story. It's a story unimaginable in an earlier non-globalized world.

We live in extraordinary times, in which rapid change and new developments mark the spirit of the age. Change affects every aspect of life, personally, nationally and globally. No one and nothing is left untouched or unaffected by it. Globalization, while opening the door for massive efficiency gains, also brings with it new challenges: increased pace of change and the rapid transfers of wealth, power and knowledge. We in Britain have shifted from Empire to modernity, and while we live in the latter, many of our assumptions and attitudes remain rooted in the former. These strain our existing systems – regionally, nationally and internationally – systems which evolved at a time when global structures were different. They put new demands on our existing institutions and, critically, on leadership.

Museums like the Museum of London, as societal institutions, have not been spared the challenges that come from being part of the globalizing world. We too are being challenged to redefine who we are, what our role and purpose is and how we understand ourselves and others. It is within this larger context that we must engage the discourse on repatriation, restitution and return.[2]

The language employed in the ongoing debate on repatriation, restitution and reparation reveals some of the inherent problems that attend this vexed debate. It is a language fraught with words such as *illicit, illegal, stolen, disputed, claim* and *demand*. It is, inherently, an argumentative and conflictual discourse, which involves responses of defence in the face of attack. These are also antagonistic words reinforcing the separation of museums from the people they serve.

We would do well to clarify the conceptual scope of what we understand by restitution, return and repatriation, all of which refer to the transfer of property to its previous location, and jointly seek to use one understanding internationally when applying these terms. Often the terms

2. The Museum of London holds one of the largest and most important collections of archaeologically recovered human remains in the world. For more information, see Lohman and Goodnow 2006.

refer to the physical transfer of objects and are rarely applied to the non-tangible benefits of repatriation such as the transfer of authority.[3] This issue is complicated by varying national applications of these words, such as the American use of the word "repatriation" with regard to so-called native or indigenous people's loss of objects to colonizers, and often with regard to claims of human remains removed from graves and placed in museums.

We urgently require a new set of words and language around repatriation shifting to the positive idea of museums and libraries sharing and presenting collections. We understand the issues around repatriation. They have been discussed, published, presented and generally thrashed to the point that has engendered in some a sense of frustration, as voiced in the words of Wojciech Kowalski, ambassador with responsibilities for cultural restitution at the Polish Ministry of Foreign Affairs: "Restitution is a reaction to a violation of law – to robbery, frankly speaking. To conduct restitution is a duty…. As a rule, however, restitution should be a straightforward restoration of the original state of affairs."[4]

The discourse has not been without its fruits. Indeed, much good has come out of wrestling with this issue, as has been and continues to be done, by members of the international museum community. Yet we are far from having reached a solution or consensus. This conference holds its place in a long line of illustrious international meetings held over many years which have moved forward the debate, albeit painfully slowly.[5] Conferences such as this are as a result of our recognition that this is not a static intellectual debate. It is an ongoing, living conversation about an ever-developing issue, which impacts upon the lives of people and nations around the world as they themselves continue to develop socially, economically, politically and culturally.

Ours is an age of deep cultural transition, in which the cultures of our national and international institutions are being challenged as never before. And, yes, even museums, those bastions of immutability, are not being

---

3. Pickering 2001.
4. Kowalski 2002.
5. For a short summary, see National Museum of Denmark 2004, pp. 11–17.

spared. Today they are playing leading roles in encouraging dialogue, civic development and economic regeneration, responding to changes in society around them, but also representing those changes.

That we continue to feel strongly enough about cultural repatriation to spend the time to meet here in Greenland is evidence of the fact that the museum community itself is involved in the global process of transformation. Ours is a time of opportunity and challenge, a time to reassess the role of institutions in the life of communities. Museums, as with all other cultural institutions, are confronted with challenges and choices. In facing these, we are profoundly aware that uniform action is difficult. We are operating in very different contexts of history, law, conventions and a multitude of factors unique to our circumstances. How are we to succeed where others are seemingly having great difficulty?

I would venture to suggest that we are facing something of a crisis in the sense that it is a time for decision making, a moment of truth. The crisis has to do with the increasing sense of alienation as experienced by many in the developing nations of our globalizing world. It is a time marked by both the *sense of loss* of a passing age and the sense of *losing out* on the coming age. It is no wonder then that the peoples of the world seek a sense of self, of identity, and attempt to piece together those parts of their history and heritage that have shaped and determined their sense of place and purpose. Entering into a globalized world and a global conversation is not just about modernizing yourself – it is about bringing a clear sense of who you are and having confidence in your own identity so that you can respond to that of others and accommodate them.

The question can therefore be put in this way: How can nations or cultural communities tell the story of their own heritage for their own people when some of the essential aspects of that narrative are in the possession of others? This is a question that goes beyond mere legal solutions. It is profoundly an ethical question and while we in the museum community are as much under the obligation to behave ethically as everyone else, we are not ethicists by training. As part of our responsibility of presenting and opening cultural meaning we should be setting a new skill set. But in the meantime, I suggest that the discourse would be greatly enhanced by the involvement of those who have such expertise. If we have learned anything from the ongoing debate, it is this: we need to open and broaden the conversation by the inclusion and involvement both of other expert voices and the public as a whole.

There is no easy answer to this. Indeed, it is not so much about having the right answers but rather asking the right questions and being in right relationship with what is happening. Jiddu Krishnamurti, the Indian philosopher of the 1960s, spoke of the need to "free ourselves from the known",[6] and Werner Heisenberg, the quantum physicist, challenged the classical concepts of science by introducing what he called "the uncertainty principle" through which he challenged the strongly held belief that the role of the scientist was merely that of a detached observer and an objective commentator.

George Soros sums it up in a recent publication:

> The Age of Reason ought to yield to the Age of Fallibility.... Unfortunately, we have left the Age of Reason behind us without coming to terms with our fallibility. The values and achievements of the Enlightenment are being abandoned without something better being put in place. Recognizing our fallibility has a positive aspect that ought to outweigh the loss of an illusory perfection. What is imperfect can be improved, and the improvement can manifest itself not only in our thinking, but also in reality.[7]

The International Council of Museums (ICOM) defines museums as "non-profit-making, permanent institutions in the service of society and its development, and open to the public, which acquire, conserve, communicate and exhibit, for purposes of study, education and enjoyment, material evidence of people and their environment".[8] This role and definition of museums has come a long way since their formal establishment 200 years ago as places for the display of artifacts and for study.

For this paper, however, I have been asked to address these questions: What are the obligations of museums in addressing the museological aspects of repatriation? How are the responses of Western museums

---

6. Krishnamurti, 1969.
7. Soros 2006, pp. 14-15.
8. ICOM 2004, para. 1.

toward this issue responsible for the formulation of international museum standards, and how are these standards being challenged when the objects are not requested for museum purposes, but to be used in a living tradition (for instance, the reuse of religious paraphernalia or the reburial of human remains)? Why is Europe so reluctant in assisting claimants in repatriation? And how do we change the debate from focusing merely on conflicts to emphasizing progress and partnerships?

The first question relates to our obligation as museums. Obligation is a strong word. It suggests duty. We are duty-bound and constrained not only to address but to act on the matter at hand.

From where does this obligation arise? We are all familiar with the origins of the obligation: Two key instruments are, of course, the UNESCO Convention on Cultural Property[9] and the UNIDROIT Convention on Stolen or Illegally Exported Cultural Objects.[10]

The UNESCO convention has a clear and conscious political motivation, and addresses the issue of repatriation from the standpoint that developed nations have enriched their cultural store with the cultural and artistic property of developing nations, leaving them the poorer in every respect, not least of all in their sense of identity. Expatriation of others' heritage, or sourcing, (interesting euphemisms) could, in this sense, therefore be regarded as national identity theft. The convention is not without its detractors who take affront at the accusation and who, as pointed out by Mira Rajan, refer to UNESCO's attitude as that of "cultural nationalism":

> The strong stance of the UNESCO Convention on repatriation ...
> has led to difficulties in securing its acceptance internationally. In
> particular, many art-market countries have been reluctant to join the
> Convention because of fears about its impact on cultural heritage
> and the lucrative art trade in their territories.[11]

---

9. Convention on the Means of Prohibiting and Preventing the Illicit Import, Export and Transfer of Ownership of Cultural Property, adopted in Paris on November 17, 1970.

10. Drafted by the International Institute of the Unification of Private Law and adopted in Rome on June 24, 1995.

11. Rajan 2002.

The UNIDROIT convention has as its distinguishing focus objects acquired through illicit trade, but its success in attracting support has been even less satisfactory than that of the UNESCO convention, which, in recent years, as shown by the UK and others' decision to participate, has begun to make some positive gains internationally.

Obligation is, therefore, tied up with being signatories of either or both of these conventions, and in the case of the UK, I am speaking primarily of the UNESCO convention to which we are signatories. By acceding to the UNESCO convention, the UK and other member states have a legal obligation to abide by all the tenets of the Convention.

The UNESCO convention is, however, more than a legal obligation.

It is also part of a wider conversation within the UN and, in particular, the UNDP on cultural liberty and human development in today's diverse world. It is in the context of this wider international conversation that the role of museums, in helping to forge the notion of national intellectual and cultural property made up of private and otherwise acquired collections in the formation of national identity, is to be understood.

Our role has been traditionally understood as conserving, studying and displaying in order that the place of cultural heritage can be understood as a fundamental aspect of our common yet diverse human story. It is precisely because of this that we cannot divorce ourselves from the significance of our role in helping to shape humanity's sense of meaning. The role of museums has been redefined since they first came into existence as institutions 200 or so years ago. The legal framework, too, has adapted to this, but often agreement and approaches have not. This extends to the way that culture is viewed generally in society and emphasizes the need to work with educationalists to build cultural literacy so that when museums have adapted, the public is responsive. The UNESCO definition of the museum requires that *we* consider our obligation legally but also ethically.

The ethical dimension of our obligation has come about as a result of the global focus on the rights of individuals and nations, which have grown in momentum and urgency in recent decades. The development of a *culture of rights* and the concomitant issue of *cultural rights* has broadened the meaning of rights beyond a legal definition.

At this point, we may pause to consider what we mean by "ethics".

The Josephson Institute of Ethics defines it in this way:

> Ethics refers to standards of conduct, standards that indicate how one should behave based on moral duties and virtues, which themselves are derived from principles of right and wrong. As a practical matter, ethics is about how we meet the challenge of doing the right thing when that will cost more than we want to pay.[12]

I prefer this to the dictionary definition, which speaks of the philosophical study of the moral value of human conduct and the rules and principles that ought to govern it. This takes us into the moral sphere of human existence. It is a place that that museums have not historically occupied and where we have been loathe to go. More, it demands of us a cost more than we are willing to pay.

Herein lies the heart of the problem regarding our inability to deal with the issue of repatriation. The problems of prevailing disparate legal conventions among source nations, our concerns over the capacity and capability of claimants to look after their own cultural property are all real and rightly occupy our professional minds. But none of these are insurmountable problems. They are challenges that provide a host of opportunities to share expertise, to build capacity, to grow a sense of global community. Culture is going to play a vital part in growing this community – it's a medium of conversation. It's how we read others and so is not only dependent on ethics, but also a crucial part of what defines us and them.

Let me return to the notion of obligation, which implies not what *is* but what ought to be. The session on Ethical Considerations is germane to this discussion and I do not wish to re-cover this ground. But I want to suggest that we may be able to begin reconsidering the costs of making ethical decisions if we are faithful to the demands and dynamics of the world of which we are part and which is rethinking itself and that *we* begin to rethink the museum and our role not as it is but as it ought to be. In other words, in order to do what we ought, we have to develop beyond what we have been and largely still are. Our Western museum tradition has given rise

---

12. Josephson 2005.

to policies and practices (including funding) that do not equip us to move easily beyond that which the museum currently is – an institution made up of collections – and our role in respect of this – that of preservers, conservers and scientific observers of such collections. We need to consciously move beyond this outdated model and way of thinking. This is why we feel so strongly about the formulation of international standards on repatriation, which are *our* standards, even when we are sympathetic to the deeply held feelings of claimants who require the return of cultural property on the grounds of living tradition. We seek assurance, often deemed beyond the current capability of claimants, that they will care for their own property. Our motives are not, in most cases, entirely ignoble. Our concerns are based upon our need to fulfil our established sense of acting responsibly as curators, as those who care about the conservation of cultural objects. The challenge we face is to move beyond this known way of being.

Quoting Wojciech Kowalski once more:

> When evoking the concepts of "national heritage" or "national ownership" we deal with a dual understanding of that law. There is, obviously, the ownership rights of individuals and that of institutions, even of the state but, from the perspective of safekeeping the heritage and fulfilling the duty to hand it over to future generations, this right takes second place to the concepts of preserving common human legacy and collections of cultural property, which together constitute national heritage. I believe this is the way to interpret international and European conventions on the subject.

The past decade or so in particular has been a period of deep crisis marked by tension and clashes between and within nations. Such conflict has variously and contentiously been described as clashes of civilizations, cultures, world views or values. It is an ongoing tension that deepens in intensity daily. The role of culture in the 21st century has become central to the discourse on how an increasingly "global" world can survive without the threat of some being swamped by the overpowering cultural force of others.

Museums exist within this complex global environment and are not spared the pressures and challenges to transform and find our role and meaning. We are not able to stand apart from the societies in which we exist, *inter alia*, to interpret and reflect diverse society to itself. In another statement on culture, UNESCO has this to say:

> A museum works for the endogenous development of social communities whose testimonies it conserves while lending a voice to their cultural aspirations. Resolutely turned toward its public, community museums are attentive to social and cultural change and help us to present our identity and diversity in an ever-changing world.[13]

I see museums as faced with the challenge which both Krishnamurti and Heisenberg presented decades ago: to free ourselves from the known ways of being a museum by exploring the role of being an actively involved participant in society and allowing society to be actively involved, not just a place where society collects its memories. We are part of the very story we tell and not just the storytellers or places where the story is told. In the case of repatriation, this means that we have to face the challenge being presented to us to respect the right of people to tell their own stories about their cultural journey and give their own meaning to those things that have shaped them as communities and nations.

Repatriation is essentially an act of justice, of right doing. As such, as we have seen in other areas of human endeavour, justice requires that truth be faced before reconciliation is possible. A part of that truth is concerned with our duty to be true to what and who we are, not only as curators of past heritage but as those who have the unique privilege of helping to cultivate the process of ongoing human development and creativity. I take strength from the example I began with and from imagining a scenario where good faith, creativity and new ideas begin to shape a new way forward.

---

13. UNESCO 2002.

Forward to Freedom

When curator Annette Day at the Museum of London approached me with a proposal to hold an exhibition to celebrate the 50th anniversary of the founding of the Anti-Apartheid Movement in London, I enthusiastically embraced the idea. This speech was given at its opening in June 2008.

In April 1990, on his first visit to London since his release from prison, Nelson Mandela made pilgrimage to a house in Muswell Hill where, in 1962, he had once been a guest. His hosts then had been Oliver Tambo, leader-in-exile of the African National Congress, and his wife, Adelaide. The three-storey North London house, which was the third London home to the South African family who had, on arrival in London, lived in Finchley and then in Highgate, was in no way exceptional – except for one thing. It had for almost three decades provided residence to what was literally the South Africa's government-in-exile. For 30 years many of South Africa's most distinctive post-Apartheid leaders were to pass through its non-distinctive front door. The house now bears a plaque commemorating its illustrious occupant, and a bust of Tambo adorns a nearby park where the Tambo children once played. Various busts of Nelson Mandela also now grace parts of the city of London, and a life-sized statue in Parliament Square is further testimony to the link between London and the nation of South Africa during its struggle against Apartheid.

By the end of the 1950s the South African government had outlawed almost all forms of public political activity and arrested or placed bans on most of the ANC leaders. So the ANC turned to the strategy of boycott as a non-violent means of protest. At its 1958 annual conference the ANC announced: "The economic boycott is going to be one of the major political weapons in the country." Together with its allies, it looked to overseas support, convinced that local purchasing power combined with that of sympathetic organizations overseas would provide a damaging if not devastating weapon against Apartheid.

Fifty years ago, on June 26, 1959, a group of South African exiles and their British supporters met in London's Holborn Hall to form the Boycott Movement to call for a boycott of fruit, cigarettes and other goods imported from South Africa. Nine months after the start of the Boycott Movement, on March 21, 1960, events in South Africa took a tragic turn as demonstrators in the township of Sharpeville were gunned down by South African forces. Within a month the African National Congress and Pan African Congress were banned and hundreds of political activists detained. The Boycott Movement transformed itself into the Anti-Apartheid Movement, taking up residence in Ruskin House, Croydon, calling for government sanctions against South Africa and for support for all those struggling against Apartheid.

But the Anti-Apartheid Movement did not restrict its activities to Apartheid. It sought to expose what it termed the "unholy alliance" of South Africa, Rhodesia and Portugal, which refused to give up its colonies of Mozambique, Angola and Guinea-Bissau, and it worked to end South Africa's illegal occupation of Namibia.

While the Anti-Apartheid Movement was born in London and was peculiarly English, it soon moved beyond being a British organization. It acted as an agent of change that sought to influence policy at the United Nations, the Commonwealth and the Organization of African Unity, as well as the International Olympic Committee and the then Imperial Cricket Conference. The Anti-Apartheid Movement has a unique working relationship with the leaders of the liberation movements in South Africa and especially the inspirational Oliver Tambo who came to London in 1960 and who helped to nurture it to become the largest protest movement in

Britain and one of the largest social movements in the world.

For 35 years, hundreds of thousands of people in Britain joined Anti-Apartheid Movement campaigns, with numerous protests held in Trafalgar Square outside the South African Embassy. What had begun as occasional demonstrations of small groups of picketers swelled to frequent and regular massive demonstrations by thousands of sympathetic Londoners and others in London at the time, many of them exiles who had relatives in South Africa. It has been suggested that as London became increasingly cosmopolitan, particularly in the later half of the 20th century, its sense of human rights and justice intensified and moved beyond the political to the almost personal.

This personal dimension of the Anti-Apartheid Movement in London found expression, for example, in initiatives by such figures as the clerics Trevor Huddleston and Canon Collins of St Paul's Cathedral, who were both instrumental in establishing humanitarian support programs including scholarships and the provision of legal defence and aid for political leaders and their families. These programs had their operations in London. (It is interesting to note that another great South African anti-Apartheid leader who has strong links with the city of London is Archbishop Desmond Tutu, who was a student at King's College London during the early 1970s.)

London, as a major world centre, provided a stage for a global spotlight to be focused on the issue of Apartheid in South Africa and other political and social hotspots. Professor Kader Asmal, a former minister of both Education and Environment in post-Apartheid South Africa (and himself an exile in Dublin, Ireland), has expressed the view that London became "the conscience of the world" by providing the space for liberation movements to keep the crime of Apartheid before the eyes of the international community. He said:

> In those years the Anti-Apartheid Movement kept alive the conscience of the world, giving the liberation movement time to rebuild. Within this international network the British Anti-Apartheid Movement played a major role, as a policy and campaign initiator setting priorities for the international movement, from sanctions to the campaign to free Nelson Mandela. The Anti-Apartheid Movement

ensured that sanctions and the campaign to isolate Apartheid stayed centre-stage.... The Anti-Apartheid Movement rose to the occasion, marshalling mass demos of almost unprecedented numbers of people, culminating in the quarter-of-a-million-strong rally to demand Nelson Mandela's release on the eve of his 70th birthday in 1988.[1]

The movement that had started in London as a boycott campaign had grown into an international demand for the liberation of an entire nation, a demand eventually met in 1994.

The significance of this 50th anniversary of the Anti-Apartheid Movement is, to my mind, not only the movement's contribution to the ending of Apartheid, but the opportunity it affords to reflect upon its longevity and its growth from a London initiative to an effective global phenomenon.

I wonder, is there something here that is particularly "London" in its nature? Did the fact that it was established in this city shape its ability to influence those in Whitehall and Downing Street and beyond to the Commonwealth and the United Nations? If so, it would be very valuable to understand this as we seek to confront new challenges requiring a global response and calling for the particular kind of resilience displayed over half a century by the Anti-Apartheid Movement. Did the work of the Anti-Apartheid Movement impact upon social developments in the city of London and encourage active citizenship and anti-racism? And does it possibly offer to the city, the nation and the world the example of what challenges can be overcome if we keep faith with each other and believe in our corporate responsibility to bring about necessary change?

---

1. Asmal n.d.

The Beauty and the Eye of Ireland

The city of Dublin had long considered creating its own museum. In November 2007 I was asked to present my thoughts on this as part of the James White Annual Lecture held at the National Library in Dublin.

In Raphael Holinshed's *Chronicles* of 1577, a ragtag Tudor history of the British Isles, he includes a fascinating essay called "The History of Ireland" by Richard Stanyhurst. Born in Dublin, the son of the speaker of the Irish House of Commons, Stanyhurst became a bit of a polymath. He published one of the first translations of Virgil into English, and like many Renaissance men, became obsessed with alchemy at an impressionable age. He published a commentary on Porphyry of Tyre when he was just 23.

But his search for the philosopher's stone did not prevent his gaze being dazzled by Ireland. And not just with Ireland, but with the city of his birth, Dublin. He describes it with all the enthusiasm of a Tudor tourist brochure:

> This citie, *as* it is not in antiquitie inferiour to anie citie in Ireland, *so* in pleasant situation, in gorgious buildings, in the multitude of the people, in martiall chivalrie, in obedience and loialtie, in the abundance of wealth, in largenesse of hospitalite, in maners and civilitie *it is* superiour to all other cities and townes in that realme. And therefore it is commonlie called the Irish, or yoong, London.[1]

---

1. Stanyhurst 1587, vol. 2, ch. 3. "The names of the civities, boroughs and haven townes in Ireland", p. 20, col. 1, ll.71–4, col. 2, ll.1–5.

Stanyhurst names this Irish London "the beautie and eie of Ireland".[2] It's a striking phrase, and one which gathers up everything from gorgeous buildings to the city's pleasing situation to the hospitality, manners and civility of its citizens.

And such a capacious view of the city, of its meaning and culture, is significant. If we are to picture the importance of any city nationally and on the world stage, we must use the widest lens possible to ensure that we leave nothing out. If we are to tell the story of a metropolis such as London or Paris or Dublin – as of course Stanyhurst himself is doing in his fashion – we need to consider every aspect of its urban personality.

City museums – those repositories of good intention – formalize such stories. They take the worthy past and try at the very least to hold on to it, and at best, to recapture it for today's citizens. But it's a risky business. If cities are viewed too narrowly, such museums can easily become mausoleums, a late attempt to capture something that has already happened, already gone. The grandfatherly sigh of "the olde days" falls heavily from each bit of text mounted on a wall or dusty display case – dreary for the best of us, fatal for the YouTube generation. Why is it that city museums often seem as if the city had departed?

It is essential, therefore, before we come to the question of what sort of institution we might want to represent a city, that we first understand what sort of a city it is that we wish to celebrate.

It sometimes seems as if two contrary principles are at play in cities. One wants to tear things down, to start over, to improve the decayed with the new. Cities, the progressivists argue, are about life, about renovation, about the living – and need to be made better.

Their opponents struggle to hold onto the past. They insist that the visionaries of renewal must understand the importance of what went before. Proponents of historical culture argue that we are nourished by the past, not just burdened by its lack of underfloor heating.

The urban planning pioneer Patrick Geddes worked in Dublin from 1911 to 1914. Like all town planners, Geddes was interested in how cities

---

2. Stanyhurst, vol. 2, ch. 3, p. 20, col. 1, ll.44–5.

worked. He had a particular fascination with communications, with the city as a network of interconnecting functions.

But Geddes was no crass utilitarian and was international in his approach. In his work in India, he quickly realized that neoclassical notions of order were certainly not the only principles of reasoned architecture and civic unity – though his colonial superiors, keen to establish the symbolic structures of their rule, tried to convince him otherwise. Unlike most of his peers, Geddes found (as one architectural historian has described it) beauty in the ragged tangles of the old towns, the narrow twisted lanes with earthen dwellings and the main streets with stylish buildings that formed what he could see was "an inseparably interwoven structure". The seeming chaos that colonial administrators sought to remove (and, if we're honest, feared) was of their own imagining – the product of a Western addiction to mechanical order. What Geddes perceived was something he called "the order of life in development".[3]

I raise this sense of urban chaos not as a way of explaining the vagaries of Temple Bar on a Saturday night,[4] but to begin a list of qualities one might wish to see in a Museum of Dublin. You can hardly get away from "the order of life" in a city as crowded and bustling as London, but it is exactly the quality one needs to hold onto in any city museum.

Geddes saw this clearly in terms of building successful cities, not just in India but in Europe. His most celebrated book on town planning, *Cities in Evolution,* was published in 1914, at the end of his time in Dublin. In it, he wrote:

> Above all things, [we must] seek to enter into the spirit of our city, its historical essence and continuous life.... Its civic character – its collective soul, thus in some measure discerned and entered into – its daily life – may then be more fully touched.[5]

---

3. Paraphrased in Kostof 1991, p. 86.
4. Temple Bar is an area of central Dublin on the bank of the River Liffey, famed for its medieval street pattern, with many narrow cobbled streets and a lively nightlife popular with tourists.
5. Quoted in Kostof, p. 86.

To understand what's there already is to see the great resource on which a Museum of Dublin can build. It may be the busiest public square where buskers jostle with businessmen on a sunny day, or the traffic roaring over the new James Joyce Bridge. But it may equally encompass James Gandon's Custom House (1781–91) and the Four Courts (1786–1803) – to cite two obvious examples of city heritage. These too are important, for they are not just grand domed buildings but convey a continuing sense of Dublin's ambitions, of its sense of itself as a city. In 1799 one writer called Dublin's Custom House "the most sumptuous edifice appropriate to such a use in Europe",[6] and we mustn't forget the scale of such an achievement.

The point is, as Geddes understood, that the city's culture is already present: it exists, both as a living past that can be explained now and as a thriving presence in the city's cultural capital. "Civic character", as Geddes calls it, is in the air, and any city museum worth its salt must never try to restrict that character by boxing it into narrow display cases called "Dublin in the 18th Century" or "Dublin Today". It must establish a living connection with the past and present environments that are all around us. It must draw power from the thriving city life we feel the very moment we step onto the streets.

There is an aspect to the city that is not the city at all. If you ask most people about London, their first description is of monuments – Big Ben, the Tower of London, St Paul's Cathedral – "gorgious buildings" of the kind that struck Richard Stanyhurst in his paean to Dublin.

But Stanyhurst recognized that cities, those fabrications of bricks and mortar, are not just marked by their most obvious difference from the countryside. Great cities share something of the beauty of their landscape. Great cities have, in Stanyhurst's phrase, a "pleasant situation". And he finds Dublin, of course, a place not just of beauty, but of a kind of pleasing moderation:

> The seat of this citie is of all sides pleasant, comfortable, and whole-
> some. If you would traverse hils, they are not far off. If champion
> ground, it lieth of all parts. If you be delited with fresh water, the

---

6. James Malton cited in Girouard 1985, p. 219.

famous river called the *Liffie*, named of Ptolomé *Lybnium*, runneth
fast by. If you will take the view of the sea, it is at hand.[7]

Well. We're all happy with that. Why bother visiting a museum at all?
But let's raise the stakes.

The river is a key feature of London's history as well, from the first
Roman settlement along the Thames bringing trade and commerce from
the Mediterranean and north Africa, to 19th-century communities of Chinese immigrants building one of London's many "small cities" in Limehouse.

Poets from Spenser to Sir John Denham have sung the blandishments
of the "sweet Thames" for centuries. But is this how people *experience* the
river – or any part of the urban setting? To get closer to the spirit of the
city, we need a keener eye. Here is Charles Dickens, for instance, in the
celebrated opening passage to *Bleak House:*

> Fog everywhere. Fog up the river, where it flows among green aits
> and meadows; fog down the river, where it rolls defiled among the
> tiers of shipping and the waterside pollutions of a great (and dirty)
> city. Fog on the Essex marshes, fog on the Kentish heights. Fog creep-
> ing into the cabooses of collier-brigs; fog lying out on the yards, and
> hovering in the rigging of great ships; fog drooping on the gunwales
> of barges and small boats. Fog in the eyes and throats of ancient
> Greenwich pensioners, wheezing by the firesides of their wards; fog
> in the stem and bowl of the afternoon pipe of the wrathful skipper,
> down in his close cabin; fog cruelly pinching the toes and fingers of
> his shivering little 'prentice boy on deck.[8]

You can feel in Dickens's language the great benighted course of the
Thames rolling beneath the foggy air of Victorian London. Here is the city,
here is what the past felt like. Not pretty, not placid: but something real and
alive. We all know what happens if you go down to the river....

If I can get this feeling across to someone coming into the Museum
of London, then I am doing one of my jobs, which is to convey to 21st-
century visitors what it was like to be a Londoner in the past.

---

7. Stanyhurst, vol. 2, ch. 3, p. 20, col. 2, ll.5–11.
8. Dickens 1996, p. 1.

London lost hold of its river for a while with the decline of the docks and boat traffic, and it is only just beginning to reclaim it as a space of leisure, of walkways and cafés and social mix. The spectacular views from the London Eye have played their part, as has global warming – though it is likely that the Charles Dickens of the 21st-century will not be writing so much about the pervasive fog, which has long since disappeared, as about floods, spilling over from the Kentish heights to the Essex marshes.

Cultural capitals have their famous buildings, their celebrated rivers and hills. But of course it is the people of the city who are to a large extent what interests visitors to any city museum. To convey *vividly* a sense of the past is to describe how the city was lived in; where people went, what they did; to find social behaviours analogous to our own lifestyles (as we would now call them) today.

Thinking of a sunny walk along the Thames (you'll forgive my chauvinism: I am quite partial to London), I can imagine the qualities of urban existence I know my visitors would relate to: the leisurely pace, the beautiful views, the social variety I encounter.

To take Dublin as our "Irish London", we can draw on a similar sense of what we might call historic leisure. Dublin's famous pleasure grounds in the 18th century were the Beaux' Walk on St Stephen's Green and Gardiner's Mall in what is now O'Connell Street. Situated on either side of the river, they competed for the patronage of the fashionable crowd. Who went there? According to a French visitor in 1796: "Worthy mothers were thin on the ground, and seemed worried. Young ladies, on the other hand, were very numerous and seemed happily occupied…."[9]

Contemporary engravings of these pleasure gardens exist, and yes, one can mount them on the wall and say: "Look. This is what Dublin was like in the past." But how much more do we need the suspicious gaze of our French tourist monitoring – or is he ogling, really? – the amorous young ladies of Dublin? How much more do we need to know that the northside rival to the Beaux' Walk was built as a speculative property develop-

---

9. Girouard, p. 188.

ment by the Gardiner family, who were hoping to draw on the success of St Stephen's Green south of the river?[10]

The building of a city is a story of strong personalities and human interests, not just one of politics and planning permission, battles and barricades. It is also one of (and I chose my example deliberately) *pleasure*. For any Londoner along the Thames, for any Dubliner or visitor who has ambled along the Liffey, catching a stranger's eye, smiling at a passing scene ... it is that quality of social life that makes cities live.

And it is that quality – the sheer pleasure of populousness – which we, who are in charge of representing urban culture, must convey with all its drama in the work we do.

I have begun this essay with high ambitions, and no little abstraction: the power of the city, its living presence, the way in which history continues as part of any present urban landscape. That's all very well as a set of ideals, you might object. But how does one attain such qualities in a museum?

Let's begin with the building. Most national museums and galleries start as buildings – or portions of buildings – in which rulers kept their collections; they developed into buildings which rulers regularly opened to the respectable segment of the public; they finally emerged as buildings belonging to the city or the nation, often on the basis of a royal collection presented to the nation, or commandeered by it.[11]

Such an inheritance suited city leaders who wanted grandly designed, central located public buildings (Corinthian columns and all) for show. Subsequent institutions imitated what we now think of as the *museum style*, in order to make a claim for their universal (they meant, of course, European) authority.

But the old hierarchies are no longer so clearly defined. The new urban settlement is more fluid, and one would like to think, more responsive to the varieties of cultural difference and change. So any new museum building needs to find a way of creating a new national and civic identity.

---

10. Girouard, p. 189.
11. Girouard, p. 330. See also Bennett 1995, pp. 17–58.

The new Capital Museum in Beijing, with its wide modernist eaves inspired by traditional Chinese architecture and its rotunda rocketing from the building's glass-roofed facade, looks very modern. Yet the enormous red columns and elaborate colours of an imperial gate that dominate the back of the foyer present a thrilling contrast. What the building does, magnificently I must say, is represent local tradition within an international aesthetic. It manages to say something old, but in a completely modern way.

The location of such buildings is equally important. A city museum will draw much of its power from just the sort of connections with the city I was discussing earlier. The Addis Ababa Museum in Ethiopia overlooks the enormous, inescapable immensity of Meskel Square in the city centre. It is hard to imagine the museum having anywhere near the same impact tucked away down a set of side streets or lost in the tree-lined enclave of an outer suburb. For here, as you enter the museum or look out from it, is the heart of the city itself, its open space, its sky. The building leads into the life of Addis Ababa, from its traffic roaring past to the aspirations and competing pleasures of its sporting stadium.

Such gestures are not merely symbolic. In the hard reality of the cultural economy, city museums need to be closely linked with the civic authority's broader intentions for tourism, leisure, housing, immigration. Museum leaders have a responsibility to support their city, and of course, can benefit hugely in return. The Museum of London, soon to be linked to the re-established Greater London Authority, hopes to ensure that its engagement with the capital remains at the heart of political thinking in terms of city development and cultural programming. We don't want to be waiting for news: we want to be part of the announcement.

Making outward contact with the capital – in terms of architecture, situation, attitude – is essential. Looking in, we can define needs that are particular to city museums. At the core of any museum is its collection. The public is at times bemused, I fear, at what's on display in museums because they imagine one just sat down one day and chose what one wanted to use to tell the history of the city.

Most people are unaware of that strange process of historic formation that goes into almost any museum collection. The first director of the Museum of London used to ride around on his horse, pointing out bits and pieces of the city he wanted. Things were donated, purchased, acquired. There was nothing so pragmatic as a collections policy. As a consequence, the Museum of London collection contains several fine views of ... Calcutta.

For historians of culture, such objects reveal the ethos of the time in which they were acquired. But pragmatically, the Museum of London has limited display space and a particular story to tell ... which is not the story, fascinating though it would be, of west Bengal.

And yet ... we need to strike a balance. Yes, the collection needs to decide what does and does not belong to it. The problem of accession and de-accession is fundamental, and one that the public is rarely aware of. It requires careful thought not just of what is needed now, but what may be needed in the future. Today's ephemera is tomorrow's rarity.

But to some extent London, like many major cities, including Dublin, is a product of many different cultures and groups. A colonial view of Calcutta may not be of immediate relevance, but a *salwar kameez* worn by women in northern India and Pakistan is. One such outfit is displayed at the Museum of London not just because it shows the shirt, trousers and *chuni* (the scarf) that can be seen outside on the streets today, but because it has become part of the capital's culture. The design became fashionable in the 1990s; celebrities from Princess Diana to Cherie Blair appeared in public wearing the *salwar kameez*, and the women's suit in the museum was in fact made in London, in Brick Lane in Spitalfields. If someone encounters such a display and walks up to it wondering what on earth it's doing in the Museum of London, I'm pleased, because it means they will discover something new about the capital, something less obvious than they might have expected, something as a tourist, for instance, they might never see.

An international outlook is therefore essential: city museums must not be parochial. Whether it is outward-looking design such as that of the Capital Museum, Beijing, or displays such as the *salwar kameez*, the aim must be to establish local interest, but within an international outlook. And our explanations, too, must mirror the largest thinking possible. To discuss the Royal Hospital at Kilmainham, built to care for soldiers and invalids, is not just to reveal the lives of Dubliners, though that may be the reason we choose to discuss it in the first place. It is equally to establish possible analogies with, among others, the Hôtel des Invalides at the edge of Paris (as it then was) or the Royal Hospital, Chelsea in London, all built on similar lines in the 16th and 17th centuries. Dublin is here, but Dublin is also part of a world culture.

There are, of course, other issues in museum life today – some might call them pressures, or opportunities. The notion that we can choose a site, construct a building, place things on display is no longer a straightforward one. I feel it's worth spending a bit of time getting underneath what some of these issues are.

The social function of *public* museums has been at their heart from the very beginning. Museums and galleries have always been places of contest, on the one hand aiming to be "temples of art" for the cognoscenti, and on the other hand looking to educate and improve a mass public.[12] This can be forgotten amid present concerns about widening audiences and improving access and diversity. This debate about who museums are for has been going on, in differing terms, for a very long time and should not be dismissed as a passing fad. Public collections should be for … the public.

There is, I would be the first to admit as I face the mountains of paper on my desk, something dispiriting at times about the rhetoric of access. The Museums, Libraries and Archives Council have produced a set of guidelines called *Access for All*.[13] This "toolkit", as they dub it, is completely well-meaning in its intentions: it really does intend organizations to find ways of scrutinizing what they do to improve their relations with their public. And that's a very good thing. But as it talks of user outcomes, community profiling, structures to enable participation, one's heart sinks. Users are people, outcomes are lives that have been changed. It's as if bureaucratic language has sunk the project before it has even begun.

But it hasn't, of course. Museums do an enormous amount of good work for the community. As the report *Museums and Social Inclusion* suggests, not only can museums create powerful places of learning that are non-judgemental and unassociated with problems and social failing – one of the most basic qualities a museum can share is its aura of success – but

---

12. Bennett, pp. 89–91. See also Hooper-Greenhill 1989.
13. Museums, Libraries and Archives Council 2004.

museums can also fundamentally "represent and express a vision of an inclusive society".[14] The ambition is high, and the standard a tough one for museums to continue to meet. Museums do an enormous amount of good to fight social exclusion, but much of the work is, as one analyst argues, unfocused and "fuzzy".[15] It may be that museums need to target more specific audiences rather than aiming for a generalized inclusiveness.

I raise the issue of access in part because cultural institutions, especially those in the city centre, are in competition in many respects with consumer culture. Commercial environments increasingly woo purchasers less with products than with their associated lifestyles. Shopping centres are now places of entertainment, whose symbolic design and atmosphere of inclusion for all, as Sharon Zukin persuasively argues, make a bid for ownership over public life.[16] The message is, especially for young people: we are what we shop. If museums are to prosper in such a competitive context, they have to assert their own definition not just of who was here, but of who belongs here now. Widening that definition broadens the basis of their claim to social importance and cultural centrality.

If widening access is as much an act of self-preservation as of social policy, it sits alongside another necessary consideration for any new museum which is *sustainability*, another word, I fear, that gets bandied about to the point of meaninglessness. But it has meaning, and an important one. The architect Richard Rogers in his search for a future architecture writes of "the sustainable city".[17] He rightly does not limit this to ecological impact

---

14. Group for Large Local Authority Museums 2000, p. 49. Museums are unusual in being able to share their attributes of success and authority with the socially excluded, in part because they lack the taint of "problem" contexts that prisons, social services and so forth are associated with through their work with the marginalized.

15. Black 2005, p. 51.

16. Zukin 1996, p. 55. See also Zukin 1995. Glenn Lowry, director of New York's Museum of Modern Art, warns of the opposite movement: that cultural competition may in fact be a blurring in both directions. How different are museums themselves from shop displays of jewellery you can buy? See Lowry 2004, pp. 129–49.

17. Rogers and Gumuchdjian 1997, p. 169.

(though he is gravely concerned about managing resources effectively in making new buildings), but understands a complex set of sustaining relationships for the city: its connections to systems of education and health, food and justice; its points of contact and creativity; its beauty and animation, in part a result of diversity thriving, being renewed, growing.

He places change at the centre of what cities are and speaks of an "active citizenship", where citizens are involved in the evolution of their cities and feel that public space is in their communal ownership and responsibility.[18] Such a vision is enthralling, because it means that a Museum of London, or of Dublin, Addis Ababa or Beijing, has a key role for the very citizens it hopes to represent. Public collections foster a sense of civic identity not by delimiting what that identity is, but by handing it over conceptually to the city. The collection is a moveable thing, possible of any number of configurations. As long as we, its guardians, keep saying to the city "who are you?", "what do you do?" and "what do you need?", our museums will remain both topical and top-notch.

I hope I have, to some extent, described the dynamism a city museum can generate by establishing and exploring its relationships to the city. Any city is much more than content for such a museum. And what content there is can only suffer by cowering fearfully in the curatorial vault, frightened that it can never make sense of the fast-changing spree that most cities are. It goes against the traditional museum mindset, to leap into the current – and that is exactly what we ought to do!

I want to conclude with a few thoughts about capturing change in city museums. I mentioned earlier two sorts of internationalism. One sort of *museum model* provides local interest and attention (as in Beijing), but remains international in outlook. Looking at museum ambitions for our time, we can see that *audiences* too (residents and visitors) are comprised of a diverse mix of cultures that provide their own international content for any city museum.

Where these two internationalisms meet is, in fact, at the very nexus of multicultural change that museums need to celebrate. In a rather witty

---

18. Rogers and Gumuchdjian, p. 16.

essay entitled "Mess is More", the architects Robert Venturi and Denise Scott Brown celebrate 21st-century urban chaos. They single out Tokyo as

> *the* city most relevant and revealing for our time. It's no longer Paris for its formal/spatial and symbolic unity, or New York for its technical grandeur.... It is Tokyo exemplified by integrated chaos involving sublime relationships engaging complexities and contradictions, and juxtapositions and ambiguities of scale, space, form and especially cultural symbolisms.
>
> There is no question concerning Japan's original genius for a cultural system, deep and broad within its dimensions, but also exclusive, and its current genius for acknowledging what we call multiculturalism – for adopting and adapting foreign influences and for juxtaposing them in creative ways that create chaos valid for today.[19]

Here, then, is a city of our time: it blends both old culture and new, and is not a mosaic of carefully placed cultural pieces but a busy, captivating, self-contradicting blur of neon lights and cultural contradictions. Are Venturi and Scott Brown troubled by this? Of course not. They're post-modernists – they're not troubled by anything! But their point about modernity in the city is right: we need to see multiculturalism as a living thing, moving and changing. Cities are fed by the influences of the world, and if a museum (the very word can begin to sound outdated in such a context) is going to feel like the city, it has to establish a dialogue with these ongoing shifts and turns, not mimic them, but know that this is how the city feels to anyone leaping into a taxi or trying to call for a drink at the bar.

People pass through cities, let's not forget. Heathrow airport has more employees than all of Newcastle – but traditionally, it's hard to get Heathrow into the museum narrative. Dublin has more Polish immigrants per capita than London. It's how the city is right now. But would a city museum here know how to represent that reality?

When you ask outsiders about Dublin, they immediately speak of its vitality, its warmth – and its Guinness. Clichés? The language of tourism?

---

19. Venturi and Scott Brown 2002, p. 153.

Perhaps, but no less potent for being so. In the end all city museums either seize or succumb to an urban brand. Such cultural identities may occur, to quote one social geographer,

> through the forging of a connection between a particular city and a personality (Joyce's Dublin, Gaudí's Barcelona), stressing the key contribution of a major landscape or prestige project (such as the Guggenheim museum in Bilbao) or highlighting a major cultural or sporting event (the Venice Biennale, the Monaco Grand Prix or the Edinburgh Festival).[20]

But here too, capturing change is important. All brands have a sell-by date,[21] and so monitoring what's happening in the city ensures that one is no longer offering James Joyce when it's really Flann O'Brien they're clamouring for.

And one isn't saying: "Look. We're a museum in a box. It's all safe and neatly packaged." Cities aren't like that, and no more should a city museum be.

If Dublin is – to return to Stanyhurst's lovely phrase – "the beautie and the eie of Ireland", it is so much more than a few old pictures hung on a wall. *The beauty and the eye of Ireland* (as a raison d'être for Dublin and its museum) is a way of thinking, a way of being in the city.

---

20. Hubbard 2006, pp. 86–87.
21. Hubbard, p. 87.

Carried Away:
The Lord Mayor's State Coach

As part of a repositioning strategy for the Museum of London, I had suggested raising public awareness of the museum's largest object, the Lord Mayor's State Coach. This paper marked my introduction to an international conference on carriages held at the museum in November 2009.

Among the many astonishing finds uncovered in the tomb of the Egyptian pharaoh Tutankhamun – the man who became King Tut, as we got to know him better – were six working chariots. Each was different, each a symbol of both military prowess and personal pastime in the life of the young ruler.

It's not every man who gets buried next to his killer. One wonders how happy poor Tut was in the afterlife to awake and see not just one but half a dozen chariots parked round him. For it is thought that the 19-year-old may have died in a charioting accident, riding alone or fatally injured alongside his racing charioteer.[1] Long before James Dean, our young Egyptian pharaoh was the archetypal car-crash teen.

The story of Tut has often seemed to me an inaugural tale for my interest in carriages, for many of its attributes penetrate so much of the history

---

1. Cotterell 2005, pp. 62–3.

of coaches and their owners: the association with power, the precarious locomotion, the final resting place as display. Tutankhamun's chariots form part of that long history of two- and four-wheeled vehicles drawn by horses or carried by men that takes us from Assyria and Ancient Egypt to China and Japan and onward, in strange metamorphosis, to the image we most often have today when the word *carriage* is mentioned – of Rococo pomp tricked out in gilded wood and plush interiors, of tall horses groomed and gleaming, proud in the bravery of their finest trappings.

Carriages are fascinating. So fascinating that they are almost the stuff of fantasy – and this may be one of the reasons that they have often been under-studied. It is as if their imagined dreamscape of high society and untold wealth, of private parks and distant castles, has rendered them invisible as real objects: mechanically contrived to travel real roads, designed and realized by artisans of the highest order. It is as if the folly of their grandeur is, more than any sturdy wheel, the very thing that helps them get away. Carriages have, for a very long time, escaped us.

I am not a carriage expert, but I would like to pause for a moment to think on a broader scale about their misapprehensions and the effect they have on the study of carriages. Carriages have been not just overlooked, I would argue, but misunderstood.

Alfred Hitchcock once famously said, "Drama is life with the dull bits cut out." I tend to think of carriages in the same way. When my mechanic begins to discuss the intricate errors of my car engine's valve system, a part of me sighs and thinks, it would all be so much simpler if I drove a carriage.

And if carriages are essentially cars – with all the dull bits cut out – what we are left with is the carapace: the ornate, the exotic, the *interesting*. So supercharged is this interest in the ornamental that in some cases, a carriage's function as a vehicle ceases – and there is more than one carriage design too heavy to be conveyed on real springs and wheels. The best term for such monstrosities – or are they aspirations to some other quality of experience? – belongs to Jacques Damase, who calls them "vast pieces of sculpture on wheels".[2] It is a just description, though perhaps too limiting,

---

2. Damase 1968, p. 54.

for are they not also paintings on wheels, furniture on wheels, architecture on wheels?

What we have in carriages is show, and it is this that dominates people's perception. And such a view is not incorrect, of course, since carriages were almost inevitably about creating a public impression. If, by extension, the spectator associates such show with power, then that too, however fixed a view, is not incorrect. Examining the social stratification evident in paintings that depict carriages – one thinks, for instance, of the broad peopled streets in the 18th-century paintings of Bernardo Bellotto – one sees the effect these elegant vehicles had. Representations of carriages dramatize class difference – between coachman and housemaid, rider and amazed (sometimes dubious) spectator. Almost inevitably, someone is watching as pomp rolls by. And these are just the most obvious amid a panoply of more subtle social distinctions.

There is much here to interest us, and yet much remains unseen. To identify poverty and privilege is to render the carriage itself a mere cipher of its owners. We need to get inside the carriage to close in on other histories: the links between carriage carving and furniture-making, for example; between carriage panels and fine art; between textile production and fashion; between decorative schemes on carriages and those of room interiors.[3] Horses and riders, coach-making and maintenance, international styles and cultural influence all merit greater attention. A study of carriage specialists and where they worked would take us away from social function and back to artistic form: when a neoclassical painter is given the surname Wagenschön, you know there is something particular about what he does and the fame he has acquired.[4]

---

3. These links have been established, if not fully studied across the world. In Germany, for example, "even on the more simple 'state and dress' carriages, much of the ornament is taken from the decorative vocabulary of contemporary wood carving and from 'throne and parade' chairs in audience chambers". (Wackernagel 2002, p. 11).

4. For a picture of the Viennese Imperial Carriage (with panels painted in 1763 by Wagenschön), see Kunsthistorisches Museum Wien, 1995, p. 12. Beginning his career as a carriage painter, Franz Xaver Wagenschön (1726–90) later became known for his allegorical oil paintings.

It may be this variety of the carriage as an art form that has made scholars nervous of studying it. It may be that the carriage is somehow too large a thing to be contained by the term "decorative art", where it was most likely to have been placed. It may be that power and show, gilding and glamour, have dazzled not just a susceptible public, but all of us. I suspect that carriages have been more noticed in representation than reality, not just because surviving carriages often have oddly dislocated histories, but because the evidence of how they were used (evidence found in paintings, tapestries, tile panels and elsewhere) has people we can actually see, rather than those we must imagine. The result has been misunderstanding, placing carriages in the roomier realm of ideas and drawing us neatly away from the objects themselves.

In Henry Fielding's final novel, *Amelia*, first published in 1751, Captain Booth, locked up in Newgate Prison, describes his wife's road accident. He laments, "The Injury done to her Beauty by the overturning of a Chaise, by which, as you may well remember, her lovely Nose was beat all to pieces."[5] Fortunately, it is this very event that leads him to woo and win her as his bride.

Representations of carriages such as this – whether in the novels of Fielding or engravings by Piranesi – have proved sturdier survivors than their source material. Yet despite their fragility, carriages have survived, and in larger numbers than most people suspect. Many were lost, too difficult to transport and so abandoned for their awkwardness, destroyed as useless, sometimes hated, relics of the past. A collection at Hatfield (in Hertfordshire, north of London) is said to have been cast out across the park to prevent enemy planes landing there during the Second World War. And there they remained, and decayed.

Yet wherever I've been in the world, I have found carriages – in Poland and Brazil, America and Scandinavia, Italy and Cuba. There are major examples and great collections: in the National Coach Museum in Lisbon, the Kremlin Museum in Moscow, the Kunsthistoriches Museum in

---

5. Fielding 1983, vol. 1, book 2, chap. 1.

Vienna, the Wittelsbach Collection in Munich and the National Museum in Rio. In Britain, the collections are little known, but there they are: the National Trust collection at Arlington Court, the Tyrwhitt-Drake Museum in Maidstone with more than 60 carriages, half on loan from the Victoria & Albert Museum and various private lenders.

There is a curious sense in which they remain both provincial and cosmopolitan. The collections have a tendency to feel local: these are our carriages connected to our history. But a more international genre would be harder to name: designs travelled from country to country, manufacturers exported widely, artists journeyed from court to court. Even in survival, carriages have been taken apart, leading to unexpected finds, such as fragments of a Portuguese royal coach turning up in Brazil. Given their iconic force as objects of the baroque – the last truly pan-European style, though by no means the only style in which we find carriages being made – carriages call for thinking beyond national boundaries, not just the possessions of kings and fiefdoms, but aspects of an international artistic culture.

As director of the Museum of London, I must be allowed a certain parti-pris toward London's own importance in this international arena. Britain was celebrated for everything from its manufacture of high-quality steel springs to the fineness of its body makers. As Dr Wackernagel points out in his essay on carriage-builders, "*body-makers* were considered to be among the aristocracy of craftsmen" in England.[6]

Examples of London coaches can be found across the world. A 19th-century drag or private coach that belonged to Prince Adalbert of Bavaria (and now in Munich) was made by Holland & Holland in London in 1870. Its robust elegance was modelled on the Royal Mail coach, and it was popular with men who liked "to drive themselves and go to the races".[7] The Kremlin Museums have several outstanding examples of English carriages, including a late 16th-century carriage given by James I to Borus Godunov, and an 18th-century coach made of maple and given to Catherine the Great by Count Orlov.

---

6. Wackernagel, p. 45.
7. Wackernagel, p. 153–55.

Britain's own examples are no less impressive. One thinks of the Gold State Coach commissioned for George III for the opening of parliament in 1762. It was described as "the most superb and expensive of any ever built in this kingdom",[8] with sculptural ornament by William Chambers and Joseph Wilton, and paintings (reminding us again of the international nature of carriage-making) by the Florentine artist Giovanni Battista Cipriani.

There are Irish and Scottish State Coaches, and of course, the Lord Mayor's Coach, on display in the Museum of London, though still appearing annually on the city streets for the Lord Mayor's Show – a rare instance of a carriage that remains in use 250 years after it was first built. Designed by Robert Taylor with allegorical panels by Cipriani, it was commissioned in 1757 and ready for the Lord Mayor's Procession that same year. It is, as Celina Fox has written, "a masterpiece of rococo craftsmanship, a tribute to the skill and artistry, the luxury production and consumption found in 18th-century London".[9] Indeed, whole histories converge – from art to economics – when we begin to examine more closely its fabrication and use, and it remains a key object in London's history.

The Lord Major's Coach is not simply an 18th-century artifact. It has a life governed by its display at the Museum of London and its spectatorship of museum visitors. The understanding – or misunderstanding, to return to my earlier suggestion – of what the carriage is, is in part an effect of its configuration as showpiece. The effect is not new. There is a long history of putting carriages on public display for visitors. When Napoleon's *dormeuse*, taken at Waterloo, was exhibited at London's Egyptian Hall in 1816, thousands flocked to see it. So great was the crush that satirical prints by Cruikshank and Rowlandson parodied the thrusting onlookers, keen for a glimpse of Napoleonica. In more recent times, the coronation coach of Queen Christina of Sweden was shown at London's Royal Academy in 1989.

There are two points to make about this fate of turning carriages into museum pieces. One is that such objects can become too narrowly asso-

---

8. Royal Archives DB 1a, cited in Marsden and Hardy 2001, p. 3.
9. Fox 1990, p. 8.

ciated with key figures and key events. Many carriages seem not only to have carried their passengers in the past, but continue to do so through a perpetuated emphasis on celebrity connection: there goes the Duchess of Genoa, here comes Boris Godunov. It is fascinating to view Napoleon's landau at the Château de Malmaison, and its value derives in part from its important link to history. And I don't mean to undermine the significant connections between carriages and leading events and figures – it's part of their appeal. But we must consider that such affiliations can distract from the carriages themselves. They are no longer objects of fascination so much as pretexts for telling the lives of great men and women.

The second point about carriages on display is that they can become too prizeworthy. The Lord Mayor's Coach is so celebrated an object that it has a tendency to become isolated from the museum itself. Indeed, the Museum of London holds another carriage – a working model of around 1702, possibly showing a coronation coach for Queen Anne. It is a curious thing, and yet almost no attention has been paid to it.

It is right that museums across the world show their prize objects, and many such artifacts are useful at telling a variety of histories and attracting people to listen to them. But from the point of view of our study at this conference, we can see a weakness in this importance. Outstanding objects stand out, whereas we may wish to embed them within their type in order to identify their nature and qualities. Glorious though the Lord Mayor's Coach is, I sometimes wish it were a little less so, if only that I could get people not just to admire, but to understand.

Having said all that, I am at one with anyone who is fascinated by carriages. As a child, I returned to Poland to visit the country estate where my mother grew up. The manor house had long since been divided into flats, and like many children, I was more interested in exploring the fields and outbuildings than the stuffy interiors that drew my mother. I remember that trip so clearly, wandering off on my own on a sunny day, poking into workshops and stables, and finally entering the coach house to find – to my utter astonishment – a carriage.

It was a far cry from the Lord Mayor's Coach on its platform: it had been abandoned, left to decay, and in fact, as I climbed inside and explored, I saw that it had become home to a variety of birds and beasts. It was for me a vision of enchantment – a glorious plaything, a fantasy house, a menagerie. And when I think of it, what I remember most is the sense of wonder, so that even today, whenever I see carriage – and yes, I admit to seeking them out – my heart jolts and something of their romance speaks to me. I am carried forward on their oversized wheels, their proud plush seats. I experience the carriage – and there is perhaps, no matter how much I learn about them, no finer than knowledge than that.

London's Historic Ties with Europe

In April 2003, Stanislaw Komorowski, former Polish Ambassador to the United Kingdom, who died tragically in Smolensk in April 2010, asked me to give the Europe Lecture at the Polish Embassy in London. I was keen to use the opportunity to reposition the Museum of London's meta-narrative to focus on migration. This paper serves as an interesting example of rescripting a museum.

London is probably the most ethnically diverse city in Europe. Latest projections suggest that around two million Londoners, around 28 per cent of the population, belong to a minority ethnic group. Anyone walking through the city along its busy streets cannot fail to notice this incredible diversity.

One hears countless languages spoken, some identifiable, others unfamiliar and difficult to place. Studies have shown that more than 300 languages are spoken in London. Sir Clive Martin, Lord Mayor of London in 1999, related that when the European Bank for Reconstruction and Development was established in the city, it required speakers of 38 different languages. It was not surprising that Londoners filled all the posts. The spoken English of many Londoners varies, betraying, through accent, intonation and vocabulary, a wide range of cultural origins. Such is the rich mix that there are at least 40 different communities of over 10,000 people who were born outside England and who now live in the capital.

About 85 per cent of refugees in the UK reside here. London has also become Europe's principal city of destination for asylum seekers. It has been estimated that around a quarter of million Londoners have been through the process of applying for asylum in the past 15 years. London is also one of Europe's most popular destinations for economic migrants, both legal and illegal.

Immigrants and refugees from the continent have helped to shape and enrich the city's development. They have made London what it is today. In 1993, the Museum of London put on a groundbreaking exhibition with an accompanying book entitled *The Peopling of London*. This set out to explore and uncover 15,000 years of settlement in London from overseas and show that immigration is not a new phenomena.

Europe's history is a tangled knot of destinations, interdependencies, influences and relationships. It is important for us not to take for granted prize British and European values such as democracy, tolerance and free speech. They came about only through the struggle and suffering of millions of people over the centuries.

With the prospect of European enlargement, it is worth reconsidering London's historical links with the continent.

It is amusing to think that in prehistoric times Britain "drifted" in and out of Europe a number of times before its final separation from the continental mainland took place around 8500 years ago. During this period, Britain achieved island status perhaps as many as five times! So much for integration....

For much of prehistory various human groups crossed into Britain by a wide land bridge now submerged beneath the English Channel. For them, it represented merely the north-western tip of the continental landmass. When Britain finally became an island, contact was maintained by ship, and here the River Thames was crucial in funnelling people, language, goods and ideas deep into the heart of southern lowland Britain.

Something of the awe in which far-flung places were held in prehistory comes across through the careful deposition of prestige items in the waters of the Thames: the offerings include a polished jadeite axehead from the western Alps found in the Thames at Mortlake, as well as other prized metalwork from both Europe and Ireland.

With the coming of the Romans, *Londinium* was founded. People came to settle in the new town from all parts of the empire – French or German people probably outnumbered Italians, but the majority were native Britons. The Roman Empire was the first European community, tied by language, laws and a monetary system. The Roman port of London grew up along the waterfront on the line of today's Lower and Upper Thames Street in the city. From here, trading contacts were established with the continent and the Mediterranean. Imports included Samian pottery from France, glassware from the Rhineland, emeralds from Egypt, amber from the Baltic, and marble from Italy, Greece and Turkey. Exports included grain, lead, tin and people (mostly military recruits and slaves). In continental Europe, when the Roman Empire collapsed, some of the infrastructure survived, but in Britain the break was almost complete. During the fifth century new settlers arrived in the London region – the Angles, Saxons and Jutes from northern Germany and Jutland. It would seem likely that they intermarried with native Britons and imposed their culture and language over most of eastern Britain (England).

The conversion of England to Christianity in late sixth and early seventh centuries encouraged diplomatic links and trade with continental Europe. Ethelbert, King of Kent, married a Frankish princess, Bertha, creating a dynastic link with the Frankish royal house. A new trading town grew up west of the ruined Roman town. *Lundenwic* was part of a European network of *emporia*, where international trade took place under royal control, with duties levied for the benefit of royal treasuries. Others included Dorestad (Netherlands), Quentovic (France, near Étaples) and Hedeby (Denmark).

Viking raids led to the collapse of *Lundenwic*'s trade in the mid ninth century and its abandonment. In 886 King Alfred founded the town of *Lundenburg* within the old Roman walls, and encouraged commercial and cultural links with Europe. The Viking wars had brought an influx of Scandinavian settlers to eastern England, and eventually a Danish king to the throne of England, King Cnut (1017–35). London became part of the Scandinavian trade network, with links as far as Novgorod in Russia.

A Norman king arrived in 1066, and many of London's commercial and cultural links switched from Scandinavia to northern France. Merchants from towns like Rouen and Caen moved to London; Jewish immigrants from the same area established a community in London. The language of the court and of trade was French.

From the reign of Henry II (1154) much of modern France was ruled by the English king – trade links grew up particularly with La Rochelle and Bordeaux. London merchants profited from the wine trade. There was considerable trade also with the Rhineland. In 1157 Henry II confirmed "the men of Cologne" in their guildhall – on the site of modern Cannon Street station. This developed into the Steelyard – the London headquarters and trading station of the Hanseatic League, an international consortium that handled much of northern Europe's trade, especially in the Baltic. The English economy depended particularly on the export of wool and woollen cloth – and not only to northern Europe. Each year a flotilla of ships from Venice, the Flanders Galleys, coasted round to the English Channel to buy cargoes, including English goods, often transhipped via Flemish ports. After Edward I's expulsion of the Jewish community from England in 1290, Italian merchants took over their role as financiers of overseas trade and moneylenders to the king. They met daily in the city, in Lombard Street (named after them). The secret of their financial power was their network of local representatives in towns and cities across Europe and their presence at all the principal fairs and markets.

In 1500, London was still sited at the periphery of the main European trade routes. But economic and financial power had begun to shift from the Mediterranean to Northern Europe, especially the Low Countries. Antwerp emerged as the commercial metropolis of Europe and its main money market. For the English economy it meant the creation of a London-Antwerp axis. Throughout this period there was transference of skill from continental Europe to London.

Henry VIII brought German armourers to teach Englishmen their skills at the Royal Armour Workshop at Southwark (1511) and then Greenwich (1515). Jean Carré, a native of Arras, arrived in London in 1567 and set up glass works in the former dissolved Priory of Crutched Friars. Later, a Venetian, Jacobo Verzelini took over the works; he was allowed to make and sell cristallo glass on the condition that he taught his craft to

Englishmen. In the 1580s, Guido Andries and Jacob Janssen set up the first tin-glaze (Delftware) pottery in London in the former dissolved Priory buildings of Holy Trinity, Aldgate.

The Reformation led to Protestants from all over Europe fleeing persecution to settle in London. From the Netherlands, then under Spanish rule, came Walloons, also known as Huguenots (who spoke a French dialect) and the Flemings (who spoke a Dutch dialect). Edward VI gave them their own church at Austin Friars and put it under the control of Jan Laski, a Polish reformer and refugee. In the late 17th century, further Huguenots arrived after the revocation of the Edict of Nantes: their churches were being burnt and their freedom of worship curtailed. It was at this time in the 1680s that the word refugee, from the French *réfugié*, was first used. Many Huguenots were poor, but some were wealthy, cultured and skilled in business and trade. They settled especially in Soho and Spitalfields and by 1700 formed about five per cent of London's population.

In the 17th century, a new commercial axis developed between London and Amsterdam, Europe's financial centre at this period. London began to copy and develop many of the features of its Dutch rival. Trade with the colonies expanded and the capital became an important European entrepôt for commodities such as sugar, tea and tobacco.

In 1656, Oliver Cromwell re-admitted the Jews into the country, allowing them to practice their religion openly. He believed that their overseas networks and financial acumen would benefit the economy. This soon became evident as their mercantile activities and their skills in bullion and gem dealing added to London's importance as a financial centre.

In the 18th century, London benefited culturally in many ways from its links with Europe. Composers and performers such as Mozart and Haydn visited and stayed for a short time in the capital. Handel made his home here in 1711, composing a series of successful operas, oratorios and anthems with Italian sopranos often singing the lead roles. The artist Canaletto lived in Soho during the late 1740s and early 1750s. In 1747, he painted the Lord Mayor's procession on the Thames in two large canvases – one showing the procession in front of St Paul's Cathedral and the other by Westminster Bridge. Count Lobkowicz acquired the paintings soon after they were painted and today they hang at Nelahozeves Castle in the Czech Republic.

In 1790, the London-based art dealers Noël Desenfans (a Frenchman) and Sir Francis Bourgeois (Swiss) were commissioned by King Stanislaus Augustus of Poland to acquire paintings to form a national collection with the aim of encouraging the progress of the fine arts in Poland. Unfortunately, by 1795 Poland had been partitioned by Russia, Prussia and Austria, forcing the King to abdicate. This left Bourgeois and Desenfans in a difficult situation. They attempted unsuccessfully to sell the collection to the British government and to the czar of Russia. In the end, after Desenfans's death, Bourgeois bequeathed it to Dulwich College. Thus, the collection once destined to be the Polish national collection is found today in South London at the Dulwich Picture Gallery.

In terms of science, the flow was more from London to the rest of Europe. In the 18th century, following on from the work of the Royal Society and great mathematicians and chemists such as Isaac Newton and Robert Boyle, London emerged as Europe's leading scientific instrument making centre. London-made telescopes and quadrants were installed in observatories all over the continent. European ship captains acquired the best maritime instruments such as chronometers and sextants in London for their voyages across oceans. The instrument makers even circulated advertisements (trade cards) in continental languages such as French, Dutch and German to promote the equipment they sold.

The occupation of Amsterdam by the French in 1795 marks that city's decline and the moment when London became the world's largest and most important financial centre. Many wealthy Jewish merchants and bankers from Europe settled in London around this time. Links to the continent and other overseas markets were crucial.

Nathan Mayer Rothschild was very successful with his network of family members based in Europe's leading cities. By 1830, he was probably the richest man in Europe. He called England (and therefore London) the financial centre of the world, the place where all major transactions go through, even those in India and China.

Many other merchants established trading houses in the City of London at this period, including the Ralli Brothers (1818) from the island of

Chios (Hios) in the Northern Aegean, fleeing Turkish persecution; Johann Henry Schroder (1818) from Hamburg, who had special contacts with the Baltic, especially St Petersburg; and Carl Joachim Hambro (1839) from Copenhagen. Merchants depended upon receiving the most up-to-date financial news from Europe. Rothschild operated his own special pigeon-post between England and Europe that brought him the latest political and commercial information in advance of his competitors.

In 1851, Paul Julius Reuter, from Cassel in Germany, pioneered a fast news service providing Paris stock market prices for London's business community. He made use of the new Calais-Dover electric telegraph.

London was now linked to Europe again, not geographically as in pre-history but by an undersea cable.

London's population rose from one million in 1800 to over seven million by 1914. In the mid 19th century, more than a third of the city's inhabitants had not been born in the capital. New immigrants swelled the population by about 10 per cent every decade. In the 1870s alone, about 500,000 migrants from across the globe reached London, drawn to the city's financial and social opportunities. One contemporary travel guide boasted that London had "more Scotchmen than in Edinburgh, more Irish than in Dublin, more Jews than in Palestine, and more Roman Catholics than in Rome."

William Wordsworth, writing in *The Prelude* in 1805, noted he could
See among less distinguishable shapes,
The Italian, with his frame of images
Upon his head; with his basket at his waist
The Jew: the stately and slow-moving Turk,
With freight of slippers piled beneath his arm!
… The Swede, the Russian; from the genial south
The Frenchman and the Spaniard; from remote
America, the Hunter-Indian; Moors,
Malays, Lascars, the Tartar and Chinese,
And Negro Ladies in white muslin gowns.[1]

1. Wordsworth 1965, verse 211.

It is worth charting the two largest groups of overseas immigrants to arrive in London in 19th century – the Irish and then later the Jews from Central Europe.

The Irish formed by far the largest immigrant community in London throughout the 19th century. Irish people had settled in the capital in the 18th century, but it was tragic blight that wiped out the Irish potato crops in 1845, 1846 and 1848 that led to many Irish families being driven from their homes by famine. Thousands travelled across the Irish Sea and tramped to London. They settled especially in Whitechapel and Southwark and in the centre of the city in the parish of St Giles, which became known as known as Little Dublin.

By 1851, there were over 100,000 Irish-born people in London as well as perhaps a further 50,000 English-born children of Irish parents (nearly five per cent of the population). It was largely thanks to Irish navvies that London's new sewers, underground and suburban railway were built. Irish workers also crossed the Channel and helped to construct railway lines throughout Europe.

By comparison, London's Jewish population numbered no more than 20,000 in 1850. The community was fairly prosperous and well established with middle- or upper-class families in a majority. There were Jewish paupers, but wealthier Jews established their own Jewish Board of Guardians in 1859 to look after them.

In the 1880s, the number of Jews in London began to rise dramatically. This reflected the exodus of refugees fleeing the pogroms in Eastern Europe. Many were forced to leave their homes and businesses in Russia and Poland at a few hours notice. London offered a refuge and the chance, for some, to travel onward to a new life in America or Australia. They arrived on ships that berthed in the docks and at wharves to the east of the city, settling close by, particularly in Stepney, which had the advantage of an existing Jewish community, plentiful unskilled work (mainly in the clothing industry) and cheap rooms.

Polish and Russian Jews, with their distinctive clothing and speech, were a conspicuous and concentrated group. London's existing Jewish community did much to help the new arrivals, with institutions like the

Poor Jew's Temporary Shelter in Whitechapel, founded in 1885 to receive new arrivals and help them find their feet.

Many found work in East London's sweated trades leading to alarmist theories that the newly arrived aliens were somehow preventing the British workman escape from poverty. Anti-Semitism simmered openly throughout the 1880s and 1890s, and in 1905 ill-founded fears about the East London ghetto produced the Aliens Act, which placed statutory restrictions upon free entry to Britain. At this period the Jewish population stood at around 140,000, about three per cent of London's total population.

The Museum of London has been recording the memories of Londoners since 1992. Its oral history archive now contains thousands of hours of interviews. These feature a wide variety of people who have lived and worked in London and who talk about their lives and everyday experiences.[3] In this way, the museum is building up a detailed picture of what it was like to be a Londoner in the 20th and now in the 21st century.

These collections have much to reveal about Londoners, especially how they came to live in the capital. There are a number of recordings that feature Jewish immigration to London. Joe Morris, a Jew born in London in 1917 to a Russian mother and Polish father, says:

> My father came to make a living here. They couldn't make a living in Poland, well none of them could, really, and my mother ran away from the Russian pogroms, they came from Russia now, as I said before. It was a lady that saved her life when she was as a child in one of the pogroms. She took her in and hid her till the pogrom was over and she came over here with her brother. Settled down, I suppose, one way or another, and eventually she met my father and got married and then the family came along.

The Irish and the Jews from eastern and central Europe were not the only migrant groups to settle in London. Many Italians arrived during the 19th century. By the 1850s, the area around Saffron Hill and Hatton

---

3. The unattributed quotations that follow in this paper are from the Museum of London's oral history archive.

Garden in Clerkenwell was known as Little Italy. London's Italians were often described as Neapolitans, but many came from other parts of the then disunited country: Sardinia, Genoa and Ticino in the Swiss-Italian Alps. Many Italians were self-employed in occupations that needed little capital: making and selling artificial flowers, plaster statuettes, small mirrors, ice-cream and chocolate. Others made a living as singers or street musicians.

One of the most successful Italian immigrants was the entrepreneur Carlo Gatti. He arrived in London in 1847 and rapidly rose from small beginnings as a confectioner to be the owner of a fashionable restaurant in the Strand, several music halls, an ice business and an electric company. By the turn of the century many Italians had followed Gatti into the catering trade and the size of London's Italian community had risen from 3500 in 1881 to 11,000 in 1901.

In the 19th century, London was Europe's political refugee capital. Beginning with the émigrés from the French Revolution in the late 18th century, there followed Italians, Spaniards, Germans, Poles, Hungarians, Russians and then further French following the brutal suppression of the Paris Commune. The Italian Count Pecchio wrote of London being peopled with

> exiles of every kind and every country: constitutionalists who would have but one chamber, constitutionalists who wished for two; constitutionalists after the French model, after the Spanish, the American; generals, dismissed presidents of republics, presidents of parliament dissolved at the point of bayonet, presidents of Cortes dispersed by the bombshell ... the dethroned Emperor of Mexico and whole swarms of journalists, poets and men of letters. London was the Elysium (a satirist would say the Botany Bay) of illustrious men and would-be heroes.[4]

It was especially after 1848, the Year of Revolutions in Europe, that many thousands of political refugees sought sanctuary in London. Many did not expect to stay more than a few months, but the months became

---

4. Pecchio 1833.

years and then decades. These refugees were permanently making comparisons between home and their adopted abode in this case London. A German term was given to this condition – *bei unser.*

A wealthy Russian reformer in London at this period, Alexander Herzen, brilliantly described life in the metropolis. Like Pecchio, he described the astonishing array of different beliefs and peoples:

> It may well be imagined how many incongruous elements are caught up from the Continent and deposited in England by those ebbs and flows of revolution and reaction which exhaust the constitution of Europe like an intermittent fever; and what amazing types of people are cast down by those waves and stray about the moist, miry bottom of London. What must be the chaos of ideas and theories in these samples of every moral formation and reformation, of every protest, every Utopia, every disillusionment, and every hope, who meet in the alleys, cook-shops and pot-houses of Leicester Square and the adjoining back streets.[5]

If one takes just one group of political exiles in London at this period, the Poles, one discovers just how difficult it was for them to campaign and promote their cause. This was because many other European émigrés were also pressing their case with the British public and government. Herzen wrote of "the army of Polish emigrants" as being

> the oldest of all and the most worn out by suffering, but it has remained obstinately alive. In emigrating abroad the Poles took their fatherland with them, and with heads erect they have proudly and sternly carried it about the world.

By 1900, London had become an essentially cosmopolitan city, with people from all parts of the globe having settled here.

The constant flow of new immigrants was curtailed by the Aliens Act and the First World War. But still more than 100,000 foreigners visited the world city each year.

The First World War brought further turmoil in Europe and thousands of Belgian refugees arrived in London, many settling in Soho. At the end

---

5. Herzen 1924.

of the war, most of them returned home, but a few stayed. Unlike in the 19th century, refugees from the Russian Revolution were refused entry to Britain (Aliens Order Act of 1920) and instead Paris became the émigrés capital of Europe for a while. Anna Pavlova, the great Russian dancer, settled in London, but she was an exception to the rule.

The victims of Nazi Germany forced the British government to relax the country's severe immigration laws, but refugees from Germany still needed to have a sponsor.

In 2001, the Museum of London acquired one of its most important 20th-century iconic items – a trunk donated by Annemarie Seelig, the daughter of a Jewish family who had fled Germany in 1939.

The Seeligs were a middle-class German Jewish family from Dresden. The trunk had been made for Alice when she went away to university to study medicine. They were non-practising Jews, who went to church rather than to a synagogue. It was not until the passing of the Nuremberg Laws in 1935 that Annemarie recognized herself as Jewish. These were the laws that deprived Jews of their German citizenship and excluded them from many aspects of German life.

In 1938, on the nights of November 9 and 10, gangs of Nazi youths had attacked Jewish homes and businesses in what became known as *Kristallnacht*. After these events, the family made plans to leave Germany.

Annemarie's mother had a cousin in London, who became the family's sponsor, and Alice, Annemarie (aged 17) and her brother, Alfred (14), left Bremen in April 1939. The family were to have their possessions shipped from Hamburg, but the Nazis embargoed them. They arrived in London with this trunk, packed with goods that they could sell and a few everyday essentials such as underwear.

Alice Seelig worked for a time as a cook before her medical qualifications were recognized. Annemarie trained as a nurse and worked throughout the country before coming back to London to work in the Department of Health from 1969 to 1983. She was interviewed by Steven Spielberg's Shoah Foundation[6], which holds the recordings of that interview.

---

6. The USC Shoah Foundation Institute for Visual History and Education.

An interview with Anna Amats, born in 1919 in Latvia, reveals the different influences on an individual's education in a war-torn Europe:

> The Russians came in 1940, which was a very bad year for us, for our country and for our people. And then of course the war started and then the Germans came in. I always laugh that I have three things: I started Latvian education, then had Russian education and then, afterwards, German education.

The reasons for her leaving her home and moving to London were wrapped up with a hatred of the Russians:

> I had to leave the country because my father said that he thought that with the Russians coming back, the way I hated them, the way I behaved when they were there, you know, he said "you better go". So I went with this Soldiers' Welfare Fund, with the last ship from Riga.

The mixed emotions at the end of the war must have been quite common among Eastern European refugee communities in London:

> It was a beautiful news when we heard about it. Except for us it was very bad news because, you know, half of Europe was given to Russians. So we knew that we can't go back now. And we didn't know what will happen to us.

Recently the Museum of London collected the fixtures and fittings from a doctor's surgery, but this was no ordinary doctor's surgery. A fascinating story emerges of a post-war doctor and his North London practice. His own history forms part of the tangled and complex web of European migrations and relationships of the 20th century.

Dr Barber had been born in Moravia (in what was to become Czechoslovakia) in 1905. He studied medicine at Vienna University, where he experienced active anti-Semitism emanating from the German students' unions. At the end of the First World War, Czechoslovakia had come into being and Barber attended the new university there in Brno, residing in a Jewish students' home. On completion of his studies, he obtained work at the Children's Hospital in Brno. When Hitler's troops invaded Czechoslovakia in March 1939, Barber was advised to leave, and with the assistance of an uncle of his future wife, Renate, he sent three crates of personal belongings to a forwarding agent in England. They planned for Renate to get a visa to travel to England as a trainee nurse, but Barber could only escape illegally. It was to be another 10 years before they finally arrived in London, following a tortuous journey that took them down the Danube in a paddleboat and then on to Cyprus, Jerusalem and Libya.

On his arrival, Dr Barber took up the lease on a shop with living accommodation above in Essex Road in north London. This he converted into a small surgery.

His ability to speak Italian attracted patients residing in the area, and he utilized his knowledge of classical Greek to communicate with Greek patients who had come to London to escape the political turmoil in Cyprus. In 1956 he began practising from a small purpose-built surgery in his home in Brookfield Park, Highgate. Limitations on space meant that the surgery's fixtures and fittings were made to a reduced scale so that they could be accommodated in a tiny room.

Perhaps because of his own experiences, Dr Barber had a particular empathy for immigrants, and he soon gained a high reputation among the communities of north London.

A large proportion his patients were immigrants, and he developed a good knowledge of the particular medical problems that they experienced, especially those from Mediterranean countries. His patients would bring him dolls in national costume when they returned from their travels back home or simply from their holidays. He built up a considerable collection of these dolls, which he displayed in cabinets in the surgery and waiting room. Children visiting the surgery were allowed to play with the dolls.

Following Dr Barber's death in 2000, his family offered the contents of his surgery to the Museum of London. We have collected most of the equipment and furniture, including the collapsible surgery bed and Dr Barber's miniature kneehole desk, along with a selection of the dolls.

Community associations and clubs are crucial places for newly arrived immigrants and refugees. They allow individuals to share their experiences with others, to stay in touch with their homelands, to speak their own language and to escape the tedium and monotony of their working lives in London.

But Zygmunt Izycki, a Pole born in Latvia in 1926, stressed the importance of learning the local language in an interview in 1992:

> There was a lot of Polish clubs. Some of those people for years and years never learned the language. And if you can't learn the language it's very difficult, if some person can't read and write. If you can't communicate, it's very difficult. My advice to anyone who comes to a foreign country, the first thing you must learn the language, you must communicate, to understand the people.

Community newspapers help to circulate information and news. After the Second World War, the Polish community in Britain energetically published the news. In 1956, Poles in Britain produced 52 regular publications and one daily newspaper. Brendan Bracken, the minister of Information at that time, was reported to have said that if there were two Poles in the Sahara, they would start a newspaper.

Building on its oral history and community-based projects, the Museum of London will be launching very soon its plans for a new gallery about 20th- and 21st-century London. This will be an exciting new multi-million-pound display that will integrate "community and people's history" within London's global multiracial, multicultural urban context. Individuals and communities that have been marginalized in London society will be given a place to express their viewpoints and have their interests heard and considered in the same way as other Londoners. The gallery will aim to show that everyone has an important and valuable story to tell.

The museum's collections of oral history reveal that all of us share the common ground of human life – childhood, family and friends, marriage, work and leisure, happiness and sadness, hopes and fears for the future. Yet each one of us is unique, with our own background and set of experiences. The new gallery will reflect the astonishing diversity of peoples, cultures and languages in London at the start of the 21st century.

Just as past generations of refugees and immigrants to London made their own valuable contributions to life in the capital, so present and future groups have much to offer. Just as the capital has been enriched historically from its ties with the continent, so, now and in the future, London will undoubtedly benefit culturally from a deeper Europe.

London's vibrant popular culture is a reflection of its receptiveness and openness to outside influences and new forms of expression. It is in all our interests that the widening of Europe proves to be a success. To secure long-term peace and security, cultural organizations such as museums have important roles to play in revealing the different ways that European identity and nationality have been shaped over the centuries.

A Final Word
to Mark the End of My Term
as Director of the Museum of London

In March 2012, having served as director of the Museum of London for ten years, I addressed the board and staff for the last time. It was not an easy speech to give as I was conscious it was a turning point for both myself and the institution.

There are occasions in one's life when words are less than adequate for the expression of the deep and mixed feelings of one's heart. This is such an occasion. However, as much for my own sake as, hopefully, for yours, I want to share with you what has been for me an experience filled with much personal satisfaction and, more importantly, learning.

When I took up the position of director of this museum exactly 10 years ago, little did I know what an extraordinary journey I was about to embark upon. Those of you who were here at that time will recall that I had come here after a stint in South Africa, where I was involved in the transformation of that country's national museum system. The challenge there was to establish a unified structure that would tell the story of a nation, previously fractured by Apartheid, embarking upon a journey toward unity and cooperation. Fundamental to that exercise was the shaping of a narrative that would be inclusive, telling the story of all the rich cultures and histories – both social and natural – of a nation in the making.

That experience contributed greatly to my still developing understanding of what museums are about. South Africa was (and still is) undergoing tremendous social change. But so is the rest of the world. We, in the UK and throughout Europe and much of the world, are experiencing massive challenges. We are facing what some are calling a massive recession. This is most marked by the experience of nations around the globe of being in the same boat. It is the experience of the interconnectedness, the shared fortunes, and increasingly, misfortunes of the global village.

Humanity has experienced many moments of great change before. History does indeed repeat itself, and while no change is the same as any other, there are indeed common elements to all historic change. The English philosopher Alfred North Whitehead once said of such times:

> It is a time when civilization is shifting its basic outlook: a major turning point in history where the presuppositions on which society is structured are being analyzed, sharply challenged, and profoundly changed.[1]

Of all that I have learned from my work in the world of museums both here and abroad, one of the most important lessons has been the power of shaping the narrative to help make sense of the often confusing and conflicting elements that is history in the making. Museums today have become less places of nostalgia and more places of reconstruction.

In a most literal sense, the recently completed construction of our new galleries epitomizes our meeting of the challenge to make physical space for the ever-developing narrative of this great city. Together we have met this challenge with imagination, energy and resilience. We proved ourselves capable of building the aeroplane while flying. Of the achievements of my tenure, the fundraising functions that raised the capital for projects such as the new galleries and the way in which everyone responded to the protracted building project give me a great sense of satisfaction. What we accomplished was a wonderful example of collaboration. Together we

---

1. Grimely Kuntz 1984.

developed the Museum of London into a dynamic evolving city museum on an international stage. It is an achievement in which we can take common pride, and I take personal pride in being the leader of such a great team effort.

The construction of the new galleries has raised the status of the museum's largest moveable object, the 250-year-old Lord Mayor's State Coach from an object once seen as somewhat of an embarrassment to the star of the museum in its own dedicated gallery.

More than having succeeded in accomplishing a challenging capital project, the restructuring of the physical Museum of London, we have, I believe, built a new culture within the museum itself. We have changed the culture of the museum from an inward looking, navel-gazing institution into an outward, open, inclusive museum with international connections.

I am reminded here of Martin Luther King's Nobel Peace Prize acceptance speech in which he alluded to the discovery of a story plot among the unpublished work of a writer. The plot, King said, was about "a widely separated family [that] inherits a house in which they have to live together". King reflected in his speech:

> This is the great new problem of mankind. We have inherited a big house, a great "world house" in which we have to live together – black and white, Easterners and Westerners, Gentiles and Jews, Catholics and Protestants, Moslem and Hindu, a family unduly separated in ideas, culture and interests which, because we can never again live without each other, must learn, somehow, in this one big world, to live with each other.

We need to acknowledge the fluidity of our century and the reality that, for most human beings, "self is my project". I venture to suggest that we think of museums as places where people reconstruct or build anew their relationships with each other. I believe that museums can mobilize their resources to assist people in the work of *narrative reconstruction* – what I might call developing and seeing my own story within the context of the shared narrative of society and indeed humanity. Our museum is a place where community can be reconstructed, story-by-story, relationship-by-relationship. I hope that if I have left anything like a legacy, it is this commitment. As former US President Dwight D. Eisenhower said: "The world must learn to work together or finally it will not work at all."[2]

As with the emergence of medieval cathedrals and their relationship to fluid, changing societies, the architecture, arts and vibrancy of those institutions, as well as the risks that they took in all of those areas are echoed in the museum of today. The cathedral in the 21st century has been described as "a medieval institution in the Wired and Fast Company world".[3] Not a bad analogy for museums. But while many of these old cathedrals have become tourist destinations and places of nostalgia, there are those such as Archbishop Emeritus Desmond Tutu's Cathedral of St George in Cape Town where new relations within society and between cultures are being imagined and fashioned, indeed being reconstructed.

As you can no doubt tell, the analogy of the cathedral is one I quite like so I beg your indulgence just a while longer.

To celebrate the restoration of Coventry Cathedral in 1966, the Dutch theologian Albert Van Den Heuvel was invited to participate in the festivities. There he offered 12 theses on the role of cathedrals. Not all of them are relevant for my purpose, but here are a few that I think find resonance with museums:

A Sign of Pro-existence – visibly existing for the whole community.

A Symbol of Diversity in Unity.

A Temple of Dialogue.

A Theatre of Basic Drama.

A Clinic for the Exorcism of Pessimism.

An International Exchange.

A Tower of Reconciliation.

A Motel for Pilgrims.

The House of Vicarious Feasts – a place of celebration.

There is some helpful imagery in the language Van Den Heuvel. He speaks of cathedrals as a sign and a symbol. The Museum of London is not merely a place or a destination. It too is a sign. It is symbol of London. It

---

2. Also quoted on page 115, but worth repeating here.
3. James Wind, quoted in Martin 2010, p. 1.

signifies London – points to it. Our advertising campaign declares: "You are here! This is us in all our long history and in all our diversity." Our museum must be understood and experienced as both a place and a community of communities.

One of the key themes that has emerged is the notion of the Museum of London as a meeting place, as a place for conversation and dialogue, as a place for unity and for reconciliation among the diverse people who are Londoners. The museum is another House of Commons, a *humanity centre.*

These goals and ideals of the museum as Commons cannot exist separately from the hard work of building relationships. We have changed the perception of the significance of this national museum by creating a strong new connection with the mayor of London and the Greater London Authority. We have established partnerships with London's smaller museums. The museum's role as an inclusive, social and learning institution has been strengthened over these past years. And we extended the Museum of London family by the opening of the museum's first outpost, the Museum of London Docklands, and joining in the Renaissance in the Regions program.[4]

Relationship building is founded upon trust. The companions of trust are creativity and imagination. Trust, creativity and imagination are all commodities in short supply in this time and so the challenge is a significant one. At the heart of this museum in this new century lies the commitment to imagine ways in which Londoners and all global citizens can discover anew the opportunities for honouring the past, engaging the present and respecting the future.

On the issue of human remains, by undertaking research and ensuring reburial, sometimes in the face of resistance, allows us, as a museum community, to be part of a Commons where we are not threatened by the ambiguities and tensions of dialogue or new encounters but approach them with delight, a Commons to which the larger community will look for safe space and for leadership.

---

4. This program is described in more detail on page 37.

In a society that will become increasingly diverse, the museum as Commons can and must be a place of reconciliation and a place of celebration, a "clinic for the exorcism of pessimism".

My time spent as part of this community, as your director, has been a rich and valuable personal experience. I can only hope that it was, for the greater part, so too for most if not all of you. We have enjoyed our own sense of being a community within the great community that is the city of London. We have shared a common journey for part of the greater journey yet to be travelled by this museum. We have reconstructed together and have ourselves been reshaped by the experience.

I am indebted to you and proud to have been a part of you all.

Do Museums Have a Role in Shaping the Global Community?

In December 2005, I gave evidence to the Mayor's Commission on African and Asian Heritage in London, chaired by Dame Jocelyn Barrow. The commission's purpose was to take stock of the issues surrounding diversity in the cultural sector.

The past decade or so has been a period of deep crisis marked by tension and clashes between and within nations. Such conflict has variously been described as clashes of civilizations, cultures, world views or values. It is an ongoing tension that deepens in intensity daily. The role of culture in the 21st century has become central to the discourse on how an increasingly "global" world can survive without the threat of some being swamped by the overpowering cultural force of others.

It is also a time in which the managing of cultural diversity has become a skill and competency sought after in just about every sphere of human endeavour. Most sensible and fair-minded people acknowledge that learning to live with diversity is essential to peace and human development. Respect for and understanding of difference, cultural sensitivity, freedom of cultural expression, cultural identity and cultural rights occupy a substantial space on the global political agenda. This is the age of identity politics, in which the conflicting interests of preserving cultural identity and that of absorbing and being absorbed by prevailing, dominant culture clash with bloody force.

These clashes are not new. It is not for the first time that people have been divided along the fault-line of cultural differences. Human history is littered with tales of cultural conflict resulting in conquest and annihilation but also of cultural encounters resulting in human development and progress. But we need not look any further than to events in the past few months and weeks to find examples of cultural tension and conflict. *Globalization*, though a modern term used to describe the consequences of extraordinary rapid technology-driven, information-based, market-supported advances over the past two decades, is not a *new* phenomenon. It is, in fact, one of the oldest processes known to humankind. It began when our forebears set out from Africa to populate the planet a half million years ago. The story of globalization is that of the development of humankind itself. It is the story of the meanderings and coming together, the exchanges, the giving, the taking and the sharing in the long process of human encounters and achievements.

Human memory is appallingly short, and the speed of change, which is the hallmark of the current experience of globalization, gives us little time for reflection, for recollection. Thus we fall prey to the amnesia of our age and ascribe uniqueness and particularity where it is not deserved. We point to the manifestations and proofs of our new global era with a sense of wonder and self-admiration – global trade, the global economy, global investments and global information systems and networks. Some of us even describe ourselves as "global citizens", members of that unique band of wanderers who consider themselves free of the shackles of nationalism and who choose to believe that national borders, passports and immigration officers are minor irritations along the global highway.

Richard Parker, senior fellow at the Shorenstein Centre, John F. Kennedy School of Government at Harvard and an Oxford economist, reminds us that, while there is much that is undeniably new about the world in which we live, there is little new about what he refers to as the "long-established patterns and achievements" upon which much of this "newness" is built.

Even those larger features we think of as most distinct about our own "global" era today – the immense trade flows, or the constant information of the worldwide Internet, or the electronic financial markets that send billions of dollars coursing around the globe – all have a longer and deeper heritage than most of us understand.[1]

Parker sites as example current US international trade which, though the total volume has increased, when measured as a percentage of gross national product, is virtually at the same level it was under Theodore Roosevelt because the US economy has grown proportionately. Similarly, in the case of international finance and global capital markets, we forget that the golden age of trade and investment happened, not in the last 50 years but in the latter half of the 19th century, when

> English investors poured money into Canadian railroad bonds, Rhodesian cattle ranches and Ceylonese tea plantations; when Americans bought German chemical firms and sold sophisticated looms to Egyptians and opened hotels in Shanghai and telephone companies in Mexico City; when the French invested in Russian and Chinese manufacturers, Senegalese farms, Caribbean plantations and New Caledonian mines.

The significance of Parker's argument is that, unlike those who would have us believe that we live in a unique and unprecedented period of human history, we can in fact look for what he calls "patterns and connections ... trends and similarities" and we are able tap into the rich traditions of the past, the experiences and values of our mutual ancestors and our faith to "shape this world as those before have tried to do".

But increasing diversity and consequent conflict mark the spirit of the infant 21st century, leaving hardly a corner of our world untouched. There is a growing sense that this is not going to go away. The times are indeed a-changin' and changing in a way that seems bent on destruction. What is equally disconcerting is the confusion created among institutions (particularly in the West) that once thought they knew the way things worked and were clear about their role in society. Religious institutions are an

---

1. Parker 2002, p. 3

interesting example of this. At the beginning of the 20th century, there was little doubt in the minds of most mainstream church leaders in the West that Christianity was strong and on the verge of spreading its message to every corner of the Earth. The spirit of optimism and faith that spurred the Church on well into the second half of the 20th century has given way (in the most part, if somewhat reluctantly) to acceptance that the world is religiously pluralistic and that the "Christian West" no longer has meaning other than as a historical definition of a bygone age that will probably never be seen again.

But despite the diminishing influence of religion in the face of the increasing secularization of many of the world's societies, religious traditions still have the ambivalent power to be agents of both healing and destruction. Fundamentalism manifests itself in almost every religious tradition, fuelling intolerance of that which is different. In recent times, the expanding plurality of cultures, values and norms has led to conflict and exclusion. Forgotten is the wisdom of theologians such as Max Muller who taught that those who know only one religion, one culture, one way of life, know none, not even their own.

This thought is echoed in UNESCO's position on cultural diversity, expressed in a recent statement:

> Among UNESCO's chief missions is ensuring space for and freedom
> of expression to all the world's cultures. It considers that, while each
> culture draws from its own roots, it must fail to blossom without
> contact with other cultures. It is not therefore a matter of identifying
> and safeguarding every culture in isolation, but rather of revitalizing
> them in order to avoid segregation and prevent conflict.

The statement concludes:

> This cultural dialogue has taken on a new meaning in the context of
> globalization and of the current international political climate. Thus
> it is becoming a vital means of maintaining peace and world unity.[2]

Because we are all by both nature and nurture cultural beings and our institutional life is an expression of our corporate cultural identity, none of

---

2. See http://portal.unesco.org for all UNESCO statements in this paper.

us is free of cultural influence, nor should we be. The events of September 11, 2001, have reminded us that ignorance of our diversity and differences, willful or not, hold the seeds of mass destruction as surely as any nuclear weapon. The world is caught between opposing currents or forces with regard to this issue. While opposing they are also interrelated.

On the one hand, there is the centripetal force of globalization, the phenomenon where the world's cultures are being increasingly thrown together, leading to an undermining of a sense of territorialism and a rise in a sense of collectivism and a shared reality. The world is thus connected through and by the global forces of media, communications, information and technology. But the benefits for some, more often than not, work to the detriment of others. The divide is clearly defined between the West and the Rest. The integrative power of the centripetal force of the West is felt by the rest of the world as threatening, overpowering, a threat to the uniqueness of the already marginalized masses.

On the other hand, we are witnessing the ever-increasing struggle for particular cultural, ethnic, religious and other identities. The centrifugal forces of narrow group identities, of blood and belonging, the deep ties of language, religion and race all conspire to mitigate against the forces of centripetalism.

Within this complex global environment, museums must be responsive to social and cultural change and reflect the identity and diversity of society to itself.

The role of museums has come along way since their formal establishment 200 years ago as places for the display of artifacts and for study. The International Council of Museums (ICOM) defines museums today as "non-profit-making, permanent institutions in the service of society and its development, and open to the public, which acquire, conserve, communicate and exhibit, for purposes of study, education and enjoyment, material evidence of people and their environment".[3] This broadening of definition has shifted our role from being merely a stage to being actors on the broader stage of life itself, where we are part of the larger cast made

---

3. ICOM 2004, para. 1.

up of societies and nations and where together we develop the plot for our future. In this sense we are more than actors. We are inter-actors who present the multiple, diverse interactions between nature, culture, history, art, craft and indeed everything that makes us who we are.

The world in which we play this role is characterized by an extraordinary juxtaposition and diversity of peoples, cultures, traditions, along with ethnic, political and religious differences, thrown together as never before. Arnold Toynbee identified this phenomenon as *Volkwanderung*, the swirling movement of individuals, peoples and cultures in pursuit of a different and better life. Within given national societies, both new arrivals and older ethnic or cultural groups struggle to express their differences, their uniqueness, while being brought face to face with others doing the same. The old hegemony of dominant cultures is breaking down, bringing with it a sense of dismay and threat. Even the United States, the only super power left, despite its own multicultural nature and the inordinate influence of its culture on the rest of the world, is finding it difficult to live in this new order. What we are witnessing today in the face of this perceived threat is a growing intolerance for difference and an increasing tendency toward conflict.

When faced by a threat of this nature, we have a choice of three responses. One is to assimilate. Assimilation is, at heart, the defeat of one by the other, a capitulation to the dominant culture. It is how many minorities perceive the dilution and co-option of their cultures, while the majority prides itself on being tolerant. In this way, much if not all of the richness of diversity is lost or driven underground, there to be perceived as undermining and subversive by the majority.

Another response is to exclude. We build borders around ourselves and our cultures and require that others stay outside them. We have given this response a name: *Apartheid* – the enforcement of ghettos and segregation. It is the cutting off of both the self and the other, more often than not leading to extreme responses.

The third choice is to coexist: to acknowledge difference as equal and as having the right to coexist in a neutral public space while pursuing difference and expressing itself in private spheres of individual social reality. Despite its best intentions, the avoidance of open conflict and the balance of mutual self-interest, coexistence can lead to isolation and fragmentation.

It depends entirely upon mutual toleration, an agreement to live *beside* each other, not to threaten each other. This itself holds the potential for threat.

In all these responses, diversity, rather than being protected, is sacrificed for the sake of a perceived unity and avoidance of conflict. None of these responses recognizes the value of diversity, the value of the other to others. We are willing to acknowledge the particular value of diversity for the other, but we are not prepared to explore the potential value for ourselves.

The commitment to promote "the fruitful diversity of ... cultures" for a more open and creative world in the new 21st-century context, expressed in the UNESCO Universal Declaration on Cultural Diversity (November 2, 2002) is based upon its conviction that "respect for cultural diversity and intercultural dialogue is one of the surest guarantees of development and peace". Yet, when it comes to cultural trade, UNESCO acknowledges that 40 per cent of the world's cultural trade products in that same year were produced by just three countries – the USA, the UK and China. The role of trade in development has taken centre stage in the international economic forum. There is also a growing understanding that development has been too narrowly defined in terms of nations achieving economic growth and needs to include "the achievement of growth in people's intellectual, emotional, moral and spiritual spheres of existence". If this is to be achieved, then we will have to move beyond an approach which may still resemble that of coexistence.

Selling culture abroad sometimes feels like selling out. But it's not. Increasingly, it's part of how we identify countries and cultures, their reputations and our responses to them. Changing perceptions has real impact – not just abroad, but for those at home too, provided we make sure cultural diplomacy not only gives but brings back the gifts of national pride.

Financial Crisis Again

Following the collapse of Lehman Brothers, a sprawling global bank, in September 2008, the world's financial systems went into meltdown. Museums found themselves greatly affected and through a process of natural selection began reducing their staff numbers and, in many cases, their operations. This presentation was given in Philadelphia in 2009 at the American Association of Museums annual conference.

The "global financial crisis" has made institutions such as ours feel particularly vulnerable. I witness among museum communities in those parts I visit around the globe a fair amount of deep brow-wrinkling and hand-wringing going on. Museum authorities meet in anxious huddles in offices and boardrooms to agonize about the tough decisions that they are being forced to make. They whisper in corridors such terms as "cutting back", "deficit budgeting", "austerity", "prudence", "redundancies", "staff reductions" (that's what we say in the UK – I think you on this side of the pond prefer the more polite term "right-sizing") and put them out there on board tables for regrettable but unavoidable consideration. There may even be talk of cutting back on services to the public, even to the closing of the doors – not permanently, mind you – but certainly until the storm has passed.

It wasn't all that long ago that we in Britain were feeling pretty good about life in our cultural sector. The Blair and Brown Labour governments as well the City of London administration displayed an encouraging and progressive attitude toward museums generally and saw the value of our institutions as centres for the exploration of such important issues as identity formation, living with and celebrating diversity and what it means to belong in a cosmopolitan society.

All of this is changing. We have a change of government in the United Kingdom and we are feeling the increasing impact of the global recession. Other cultural institutions in the UK – such as English National Opera, the London Symphony Orchestra and the London Philharmonic Orchestra – have all recently received the news that their budgets have been significantly cut. It is very tempting and really quite easy to feel victimized. Cultural institutions can be easy targets for cutbacks, as we are more often than not considered a bit of a luxury at the best of times, and in times of trial we are vulnerable to those wielding the axes. But it is not only government funding that is being cut – philanthropic giving is also under pressure.

There have been claims made that the golden age of philanthropy is well and truly over. The days when wealthy patrons supported the arts almost as a matter of course are no more. And even if philanthropy is not yet quite dead or even in the process of passing away, it is clearly not terribly healthy either. So what would be the point of pursuing this course of funding? What are we to make of philanthropy that, when significant financial crises hits, is redirected to what the donor considers to be of greater importance? Why should we continue to develop a dependency upon that which patently cannot be depended upon? And do we really understand or attempt to understand how and why donors (including governments) make decisions that do not help us but favour others?

The past 20 years has seen a 25 per cent rise in personal incomes in the UK. Yet despite the fact that personal wealth has more than doubled, there has been a 25 per cent drop in charitable giving as a percentage of gross domestic product. Private giving in the United States is double that of the UK by comparison.

So we have had to think particularly hard as to how to bring about change and support for a culture of giving in the UK. The promotion of philanthropy for our sector calls for a coordinated approach that includes a celebration of philanthropy as being commendable and noble, the public recognition and honouring of the contribution made by philanthropists, and incentives such as tax breaks to encourage a culture of giving. You here in the US have a huge amount of experience in this regard.

UK museums were founded through the contributions of individual philanthropists, driven by the conviction that the quality of life for all citizens would be enhanced by access to important objects, imaginatively interpreted within a core educational purpose. Building on this legacy, we are committed to promoting civic engagement and renewal through encouraging individuals to strengthen the great public collections for the benefit of all. This engagement is not just with the traditional sector of society who has either inherited wealth or has created new wealth.

There is another source of support, one where the engagement of audience members, gallery goers and museum visitors is more than the price of a ticket. It is about developing this group into becoming philanthropists and debunking the idea that philanthropists have to be the wealthy class only. We are committed to making the long-term link between the private individual and the public good.

In April 2008 Britain's major cultural institutions came together to launch a new manifesto, *Private Giving for the Public Good*, opening a nationwide campaign to encourage a culture of giving to the arts and heritage.

The campaign calls for greater support to encourage a culture of giving and wider recognition of the contribution made by cultural philanthropists. Many UK cultural institutions were founded through the contributions of private benefactors who wished to give something back to their communities. The aim is to encourage the philanthropists of the future by making it attractive and possible for them to be involved now.

Cultural organizations have to lead a social change that will create a national culture of giving. Private interest has to be reconnected with the public good. Philanthropy plays a key role in civil society: it makes the link between the private individual and the public realm; it generates a positive gain for the giver and for those who benefit, directly and indirectly, from private generosity. A citizen that gives back is an engaged citizen, part of a renewed society.

Here are some examples:

Independent Opera was established by fund manager Bill Bollinger. Giving more than simply money to the arts, he created his own charity to help music college graduates make the transition to a professional career. In his words:

> If all that was done in the name of charity was to redress dire need in the world, we wouldn't have the Sistine Chapel or Handel's Messiah. Those beautiful things might seem frivolous to some people, but they touch our soul, and if you don't engage with things that touch your soul, what are you doing here?[1]

In 2003 Candida Gertler and Yana Peel created the Outset Contemporary Art Fund, dedicated to supporting new art. This charitable foundation focuses on bringing private funding from its supporters and trustees to public museums, galleries and art projects. It has supported most of London's leading visual arts institutions with their capital campaigns, education, outreach and programming needs and has donated nearly 100 works of challenging contemporary art to public institutions across Britain. In a new development, it has recently set up Further Outset to develop similar initiatives across the country.

Talking about creating and developing initiatives across the country, if we have learned anything in recent weeks and months, it is that the world is wondrously connected by technology, and that when people are motivated to ring the changes by getting involved in the determination of their own future, little can thwart the power of such mobilization of a cause that people believe to be intrinsically good and right.

We could learn some valuable lessons from this. Inexpensive technologies such as social media provide us with powerful means of connecting, building relationships and growing communities of common intent around a common cause.

Such is the cause of philanthropy. The enduring fabric of British cultural life is built on the foundations of private generosity. Our national institutions have their roots in individual philanthropy. The British Museum

---

1. Bill Bollinger, quoted in *Wealthclick* 2013.

was founded on a legacy, the British Library on a royal gift of books. The Royal Shakespeare Company has its origins in the generosity of the Flowers family of Stratford-upon-Avon; the National Theatre, English National Opera and the Royal Ballet can all trace their history back to the charitable inspiration of Lilian Bayliss.

It is the same here in the USA. This society's enduring fabric is made from similar stuff. So it is for all the nations of the world.

I believe that ensuring the enduring fabric of cultural life the world over should be the task not only of the wealthy few but of us all.

This is the beginning of a fundamental change.

Together, private individuals of all degrees of wealth, existing trusts and foundations, business sponsors, and local and national governments can rediscover the core values that created the cultural fabric of a nation.

Those values are imagination, creativity, cooperation, generosity – and a willingness to invest in the future for the love of humanity. Which is, after all, what philanthropy means.

Ars Homo Erotica
at the National Museum in Warsaw

The opening of the National Museum in Warsaw's exhibition *Ars Homo Erotica* in June 2010 was controversial. Professor Piotr Piotrowski, then director of the museum, and his deputy Kasia Murawska-Muthesius led with a challenging concept, one that finally shook the National Museum into the 21st century. The exhibition helped pave the way for future changes. This speech was written for its opening.

My contribution to the discussion evoked by this important exhibition was initially intended to focus purely on the issue of human rights. The human rights struggle of LGBT people in Poland is a story of mixed success, of some important legal victories but also of political failure and continued outright violations. This is a struggle that must be continued by those best equipped to do so, those in the front lines of the struggle here in Poland. As a member of the EU, Poland has to face the realities of being a part of a community built upon principles of democracy, not least those of equality and respect for all and of indivisible human rights. I fully support this struggle and have absolute faith that it is a battle that will be eventually won. But my focus here is more on the *human* part of human rights and what this aspect is concerned with. I will endeavour to draw an analogy from my personal experience that I hope will add to our common understanding and resolve to achieve our rightful place in not just this country but the global community. For this is the true extent of both the struggle and the claim of our humanity.

My thoughts on this, I acknowledge with gratitude, were initially stimulated by my reading of a paper by Pawel Leszkowic and Tomasz Kitlinski, the short title being "Toward a Queer Alterity, Faith and Democracy".[1] In this important contribution to this exploration of human rights they make the simple yet profound point that "human rights refer to our *shared humanity*", "not only to individuals but to groups", not only to us but to the *other*. I was struck by the depth of meaning of "other" excavated in the paper. This *otherness* is what is referred to as "alterity" and the paper is a wonderful exploration of how the *other*, the *stranger*, the *alien* is dealt with within both religious and philosophical traditions. The writers unpack the almost universal thread of hospitality in these traditions and, when reading it, I was transported, so to speak, in my mind to my own experience of being the other in a land which had just come through one of the most famous political transitions in modern times. That land is South Africa. Hospitality is a fundamental concept and practice on the African continent. In South Africa, even during the most repressive periods, white South Africans prided themselves on their ability to extend hospitality, though it needs be said to everyone but *other* South Africans! Foreigners who visited South Africa before the transition attest to experiencing this hospitality and the remarkable irony of the Apartheid situation.

I went to South Africa to take up the position of chief executive officer of the Iziko Museums of Cape Town after the transition in 1994. I had visited there previously at the invitation of the Desmond Tutu Peace Trust to consult on the design of the Tutu Peace Centre. My job at Iziko entailed, among other things, the creation of one truly national museum out of 13 independently run institutions all of which told, in one way or another, the story of the superiority of white culture.

---

1. Leszkowic and Kitlinski 2005.

South Africa was a country torn apart along just about every possible divide one could think of. The struggle against Apartheid was not simply one of racial discrimination. It was essentially a fight for justice and equality, the same fight we are fighting here today. It was a fight against exclusion, a fight against the reduction of the other to less than human, thus declaring them free game to commit violations of their rights and violence against them. It was the attempt to assume the right to expel those who are different from citizenship and from humanity itself.

One can barely begin to imagine the extent of the marginalization of such minorities as the gay and lesbian communities in such a fractured society. I saw first-hand how the Apartheid regime engineered the Apartheid construct through art and culture. The museum system that I was hired to transform had been entirely designed to tell the story of superiority of one race over all the others. One particularly offensive exhibition was a diorama depicting "primitive" Bushmen tribes located not in the cultural history museum but in the natural history museum.

Yet South Africa today, despite its ongoing challenges, has one of the world's most progressive constitutions and a bill of rights second to none when it comes to the protections and rights afforded to minorities, to those others. In particular, the rights of gay and lesbian people are protected under both the South African Constitution and the Bill of Rights.

Is there something that we can learn from this experience? I like to think so, and I offer this also as a response to the challenge set by Pawel Leszkowic and Tomasz Kitlinski when they encourage us to explore the idea and practice of hospitality, of *philoxenia*, which means literally "love of the stranger." The *Ars Homo Erotica* exhibition of homo-erotic art will no doubt be regarded by many as representing "strange love", of a love other than "normal", "right" or "good", indeed even "alien and other." I want to suggest that there is almost a futility in the expectation on the part of those who are alienated that they will eventually win this battle for justice and equality mainly because those who exclude them and deny them their rights decide to ring in change as a result of enforcing legislation, imposing penalties or a lengthy and arduous re-education.

I believe that the South African story brings a further dimension to our understanding of hospitality and it is one that turns everything on its head.

It is a re-interpretation of the dynamic of alterity in which the stranger is the one who includes, who makes it possible for those who would exclude to see themselves for who they are, for what they have become through their practice of and belief in their rightness and superiority, whether racial, moral or whatsoever. The philosophical and political principle at work here is that of *ubuntu-botho*, which literally translates into "the quality of being human and humane". It is a principle resuscitated out of African tradition by Archbishop Tutu. One who practices *ubuntu-botho* displays compassion, gentleness and caring. Such a person uses their strength on behalf of the weak. A person, no matter how rich or powerful, is regarded as deserving of pity (sometimes even contempt) if not possessing *ubuntu*. It is an indispensible attribute, even a hallmark of humanity. Without it, one is less than human. You may have the power, wealth and numbers, but without *ubuntu* you do not amount to much.

Ubuntu can also be translated as "I am because you are; you are because *we* are" or "A person is only a person through other persons". *Ubuntu* equips one to look at one's persecutors and recognize that they need your help in order to regain their humanity. You do not need their help to gain acceptance or respect to claim yours. Such a philosophy scandalizes the world (and the word *scandal* comes from the Latin word for a stumbling block). But having *ubuntu* is enormously empowering to those who practice it for it enables them to take control of their lives rather than allowing themselves to be imprisoned by others in a state of victimhood and depending upon them for their liberation.

We are all *other* and in this respect we are all the same. When, as in this exhibition, we present ourselves to each other in acts of erotic love, we offer an invitation for the other to experience their own possibility of wholeness. We help them to recognize their incompleteness and the potential available to them when they open themselves to the other in love. This may be very hard to appreciate, but as G.K. Chesterton said, "Love means to love that which is unlovable, or it is no virtue at all." And William Blake may not quite have had this exhibition in mind when he said, "Art can never exist without naked beauty displayed." But the artists whose works are set before the people of this nation are making possible a singular opportunity to engage their shared humanity through art.

Ars Homo Erotica offers a rare and unique opportunity to invite into community rather than to protest exclusion from it, to offer an opportunity to experience fuller humanity rather than only to plead acceptance of difference, and to display human love as possible in countless forms of expression:

as *agapé* – as contentment and holding in high regard;

as *philia* – as virtuous, communal and befriending;

as *storge* – naturally affectionate and accepting; and

as *eros* – passionate and beautiful.

Ubuntu is nothing if not all of this and an invitation for all humanity to be at home with each other. It is another purposeful step toward claiming our full humanity and dignity and right to expression of who we are rather than asking for acceptance and recognition. It is a call to all to recognize that without the other we are *all* less than we could be.

Fast Forward: Brazil's Museums Today

Early in 2011, through the generous sponsorship of HSBC, I invited
directors of Brazil's leading museums to London to help create new
partnerships and develop relationships. This introduction helped set the
context for the meeting.

Brazil has frequently evoked images of earthly splendour, no mere country,
but a vast continent all of its own, a land of mysterious forests and powerful
rivers, of lushness and superabundance, of brilliant sunlight and dazzling
sea. As the historian Robert M. Levine reminds us, descriptions of Brazil as
a tropical paradise circulated widely in Europe from the beginning of the
16th century.[1] Over four centuries later, the writer Stefan Zweig was still
amazed at "this land [that] comprises everything at once".[2]

Yet beauty, mystery, grandeur or whatever it is that our notion of paradise might demand by way of definition, are as much a distraction as a
vision if we are to understand contemporary Brazil. As a place of the mind,
Brazil can blind us to its realities. However tempting, it is a lazy view that
sees a Brazil no different today than it was 50 or 100 or 500 years ago. For
the country has changed, like any modern state. It has developed its own

---

1. Levine 2003, p. 38.
2. Zweig 1943, pp. 80–81.

style of national presentation and elaborated contemporary cultural forms that are not merely reflections of familiar tropes – of carnaval and bossa nova, barbecued *churrasco* and pictures of Pelé – but active forms of self-definition suitable to changing times, new political climates and advancing social needs.

Brazil's museums, and there are now more than 2000 of them,[3] are among the most potent of these cultural forums, for they are both experiences to be had and a set of arguments put forward, marshalling their content into spaces that makes sense in 21st-century South America. Take the Fundação and Casa Chico Mendes in Xapuri. These are not merely cultural repositories of the sort witnessed in the past. Honouring the life of the environmental activist and union leader Chico Mendes – now known worldwide as a leading figure in the movement to preserve the Amazon rainforest – the museum is a vivid portrait of political activism as we know it today. It is modest in its fashion, for the house where Mendes lived with his wife and two children, and where he was gunned down in 1988, is very much a moving testament to his quotidian life. And yet the museum is global in its impact. This is not the Brazil of brashness and beauty, of the long untroubled view. It is a moving symbol of the complex forces at play in the country, a close-up of one man who believed in a better future and who, commemorated in this way, represents the new contested territories at the heart of Brazil today.

In his book *The Portuguese and the Tropics*, the Brazilian sociologist Gilberto Freyre identified a quality in the Portuguese that he rather wonderfully called "Ulyssism".[4] The attribute is not merely one of wandering or exploration – like Homer's protagonist Ulysses, cast upon the Mediterranean Sea after the Trojan War – but the wilier ability to adapt to one's surroundings. It is an artful term to distinguish the Portuguese colonial approach from some of its frostier competitors.

Up to the 20th century, Brazil remained a *terra incognita*. The popularity of Theodore Roosevelt's post-presidential travelogue, *Through the*

---

3. Brazilian Ministry of Culture 2007, p. 98.
4. Freyre 1961, p. 50.

Brazilian Wilderness (first published in 1914 and still in print), captured an
ongoing sense of mystery:

> When we started in the morning, the day was overcast and the air was
> heavy with vapour. Ahead of us the shrouded river stretched between
> dim walls of forest, half-seen in the mist. Then the sun burned up the
> fog, and loomed through it in a red splendour that changed first to
> gold and then to molten white. In the dazzling light, under the bril-
> liant blue of the sky, every detail of the magnificent forest was vivid
> to the eye: the great trees, the network of bush ropes, the caverns of
> greenery, where thick-leaved vines covered all things else.[5]

Roosevelt would be credited with the discovery of an unmarked river
in Mato Grosso, now named the Rio Roosevelt, and his memoir carries all
that sense of wonder Brazil inspired in him and those earlier travellers.

Less mysterious were the recommendations on clothing from him
and his son: "Knicker-bockers with long stockings and leggings should be
worn; ordinary trousers tend to bind the knee. Better still, if one's legs will
stand the exposure, are shorts, not coming down to the knee. A kilt would
probably be best of all. Kermit wore shorts."[6]

That the landscape of Brazil should merit not just Dutch-descended
Americans wearing kilts but stupendous admiration is undoubted. But the
difficulty of such perpetual adoration is that it removes the possibility of
other types of cultural formation. Where does it leave that which is not
abundant or beautiful? What prospect is there for an evolving, complex,
living culture when all anyone sees is an endless, almost suffocating, paradise? Does one see at all, or is one defaulting to a pre-existing categorical
definition of the country?

Such limiting fantasies about Brazil are not merely the hyperbole of
tourists and travellers. Geographers are always keen to remind us that the
land mass of Brazil is greater than that of the continental United States.
Historians recall that the sugar trade between Portugal and Brazil became
at one point the largest in volume of all European trans-oceanic trades.[7]

---

5. Roosevelt 1914.
6. Roosevelt.
7. Parry 1974, p. 50.

We are encouraged to remember that Salvador (Bahia) was the second city of the Portuguese empire. I am not disputing the truth of these facts, but the need to raise and repeat them may indicate an underlying desire to hold on to these very images of Brazil's size and potency – images that, I would argue, need finally to give way to newer cultural forms that scale not just the heights but the byways and shoals of the country's history and present condition.

Indeed, the principle applies more largely to the contemporary risks of cultural cliché brought on by tourism and globalization. Generalized ideas about Brazil are certainly not an out-moded thing of the past that we've now got beyond. "Paradise" is still with us, though less as holy reward than holiday destination. Should we celebrate the fact that people across the world can sing along to "The Girl of Ipanema"? Of course! But we should also ask: what songs are they missing? Or is Brazil just one big beach, one glorious bossa nova, and we can leave it at that?

The inverted form of this paradisiac cliché takes us symbolically from samba to Sampa (as São Paulo is familiarly known). The French poet Blaise Cendrars captures the anti-mood in his 1924 poem "Saint Paul", in which he praises not the city's beauty, but its "furious hunger" and applauds its plethora of styles: "ridiculous grotesque beautiful large small north south egyptian yankee cubist".[8] His praise of the chaotic justly seeks to rescue the overlooked, particularly in light of a desire to shuck off the oppression of colonial attitudes and European cultural hierarchies. But is he merely installing another sort of cultural cliché? One that replaces abundance with loss, natural order with urban disorder? Is he romanticizing the difficult without really understanding it, let alone seeking to remedy it?[9] Stefan

---

8. French original from Blaise Cendrars, "*Feuilles de route*", 1924, cited in Louyot 2005, pp. 22–23. Louyot notes that Cendrars was invited to São Paulo by a group of modernists that included the poet Oswald de Andrade, the painters Tarsila do Amaral and Anita Malfati, and the sculptor Victor Brecheret.

9. The problem of such clichés persists, particularly where race is concerned. Silence can give way to a spurious "cool" no less unreal than its precursor. See Sepúlveda dos Santos 2005, pp. 51–65.

Zweig on the narrow streets of Rio de Janeiro 20 years later finds himself equally caught up in the spectacle of poverty:

> Even the poorest [thoroughfares] – or rather, just these – are full of colour and life and movement. Nothing about them is specially prepared for the foreigner; nothing obvious enough for the camera; nor does their charm lie in their architecture, their structure, but in just the opposite – in the animation and disorder, the casualness, which go to make each alley attractive.[10]

Indeed, preparation for the foreigner is just about the last thing these streets are or ought to be about. But Zweig, like Cendrars and others, has inverted his categories of praise with little sense of his own mistaking of what he sees. It is not that all such interest is misintended. When the Anglo-American conductor Leopold Stokowski asked the Brazilian composer Heitor Villa-Lobos to gather samples of Brazilian music – sambas, batucadas, marchas de rancho, emboladas – for a series of pan-American recordings and performances in 1940, his interest in Brazil's particular cultural history was genuine,[11] just as Cendrars and Zweig were trying to gather something authentic. But the risk – and I would argue that it is a risk that can imperil even highly nuanced cultural spectacles, such as the Guggenheim's 2001–02 exhibition, *Brazil: Body and Soul* – is that cliché and fantasy limit certain ways of seeing and crucial subject matters, and it is this missing content that Brazil has on its own terms sought to explore.

Cultural reality – if this is what we are opposing to cultural fantasies about Brazil – has a long history. It is not merely that one can jettison the past and move to a new position free from old influences and longstand-

---

10. Zweig, p. 189. To be fair to Zweig, rescuing the dignity of the disenfranchised by speaking on their behalf is always problematic, particularly in art where representation inevitably shapes and aestheticizes its subject matter. Even today, a film such as Héctor Babenco's *Carandiru* (2003) creates a troubling effect of beauty out of the gritty realities of the famous prison of São Paulo.

11. On 16 July 1940, Villa-Lobos wrote back enthusiastically about Stokowski's *"plans d'échange folklorique entre les nations des continents américains"*, but the project seems never to have been realized.

ing concerns. Nor would one wish to erase memory: one seeks rather to understand it.

Past culture is both content and framework in this context. To visit the Sanctuary of Bom Jesus do Congonhas (a UNESCO World Heritage site) is to see a continuity of value with the great baroque churches of Europe. One can, if one is minded to, read the building within its own aesthetic terms, taking its religious and artistic intention directly without recourse to the instrumental effect such a structure had by being built in Minas Gerais rather than Lisbon. More broadly, one can examine historical towns such Diamantina or São Luís, or the ruins of the Jesuit missions of the Guaranis (all three are also UNESCO World Heritage sites), for evidence of a certain type of artistic elevation, but also for a much richer tapestry of history. One finds the Portuguese making their way as one expects, but also the French and the Dutch. There is a fascinating tension between Old World ambition and New World intractability, elegant facades in mountain settings, fluted columns competing with tropical trees. These sites represent an essential record of Brazil's complex past that needs to be maintained.

The initial impact of such buildings is historically specific. While their lasting influence over later centuries is more tenuously construed – sometimes objects of disdain and destruction, sometimes the seat of new formations of power – its enduring potency is nonetheless a fascinating component in any present-day cultural understanding. Past culture continues to live in some form or other in any society's make-up.

This is most concretely realized when old buildings are used to house present-day institutions. The Royal Museum, established by the Portuguese Prince Regent João VI, opened to the public in 1821. Soon to become the National Museum, it was housed in a new colonial-style building on the Campo de Sant'Anna (today the Praça de República). The museum became an important arena of research, and part of its modernizing mission throughout the 19th century was to present the collection (a hybrid of cultural objects and natural history) in a more rational, less collectorly fashion, using internationally agreed categories of scientific investigation. As part of a larger world movement toward such universal systems of knowledge – similar transformations were occurring in museums across America and Europe – museums like Brazil's were national "not because they showcased the nation-state, but rather because they represented its capacity to represent".[12] What was on display was Brazil's capacity to speak the master-narrative of scientific authority.[13]

Such symbolic meanings change over time. The National Museum began to be challenged by other museums in Brazil, such as those founded in Belém and São Paulo after the overthrow of the monarchy in 1889. Their claim was very strongly staked on the authority of regional identity, and they staged particularity of people and place against larger universal histories (though their classicised architecture did not reflect as innovative a local stance).[14] The National Museum itself moved to a new location in 1892, inserted into the former imperial residence in the Quinta de Boa Vista, where it resides today. The palace interiors were stripped out and placed in other museums. Even today, these historical buildings continue to carry the weight of national identity: understood in different terms, but a kind of vision themselves of cultural evolution, displacement and ongoing meaningfulness.

If historical buildings represent a will to power, both in terms of their original intent and their later use, the turn from classical to modern architecture constitutes a developmental shift toward self-definition and a new confidence in national outlook. Indeed, confronted with the zany modernism of a building by Oscar Niemeyer, one is less able to speak of self-definition than dramatic insistence. It is as if the Brazilian character people have been trying so hard to define has been taken up intellectually and given new form.[15]

---

12. Andermann 2007, p. 33.

13. Paradoxically, the development of such scientific approaches came at the expense of general access to that learning and its processes. Specialized knowledge created an elite whose newly required laboratories and research centres were, unlike generalist museums, no longer open to the public. See Lopès 1996, p. 262.

14. See Andermann, pp. 41–45, and Lopès and Podgorny 2000, p. 115.

15. The importance of these buildings for Brazilians, and their pride in the country's architecture, is borne out by audience figures. An exhibition about the

Architecture is one of the cultural platforms for which Brazil has become celebrated. Brasília is like no other city on the planet. Indeed it is the only 20th-century city listed as a UNESCO World Heritage site. As a townscape it shows big thinking, setting out an urban plan, setting down architectural masterpieces, taking care that setting itself – the very land on which the capital city sits – is integral to the vistas of the built environment. These are not just buildings of Brazil, they are very much *in* Brazil and gather the landscape of the interior round them to ensure we do not forget. It is a tribute to the collaboration of Lúcio Costa and Oscar Niemeyer that Brasília can still present itself in all its enduring newness and civic importance. They have built as much as anything not a solution but a stage, in which the passerby is very much alive to his or her surroundings.

Museums and other cultural buildings benefited from this 20th-century architectural efflorescence. There are any number of them one might discuss. One of the most pleasing to my mind is Affonso Eduardo Reidy's 1954 design for the Museum of Modern Art in Rio de Janeiro's Parque do Flamengo. Designed initially as a composite space (gallery, theatre and school), Reidy's building was as much about the artistic education of the public as art itself. With its open views that encourage the spectator to regard the landscape outside as part of the visual narrative, Reidy drew on the Museum of Modern Art's founding purpose:

> The cultural influence of a museum on modern art is derived not only from the collection of works of art and from the study courses and lectures held there, but more particularly from the creation of its own intellectual atmosphere in which the artist finds enrichment for his own work and ideas and in which the public can assimilate the artistic culture required by the mind of modern man.[16]

Here an "intellectual atmosphere" is created that draws on an inspiring collection of art, a building of great rhythmic pronouncement – with its

work of Lino Bo Bardi, first developed for the Venice 2004 Architecture Biennale and then exhibited at the São Paulo Art Museum in 2006, attracted 83,000 visitors in Brazil.

16. Franck 1960, p. 66.

frame of crisply angled ribs spaced at ten-metre intervals – and a prospect of sky and sea that inspires both spectator and artist. Challenging the view of the past that gallery spaces need to be enclosed, Reidy creates a space that is not just modern but is modern in a way that makes sense for Rio.

The modernist style of Le Corbusier found many proponents. Perhaps the most famous among them was Brazil's own Oscar Niemeyer. What was innovative in Niemeyer can be identified firmly as a Brazilian aesthetic, as David Underwood writes:

> While the European rationalists from Gropius to Le Corbusier had sought a sober, hard-lined architecture based on the machine aesthetic, with its mass-produced materials and standardized forms, Niemeyer proclaimed a new Brazilian aesthetic based on the physical geography of Brazil and the suggestions that "form follows feminine".[17]

As Niemeyer himself confessed:

> It is not the right angle that attracts me, nor the straight line – hard and inflexible – created by man. What attracts me is the free and sensual curve, the curve that I find in the mountains of my country, in the sinuous course of its rivers, in the body of the beloved woman.[18]

Perhaps the most telling instance of this dialogue of curves is Niemeyer's Museum of Contemporary Art in Niterói, a flying saucer perched on a promontory above the Praia de Boa Viagem. You enter via a sinuous ramp to find a circular building again as wedded to its impressive views – Rio across Guanabara Bay, the Sugar Loaf and Corcovado Mountains – as it is to its dynamic displays of modern art. The building succeeds as modernist statement, self-sufficient and pure, and yet insists on a vital relationship with art and nature. Brazilian display here becomes something quite different from the usual modernist response: it wants to draw power from Rio's watery curves and mountain peaks, not just as remembered forms, hidden away once one has entered the temple of art, but as energising shapes that are as inherent to aesthetic perception as any man-made artistic traditions.

---

17. Underwood 1994, p. 42.
18. From *Meu Sósia e Eu* (1992), cited and translated by Underwood, p. 41.

To be in Brazil is to see in a Brazilian way, and Niemeyer's building encourages that interconnected gaze.

There are of course larger discourses of contemporaneity. One doesn't want to identify too narrowly a national style without recourse to its international context. Architects like Niemeyer worked worldwide, and Niemeyer in Le Havre, France (where he built a Maison de la Culture), has some of the sensual fluidity of Niemeyer at home. Indeed, for Lina Bo Bardi, another of Brazil's architectural inventors, national style is something to be addressed rather than assumed:

> The architect doesn't need to be born in a certain country or to belong to a certain race to attend to the specific needs of a region.... Modern architecture resumes the contact with what is most vital, primary and non-crystallized in human beings and these factors are linked to different countries. The true architect can solve, when called upon, the realities of any country.[19]

Bo Bardi rightly sees the risk of identifying an indigenous style from within, for it is too limiting if one wishes to pursue diversity and cross-cultural influence, and perhaps a different sort of national style. Better to have the whole panoply of possible effects nourish one's designs and the possibility of change within cultural identity. Her notion of contact is borne out in one of her most admired buildings, the Pinacoteca do Estado de São Paulo. Here is a building made in two parts – one elevated, the other half-buried – to create a third space, preserving rather than blocking the visibility of São Paulo between the two constructed elements. In the words of one critic, "the city is given refuge in the empty space".[20] Here the principle of welcome adopted by Reidy, Niemeyer and others in terms of natural surroundings applies equally to the built environment, what we might think of as the landscape of man. It is a fitting architecture for one of Latin America's greatest and wide-ranging international art collections, spanning European, African, Asian and American art, housing on an equal footing Renaissance Italy, 21st-century Brazil and just about everything in between.

---

19. Bo Bardi 2002, p. 213.
20. Bo Bardi, p. 213.

In 1925, the Brazilian poet Oswald de Andrade captured the strange one-sided direction of colonization in his poem "Mistake of the Portuguese":

When the Portuguese arrived
In a heavy storm
He clothed the Indian

What a pity!

If it had been a sunny morning
The Indian would have undressed
The Portuguese[21]

To read the cultural commentary of European visitors to South America over the centuries is to find oneself confronting a lot of clothing and nowhere near enough undressing. Moreover, one is faced with two forms of invisibility in relation to indigenous peoples or what Andrade succinctly calls "the Indian". The first results from a gaze so enamoured of its own superiority that it cannot see anything equal – let alone superior – to it.[22] The second disappearance arises from an attitude, like that of the French philosopher Montaigne, equally blinded to reality by an idealized vision of noble purity, of "innocent savages" living an Edenic existence on the land. Such a romanticizing view translates what it sees into something quite unreal, so unreal that "seeing" is not really what the writer is doing. In both cases, as Andrade pithily expresses, the European "clothed" the Indian to the point where he was no longer recognizable or, more troublingly, he ceased to exist.[23]

---

21. Quoted in Bethell 1995, p. 21.

22. Myrian Sepúlveda dos Santos captures the haughty tone of such commentators very well: "Rather than advocate a romantic view of the tropical forest and its heroic inhabitants, most of them considered Brazil a land inhabited by savages or uneducated people, who were very distant from the high values of Western civilization". See Sepúlveda dos Santos 2003, p. 188.

23. Andrade was very much at the forefront of defining a Brazilian cultural sensibility distinct from its European influence. His *Manifesto pau-Brazil* and *Manifesto antropófago* were part of a larger 1920s movement to locate a modern Brazilian identity. See Amaral 1995, pp. 19–20.

These two aspects of the "orientalist" gaze have both been much discussed. But such discussions can suffer from remaining too wed to the gazer and insufficiently attentive to the gazed upon. The limits of thought are privileged worries when set next to actual deprivation. In a country such as Brazil, the long-term implications of colonial expansion, racial policy and material exploitation remain very real concerns. And it is by facing such concerns, by drawing on them and exploring them, that some of the country's most interesting recent cultural forums have arisen.

The Afro-Brazilian Museum in Salvador takes up the important relations between Brazil and Africa. If dominant historical narratives tended to view the Afro-Brazilian connection as instrumental, blurring the slave trade not quite frankly into discussions of immigration and saying little about the lives of Africans themselves, this museum turns such parochialism on its head. It does not simply discuss the life and legacy of Africans in South America but connects the two continents as distinct entities, not treating one as a mere aspect of the other. Here is a building where an iron figure from Benin can share space with three-metre-high carved tablets by the 20th-century Argentinian-Brazilian artist Carybé with no loss of purpose or pleasure.

Other lost stories are similarly retrieved. The Museum of the Indian in Botafogo in Rio displays materials ranging from period photographs to feather headwear, as well as reconstructed traditional environments, including a Guarani fazenda and Xingu kitchen. As a keeper of records, its holdings are impressive: 16,000 ethnographic artifacts, 16,000 publications, 125,000 historical documents. Yet it has a social purpose: to improve how indigenous peoples are perceived in Brazil, correcting misconceptions about them and enlarging people's understanding. Its holdings are not merely archival, but potent devices to instill knowledge and awareness and shape Brazilian social attitudes in the future.[24]

---

24. The National Museums Policy of Brazil supports such work and looks to establish "integrated policies of exchange, acquisition, documentation, research, preservation, conservation, restoration and diffusion of collections from indigenous and afro-descendant communities and from the varied ethnic groups that constitute the Brazilian society". (Ministry of Culture 2007, p. 95.)

The cauldron of São Paulo is a likely venue for the recentring of alterity,[25] and unsurprisingly, the city has over the decades witnessed new forms of attention given to what might once have been overlooked. The Museum of Japanese Immigration presents not just traditional Japanese exhibits: it reproduces the very boats on which Japanese migrants formerly travelled to Brazil. The museum takes journeying as an important cultural metaphor and, with the arrival of the Japanese in Brazil as its particular instance, reveals that process of accommodation that any outside culture must make when it encounters another – a point whose application is no less relevant today than it was when such cross-cultural encounters first occurred.[26] Nor are such migratory movements limited to questions of cultural absorption and degrees of assimilation. As Emanoel Araújo, former director of the Pinacoteca do Estado de São Paulo, has said, bringing Rodin sculptures to the Pinacoteca in 1995 gave an important signal that the museum's Brazilian art belonged side by side with the best European art. The point was not merely Rodin's astonishing draw for the city (150,000 visitors in 38 days), but that people came and saw the building and its collection as an important cultural monument: it situated the Pinacoteca and elevated its importance.[27] Cultural relationship is not just a question of influence or interpenetration: it is about the symbolic value we place upon other cultures, and in so doing, create the value of our own.

Extending the boundaries of cultural perception is a key function of museums. Retrieving what was lost, revaluing what was once overlooked,

---

25. See page 200 for more on *alterity*.

26. For an account of persistence of ethnic identity in Japanese immigrant groups in Brazil, and the degrees to which it was shaped by choice or constraint, see Reichl 1995, pp. 31-62. A related cultural reading of the immigrant discussion can be found in da Costa Leitão Vieira 2007, pp. 117–26.

27. From "*De Rodin à l'Héritage Noir*", an interview with Emanoel Araújo, in Louyot, pp. 142–49: "*Les gens ont recommencé à s'intéresser à la Pinacothèque. Et c'était un signe important, de fêter la renaissance d'un musée d'art brésilien par une exposition d'un grand sculpteur français: ça situait les choses, leur donnait de la hauteur. L'art brésilien a sa place aux côtés du Penseur du Rodin.*" The impact of blockbuster exhibitions on the Brazilian cultural scene, as elsewhere in the world, merits close attention. See Sepúlveda dos Santos 2001, pp. 29–45.

giving voice to the silenced are all important uses of the past that enrich the future. In particular, as we move into an age of virtual chat and digital identities, we see increasingly that museums need not be about objects alone. Audiences' expectations have altered, not for the worse (as doom-mongers in certain cultural quarters would have it), but in terms of fluidity, the current visitor moving seamlessly between the sensual actuality of his iPod and the vast immaterial catalogue of music it can hold.

Preserving the evanescent matter of our lives is a new challenge for museums and an opportunity for new approaches. Displaying the technology of an MP3 player to an audience in the future, rather than the use or experience of it, would hardly be the point. The Museum of the Portuguese Language in São Paulo, opened in 2006, takes Brazil's *lingua franca* and creates an opportunity for exploration and experiment. Culture here is addressed through participation – appropriately enough where the subject matter is that bond that unites us, language itself. Interactive exhibits are the means to venturing through history and culture, from Brazilian dialects to language in sport, dance, food or music to a giant planetarium of poetry and prose. Porto Alegre's Museum of Science and Technology is a similar celebration of activity in museums, with more than 800 interactive experiments that explain science but also stimulate curiosity and awaken the scientific spirit. For younger visitors especially, the museum is science and a great gateway not just to learning, but to opportunity.

Such museums can preserve important cultural meanings. The Museum do Mamulengo in Olinda (a former Brazilian capital and World Heritage site) is devoted to a popular tradition of travelling puppet shows from north-eastern Brazil. It displays the traces of puppetry with a rich array of often satirical, sometimes scary figures propped up for visitors to see. But it is very much a living place, where aspects of making and performing can be seen, and the continuity with the past – of the living tradition of the *mamulengueiro* – is maintained. Indeed, it is this intangible heritage – not just culture as display, but its power and meaning for people, culture as activity and ambition and ongoing process – that unites all aspects of culture, from the clichés we might want to get beyond (all the more potent for their ubiquity) to the byways few might have thought to explore.

This intellectual thrust to capture meanings still current in society enables Brazil's contemporary museums to sweep up much of what could be dismissed as historical relic or outdated fantasy. The Carmen Miranda Museum in Rio de Janeiro, designed by Affonso Eduardo Reidy, is a circle crowned by palm fronds that thrust up as joyously as any of the actress's own fine and fruity headwear. What might at first appear as absurd cliché is in fact a witty tribute to a much-loved personality, and can be aligned to museums perpetuating the reputations of Oscar Niemeyer (in Curitiba), Jorge Amado (in Salvador) and other influential cultural figures. Indeed we are not so far from the organizing principle that uses an iconic person to present ideas and debates still significant to audiences today, as the Chico Mendes Museum accomplishes in a very different context. The subject matter may not be as ostensible as one imagines, and the politics of any cultural form may be found as one looks beyond the glitzy surface. Miranda leads, in one line of argument, to Brazil's current push to install a series of film and music museums, many of which are allied to programs of urban regeneration, such as that along Copacabana beach.[28] What might be dismissed as popular is in fact something very much for the people.

More traditional forums for the recorded past are no less significantly recuperated than fantasy elements of cultural identity. At Igarassu in Pernambuco, in the former Franciscan Convent of St Anthony, the Pinacoteca beautifully displays paintings that once hung in Igarassu's Church of Saints Cosmas and Damian, Brazil's oldest church, built in 1535. The sacred art is in one respect traditional. But here in fact are some of the movements of Brazil's past encapsulated: four paintings of 1729 show colonization and the devastating arrival of yellow fever in Pernambuco; the convent itself, built in the late 16th century and later expanded, became during the Praieira revolt of 1848 the base of revolutionary troops. The point again is that institutions ostensibly relegated to familiar categories thrive in new times and new environments by exploring the rich historical meanings relevant

---

28. Cesar Balbi, director of the Carmen Miranda Museum, interviewed by the author in July 2009.

to Brazilian society today. Successful museums awaken the past – sometimes with new means, new emphases; at others with the most traditional of forms – for each new generation that comes through their doors.

The prospect is not always straightforward, and Brazil no less than any other country cannot afford to take its culture heritage for granted. Dom Irineu Marinho, director of the Sacred Art Museum in Olinda, warns of abandoned deposits and a failure to grasp older traditions, such as that of sacred art and its important link to Brazil's European past. More tellingly, he relates two very real concerns in Brazil today: security and conservation. When you see live bats in the Museu da Camara Cascudo in Natal, there's a wonderful conflation of collection and living context. But the symbolism is potent, for as Dom Marinho points out, bat infestation is a major threat to the preservation of Brazil's historical artifacts.[29]

The living traditions of Brazilian culture are nonetheless flourishing. A 19th-century colonial mansion in Rio houses some of the earthiest art you can find in the expansive International Museum of Naive Art. Álvaro Siza's new building in Porto Alegre for the Iberê Camargo Foundation, opened in 2008, builds on the exciting history of architectural statement viewed in Niemeyer, Bo Bardi and others. Like his predecessors, Siza is determined to understand the Brazilian cultural space as an interface between art and environment: "Architecture should never be an arrogant transformation of landscape or space. My wish has long been that the buildings I design have somehow always been there. I want them to be necessary, never forced."[30]

In creating what architectural critic Jonathan Glancey called "a magnificent mixture of sensual curves and glorious swoops, of galleries that samba out of the main building and then samba back in again", Siza affirms the genuine vitality at the heart of Brazil today.[31] Not paradise, not the past, but something larger that sweeps up the two together, mixing high and low, the popular and the recherché, politics and culture. Where the country is

29. Dom Irineu Marinho, interviewed by the author in July 2009.
30. *Guardian* 2009, p. 20.
31. *Guardian*, p. 21.

growing economically, and facing the social and environmental impact of such growth, new cultural realities need to face such issues, debate them, make sense of them. As the Brazilian financier and patron Edemar Cid Ferreira said, "To be a great economic power, we must become a great cultural power".[32] Given the diversity and richness of Brazil's museums today, one can only imagine that success is assured.

---

32. Louyot, p. 177.

Creating a Future
for Our Cultural Institutions

Developing an international network organization like the International Council of Museums (ICOM) is a daunting process, not least because members often cannot find consensus on priorities. This address was given at the National Museum in Wales in 2010 to conclude my chairmanship of ICOM UK.

On November 12, 1936, Winston Churchill addressed the House of Commons and in a famous speech warned the British people of the inevitability of war with Germany. He admonished the political leadership of the day in these words:

> They go on in strange paradox, decided only to be undecided, resolved to be irresolute, adamant for drift, solid for fluidity, all-powerful to be impotent.... Owing to past neglect, in the face of the plainest warnings, we have entered upon a period of danger. The era of procrastination, of half measures, of soothing and baffling expedience of delays, is coming to its close. In its place we are entering a period of consequences.... We cannot avoid this period, we are in it now.... I have been staggered by the failure of the House of Commons to react effectively against those dangers. That, I am bound to say, I never expected. I never would have believed that we should have been allowed to go on getting into this plight, month by month

and year by year, and that even the government's own confessions of error would have produced no concentration of parliamentary opinion and force capable of lifting our efforts to the level of emergency.

I was appointed director of the Museum of London and chair of ICOM UK in 2002. These appointments were somewhat overshadowed by events reverberating around the world during this period. It was post-9/11. The drums of yet another war were beating. The internet bubble was bursting and global stock markets were in crisis.

I wonder if Churchill would have seen the coming of those events, had he been around. There were more than enough indications that the American hegemony and the hypergrowth of the world economy could and would not remain unchecked. But not many world leaders paid any attention to the warnings of those who did see the impending danger. As Churchill had said of members of the Commons: "They go on in strange paradox, decided only to be undecided, resolved to be irresolute, adamant for drift, solid for fluidity, all-powerful to be impotent."

Six years on and the global financial system is in a state of breakdown and disastrous collapse. Governments around the world in once buoyant economies have rushed to bail out the institutions that control national economies in a bid to support the unpredictable and fragile global financial market.

How did Churchill's Britain fail to see what was coming? And how is it, that with all our technology, our access to information and prodigious knowledge, we failed to heed the signs of our own times and now find ourselves facing a series of crises of such magnitude – economic, environmental, social – that some have described as "the making of the perfect storm"?

This question concerning our almost universal predisposition not to see the obvious has many answers: short-sightedness, naivety, poor leadership – the list goes on. Max Neeff, the Chilean philosopher, not flippantly, ascribes it to mankind's stupidity – a quality as real and influential as our intelligence.

We have entered another Churchillian "period of danger", but one of an unprecedented nature. We live in an age of profound cultural transition, a time in which the complexity of our multicultural world confronts us with challenges that have taken on an urgency and intensity quite unlike anything we have experienced in history. It is a time when hardly any of our public institutions are free from having to undergo deep soul-searching as to their meaning and their role.

I have expressed this sentiment on a number of occasions over the past six years – at the Museum of London, in my work with UNESCO and in my role as providing leadership to ICOM UK. The more I say it, the more I appreciate its significance. I have used it to argue for a deeper comprehension of and commitment to the issue of cultural diversity in our cultural heritage institutions. I have also used it to argue for greater appreciation of the vital (life-giving) benefits of partnerships and collaboration between national and international cultural institutions.

But mine is not a unique sentiment. Other voices across a wide range of institutions can be heard expressing the same sensing of a profound emerging historical reality. Cultural institutions around the world have been left wondering in recent weeks what will become of some of their largest financing sources as the global economic crisis unfolds. In the US, Lehman Brothers, Merrill Lynch, Bear Stearns and Washington Mutual are no more or are under seizure by regulators. All were significant supporters and funders of the arts and generous contributors to museums in America. Here in the UK, it is yet uncertain how the forced fixation with the global economic crisis will affect our cultural institutions.

Western museums, once relatively secure from the vagaries of political and economic turbulence, are now as affected as any institution by the shifts in both nation and world as a result of increased mobility of people, objects, knowledge and capital, new technologies of communication, and transnational forms of governance. These are aspects of globalization germane to museum developments.

We may not know what the impact of the financial meltdown and subsequent slowdown of the economy will have on cultural institutions until much later this year, but there is bound to be a re-evaluation of contributions and donations by both individuals and governments. The impact upon memberships and visitors and the future of collections as means of raising capital awaits analysis. Museums in developed nations may become more like our developing nation counterparts where they are prone to be perceived as a distraction in the face of other scarce essential resources.

There has been a profound shift in the way museums understand themselves and the way they are perceived in the 21st century. The typically Western concept of collecting, conserving and presenting objects in a museum has experienced radical social and political changes during the past half century has led to a transformation of the concept of the nature, intention and role of museums. In non-Western countries the emergence of new audiences and of museum networks are breathing fresh life into our industry and challenge our Western notions of what we are and should be in a world of increasing interconnectivity and interdependence.

Museums play a crucial role in reflecting our understanding of the world in which we live, move and have our being as well as the values and norms which influence our increasingly cosmopolitan and multicultural societies. The future of museums in playing this critical role of grappling with unfolding history could be severely compromised by these current events. At the very time when museums worldwide are playing an elevated role in the formation of cultural identity and are receiving increased public interest and participation, they are under threat by major global economic downturn. All our old insecurities and crises of identity begin to resurface and the hard-won lessons of our recent past are in danger of being jettisoned as we struggle to ensure our individual survival.

ICOM was formed to ensure that we museum professionals remain committed to "the conservation, continuation and communication to society of the world's natural and cultural heritage, present and future, tangible and intangible".[1] If it is to do so under the present circumstances, circumstances which in all probability will not quickly disappear, then we who make up this organization will need to make a Churchillian assessment of the present and future. Such assessment must be done together and with urgency. We cannot watch from the sidelines and wait for events to unfold. We will have to increase and accelerate our partnership work. As single institutions, our chances of overcoming these challenges are slim indeed. Collectively, in partnerships of mutual collaboration we can meet our mutual responsibility to fulfil our role in society.

---

1. See the ICOM website: http://icom.museum.

The old notions and sentiments of empire and nation no longer provide the energy for a world of interconnectedness and mutual codependence. Museums attempt to display the world to the world. The world in which we live is increasingly a world in which the idea of the global commons is as pertinent to culture as it is to place. Our human destiny is a common one. Our diversity is a communal asset. The irony of Churchill's world was that it took the extreme circumstances of a world war to begin to shape the notion of a united Europe. It is the irony of our own time that the crisis in the global economy may well be the impetus for the realization of the benefits of collaboration and partnerships in the museum community, nationally and transnationally.

When the events following the global financial meltdown of 2008 are recorded and presented to future generations, I wonder whether any mention will be made of what museum professionals did. Will history record that this was the beginning of the end for cultural institutions? Was this yet another time of "strange paradox", of indecision, lack of resolve, drift and fluidity, impotence and neglect in the face of the plainest warnings? Will ours also be "the era of procrastination, of half measures, of soothing and baffling expedience of delays" or will we museum professionals seize the opportunity to recommit ourselves to ensuring the custodianship of the natural and cultural heritage of the people of the world. If we are to do so, we will need to take some very courageous steps out of the sanctuaries of our jealously guarded institutions.

The intensifying tensions and conflicts between cultures and world views that have been the hallmarks of international relationships particularly over the past decade, must be ameliorated and indeed countered by our heritage institutions modelled upon global cooperation, honouring of diversity, respect for cultural identity and cultural rights. To put it crudely, the opportunity exists for us not merely to record the past but model the future.

Today, as a result of extraordinary technology in communications, we are overloaded with knowledge of how things are, particularly how bad they are. We are burdened by bad news of conflict, disaster, poor leadership, failing economies.... The list is endless and the scale is global. This is part of the historical legacy we will leave for our children's children. We cannot rewrite what we have written. But we can add a critical footnote that has the power to shape the future. As the US electorate has just discovered, the desire for positive change and the power of hope are not idealistic dreams. History can be made when, in a crisis and in the face of danger, people are prepared to break with the past, to do the untried, to test the unknown, to be resolute and decisive, to seek the way of global collaboration and international partnerships.

The Museum of Life:
Driving through Gdansk
in Pawel Huelle's *Mercedes-Benz*

This paper was given as part of European Literature Night at the British Library in May 2009, and it gave me an opportunity of sharing my passion for Polish contemporary writing. Pawel Huelle and his superb translator Antonia Lloyd-Jones were both in the audience, which was rather daunting. It was this book and its theme of life at the crossroads that provided the inspiration for my own.

Pawel Huelle is a true European. His novel *Castorp* pays hommage to the great German writer Thomas Mann.[1] It is Mann's 1924 novel *The Magic Mountain* that provides a passing reference to the young Hans Castorp's time as a student in Danzig. Huelle grabs this throwaway remark and with great invention and realism elaborates the back-story of this naive young man, studying shipbuilding at the Polytechnic, falling in love with a stranger, already finding the world too large, too mysterious for his understanding. *Mercedes-Benz*, the novel I want to introduce here, is another

---

1. Huelle 2007.

hommage, this time to the wonderful Czech writer Bohumil Hrabal, whose story "Evening Driving Lesson" seems to have prompted Huelle's own comedy centred around a series of wayward driving lessons.[2]

But Huelle is also something quite specific – not just a European man of letters (among the many hats he wears), but a Polish writer, and most particularly, a city writer. For me, as director of a city museum, the Museum of London, it is this commitment to a particular city that first drew me to his novels.

The city in question is Gdansk, the great port on the coast of northern Poland, where Pawel Huelle was born in 1957. He graduated from Gdansk University and has worked in the city as a university lecturer, journalist, playwright, director of the Gdansk Polish Television Centre and most recently, as a columnist for *Gazeta Wyborcza*. He has been a part of that city's immense history in the second half of the 20th century, growing up under the communist regime, and later working for Lech Walesa in the press office of the Solidarity movement. His most recent novel, *The Last Supper*, like his previous books, is also set in Gdansk, though this time not in the past but in a distant future, where the city's traffic jams are less to do with poor town planning (something the hero of *Mercedes-Benz* complains about) and more to do with terrorist attacks.[3]

It is therefore not just as a European or a Pole, but as a man of Gdansk that I wish to introduce Pawel Huelle. And there is perhaps no better book to look at than his 2002 novel *Mercedes-Benz*, a book seemingly about a man called ... Pawel (make of it what you will) taking driving lessons from a pert young woman called Miss Ciwle, "the only lady instructor at the Corrado driving school".[4] It is, however, a novel that is really – as we drive through Gdansk and witness its monuments and messes – about the city itself and what it means to be alive in such a place.

---

2. Huelle 2005. Hrabal's story is referred to on page 4 of *Mercedes-Benz*, where its title is given as "Evening Driving Lesson". According to a source in Oxford, this story does not appear to have been translated into English. Its Czech title is *Vecerní Kurs*, literally "Evening Class".

3. Huelle 2008.

4. Huelle 2005, p. 1.

Here's how the story begins:

> "Goodness how beautiful," said Miss Ciwle, neatly sliding herself across the driver's seat over my knees, while I deftly performed a similar movement in the opposite direction beneath her. "God, how well you tell a story," she went on, checking the gears and the ignition, "but why doesn't it work in my dual control either? Hmmm, I wonder…." She finally got the engine started and, showing our entourage of drivers that most mannish and indecent of signs with her middle finger, she slowly advanced along the human avenue, masterfully weaving her way among the throng of our would-be tormentors, eager to flog us on the spot at that dreadful crossroads, that first car-driving Calvary of mine.[5]

There is so much pleasure in the opening pages of this book, I hardly know where to begin – or even if I have to! Here, in short compass, are Pawel Huelle's great strengths as a writer: the ability to tell stories (and stories within stories), the light touch, the playful self-consciousness, the delicious comedy. As a Pole myself, I find it deeply funny. But I'm assured by my friends (to whom I am always passing Huelle's work as it appears in English) that the humour travels extremely well.

But Huelle's writing, like the greatest works of comedy, has an underlying seriousness. For, viewing the narrative set-up of *Mercedes-Benz* philosophically, what is it we need in life but "driving lessons"? Who is it we might long for, if not the divine Miss Ciwle, with her roll-up cigarettes and infallible ability to take on the angry crowd? Which of us does not require the precious attention an "instructor" can give us?

And there is, of course, however comically we stall and escape ... the driving. *Mercedes-Benz* is prefaced by an epigraph:

> This is the way you are going
> even before your heart fell silent.

We sense the importance of the heart within the novel's opening pages. The nascent eroticism of Pawel's relationship with Miss Ciwle is both funny and very real as they slide, she over, he under, to exchange seats in

---

5. Huelle 2005, p. 4.

the middle of the traffic jam they've caused. "How well you tell a story!" she pants. "How well you drive!" he replies.

But there's an underlying melancholy as well, a sense that not all fatalities – unlike grandmother Maria's – can be avoided. Can the heart that falls silent find its reward? Not all histories are so simple, and as Huelle's Polish readers know, the author of that epigraph was the poet Józef Czechowicz, who was killed by a German bomb in 1939 at the age of 36 – a tragic loss to both life and literature. (There is a museum devoted to Czechowicz and his fellow writers in Lublin, where he died.[6])

"This is the way you are going." Is one too old to learn something new, to change course? As Pawel says, "The whole idea of learning to drive made no sense at all, because it was too late in life, and I'd already missed the moment." And look, even if you are willing to try, how quickly it all descends into chaos!

But the wondrous thing about *Mercedes-Benz* (a serious car, by the way, much flattered throughout the book) is that it suggests – and this is what interests me profoundly given my own concerns with the cultural environment – that meaning is very much about how individuals make contact with their surroundings. The car is both a focal point for the book and an outlook on the world. And just as Hrabal described "those Prague streets and crossroads, first up the hill toward Hradcany, then down toward the Vlatva", so will Pawel take us through Gdansk, getting stuck in traffic (again) on Warsaw Insurgents Street, "driving fast alongside the Napole-

---

6. The Józef Czechowicz Museum of Literature, Branch of the Lubelskie Museum in Lublin (Muzeum Literackie im. Józefa Czechowicza w Lublinie, Oddział Muzeum Lubelskiego w Lublinie) www.zamek-lublin.pl. The museum commemorates the lives and works of well-known Lublin novelists and poets: Józef Czechowicz, Konrad Bielski, Józef Łobodowski, Kazimierz Andrzej Jaworski, Antoni Madej and many others. Józef Czechowicz (1903–39) was one of the most distinguished Polish poets of the 20th century. His poems, and especially "The Poem about Lublin", capture the magic and charm of the town during the period between the world wars. This avant-garde poet, participant of the Polish-Soviet war of 1920, was killed in the prime of his artistic life in his native Lublin by a German bomb that hit the building near Litewski Square.

onic forts", visiting Miss Ciwle's brother and friends on the allotments on the hills.[7]

What we see as we drive, in the privileged space of the car, is the setting for our lives, framed by the windscreen we are looking through. It may be a picture frame, given those static Gdansk traffic jams. But it is of course, as we *drive* through the city, a *moving* picture, the cinema of urban life.

In *Mercedes-Benz*, Huelle offers us the rich texture of being alive. The city, like any culture, can be threatening, chaotic, inapprehensible. But it can also be knitted up and brought together – and Huelle shows us how. For the city – its forts, its churches, its hills – is a real place, with its own history and (as we shall see in a moment) its own journey. But it is also, for each of us, a personal place, a place of sentiment. We each have our own Gdansk, our own London. And if Huelle warns that the city is perilous with trams and trucks and angry drivers, if he worries that we have left it all too late, he consoles us with the knowledge that what is to be cherished is not some external measure, but what the city *means* to us in all its aspects.

It may be a place of marvels. When Pawel walks past a traffic accident, he sees the firemen "busy cutting the interlocked cars apart, causing an even bigger traffic jam than before". Is this just horror, an urban nightmare? Partly, for Huelle is no innocent as a writer. But Pawel our narrator continues: "I tell you, it was beautiful, with great plumes of sparks flying from under the whirling blades like tresses of Berenice's hair, so very beautiful that I slowed down and, despite my own principles, joined the dense crowd."[8]

The city is also a literary place, a place of stories. What we bring to our perception – and this is exactly what happens in a museum – is the wealth of memory. Such recollection may be literary, and Pawel's delicately formal address to his "dear Mr Hrabal", and the way he reiterates Hrabal's own tales, honour the way in which what we have read becomes a part of who we are, how we see things, how we talk about them. The stories we

---

7. Huelle 2005, pp. 2, 32, 38.
8. Huelle 2005, p. 42.

learn become our stories, ones we pass on and tell. And this no less than personal memory, as the book's wonderful collocation of family tales and photographs – for there are pictures included – illustrates. Pawel stalls, he is embarrassed. What can he say, or do? He turns to Miss Ciwle: "You know ... my grandmother Maria ... had a similar experience...." And off we go.

Where narrative meets romance is in the telling of tales. Perception is one thing. Communicating what we see is another. "Who could I tell?" asks Pawel at one point, as if that were the essential thing.[9] Pawel's long opening sentence (it runs for a page and a half) is part of his hommage to Bohumil Hrabal, whose *entire* novel *Dancing Lessons for the Advanced in Age* (more lessons!) is constructed out of a single sentence. For both writers, I suspect, such a sentence is proof of how all things are connected, how everything can be taken up and included as worthy matter. But it is also, and we see this in Miss Ciwle's warm response to Pawel's storytelling, about making contact with a listener. The role of instructor is one thing. Pawel's less certain role – lover? entertainer? guide? – is another. But he is – and that heroic opening sentence announces it clearly – a master storyteller.

Here's a second extract, from later in the book, during another of Pawel's lessons with Miss Ciwle:

> My dear Mr Hrabal, there was a very long silence; now we were driving slowly along Horseback Way, down the avenue of old lime trees that were planted here over two hundred years ago at the expense of Daniel Gralath, and it occurred to me that if only Spanner and Elephant had been fond of freemasonry like Mayor Gralath they might never have disgraced their medical vocation, remaining loyal to Hippocrates instead, because the spirit of freemasonry calls for self-sacrifice and brotherhood and forbids one from thinking of one's fellow man purely in terms of bars of soap or nine-figure sums in one's bank account. But then again that same Masonic spirit vanished from this city long ago, as the name of the road we were driving down shows, for example: first it was called Hauptallee, then Hindenburg, then Hitler, after that Rokossowski, and finally Victory, just

---

9. Huelle 2005, p. 56.

as if all the successive rulers of the city were afraid of Gralath, if only of his memory.[10]

Here, as I mentioned earlier, is the story not just of our narrator, but of the city. Indeed the novel as a whole carries us through the 20th century, from grandmother Maria demolishing her fiancé's Citroen in 1925, to Pawel's father after the war, to Pawel's own driving lessons in the recent past.

One street in Gdansk becomes the history of a country, and Huelle reminds us that the city has its own evolution (to reiterate Czechowicz), its own "way it is going". Pawel is notably silent on these topics, unable, or unwilling, to speak to Miss Ciwle, who notices and asks him what he is thinking about. Perhaps some matters are not so easily spoken.

But the novelist, of course, is not his character, and he can list the successive rulers so keen to impose their names on this fine "avenue of old lime trees". Their own horrors, and those of Doctor Spanner at his infamous Anatomical Institute in Gdansk in the Second World War, are set next to Pawel's lingering anger at what he has learned from Miss Ciwle, whose dependent brother has been the object of greed and abuse by Doctor Elephant, "a past master at making money disappear [who] always knew how to squeeze it out of desperate people".[11]

Satire is one of Huelle's sharpest tools, and it ranges from the savage indictment of "pure profit" here to some very funny set pieces against contemporary art, including a long section told by Miss Ciwle's friend Physic about his bogus, but highly lucrative, success in California producing installation art.[12]

But there is something else as well. To name the city's past is to honour the experience of all citizens. It is to uncover the complexity of civic identity, of nationhood. A drive with Miss Ciwle down Horseback Way is a far cry from parades and propaganda. But as Pawel thinks, somehow "all those

---

10. Huelle 2005, p. 73.

11. Huelle 2005, p. 70.

12. Huelle 2005, pp. 104–14. This satirical impulse can cut against the city, too. In *The Last Supper*, more bogus contemporary art appears under the guise of "City Air", empty glass cubes of air from different sites in Gdansk, and from other cities, set in a modern art gallery.

brass bands, swastikas, hammers and sickles got mixed up together", not just to produce the modern age in Huelle's satirical climax, but as a potent description of how history infiltrates the present. To name the past is to clarify its effect.

Importantly, the story of the physicist Daniel Gralath, who was indeed mayor of Gdansk in the 18th century, is inspirational.[13] His lime trees survive along their wide avenue and carry on. In a cynical age, his generosity is at first incredible to Miss Ciwle, and then so inspirational that she suddenly realizes she has not been paying attention to the car and they are almost out of fuel. She is quite literally *transported* – as much by the power of words as by her Fiat's combustion engine.

We stall. We forget to indicate. We run out of fuel. To be distracted in *Mercedes-Benz* is to have submitted to the storyteller's spell. It is to have been *moved* out of one's present into a larger realm of memory and feeling.

And while there are many realms in which such largeness subsists, one of them is the city, that potent source of inspiration and distraction itself. In Pawel Huelle's most recent novel, *The Last Supper*, he describes a man "who breathed to the rhythm of this city, just as a child in its mother's womb lives by her pulse and breathing".[14]

When I think of London, I find it is this complex rhythm of the city that inspires me, that feeds me. Who I am emerges from the city and is reflected in it. When I invite the public into the Museum of London, it is to make that experience which is common to everyone a more meaningful one: to elucidate the richness of the city's past, to find stories that can not just be told to them, but shared by them, passed among them, stories that become a part of the city's currency. To preserve a Roman head of Mithras found in London, an Anglo-Saxon ring, an 18th-century costume is as important as Daniel Gralath's trees in Gdansk. For what these objects represent are the people of the city, the citizens of the past we live alongside, in effect, and this is how we remember them.

---

13. Daniel Gralath (1708–67) was a German physicist and mayor of Gdansk (Danzig). He also founded the Danzig Research Society. He published a *History of Electricity* in three volumes, 1747–56.

14. Huelle 2008, p. 109.

Huelle's sense of this in *Mercedes-Benz* is captured in the grandfather's photographs. Karol not only records the past, but he later goes back and (in good museum fashion) writes captions, "putting his archive in order, writing the missing dates and places and names of people on their cardboard backing".[15] But Huelle understands – and it is this philosophical understanding where I find his subtlety as writer moves me – that there is no simple fixed position: of past or present, of national or personal identity. He describes Karol's photographs, ostensibly a very distinct record of specific events, as images that themselves keep changing, taking on new meanings, not just for different spectators, but for Karol himself, as time passes and experience alters him.

Huelle describes this wonderfully:

> As he unrolled it again, this particular reel of time felt like something very different from a catalogue of ordinary memories; it felt as if those moments captured in the past by the cold shutter of his Leica now made up a completely new volume that he'd never intended to create, consisting of chance moments, twists and turns of light, bits and pieces of matter and voices that stopped sounding long ago; it was like a suddenly open vista to the astonished passer-by, a wonderful spectacle of phantoms of time and space, swirling like golden pillars of dust in a dark old granary.[16]

"The astonished passer-by". Is that not what we all are, whether gazing at photographs, standing in a museum, driving alongside Miss Ciwle, reading a novel by Pawel Huelle? These golden swirls of time make museums versions of Huelle's city drive: the gaze outward, the reflection inward. Together they comprise not just knowledge of a place, but engagement with it. What *Mercedes-Benz* may ultimately teach us is that every drive is a potential *romance*, not just with a person (though that's certainly on the cards here), but with the world.

There is only one problem with Pawel Huelle's *Mercedes-Benz.* That problem is ... that it comes to an end. Because it is the sort of book one

---

15. Huelle 2005, p. 96.
16. Huelle 2005, p. 96.

wants to go on forever: we want more stories of grandmother Maria and grandfather Karol turning fox-hunting into an annual automobile chase after an inflatable balloon; more tales of his father's disappointment each time his rescued Mercedes *doesn't* break down and require a loving repair. We want the simmering Miss Ciwle to continue to take Pawel through his paces, commanding him to turn left, to release the clutch slowly, to indicate even in the wilderness!

And the book promises that: that life, like the best sentence by Bohumil Hrabal (and it would be hard to choose), is an endless sequences of stories; that any place can prompt its own memories and meanings; that the very joy of existing is like driving a car through a city, with its parade of citizens and events, its cranes and congestion, with its driver and passenger looking out and discussing what they see. It's about making contact – with people and places; it's about falling in love.

Just get in the car, as Miss Ciwle says, and look how neatly we shift into a higher gear.[17]

---

17. Huelle 2005, p. 61. She actually says: "Look how neatly we shift into fourth."

Museums at the Crossroads?
Knowing Your Limits

From the outset of my arrival in Canada in 2012, I was involved in a number of UNESCO-related activities. This address was prepared for the AGM of the Canadian Commission for UNESCO in 2013 and inspired by the evolving vision for the Royal British Columbia Museum, one of the world's great treasure houses.

Allow me to begin by taking you on a journey. The year is 1585. Captain John Davis has sailed from the south coast of England in search of the Northwest Passage. His ship is the rather worryingly named *Moonshine*. He's rounded Greenland and is coming up an inlet which would eventually be called after him, the Davis Strait. This is a description written by one of his crew:

> The people of the country, having espied us, made a lamentable noise, as we thought, with great outcries and screechings. We, hearing them, thought it had been the howling of wolves.... When they came unto us we caused our musicians to play, ourselves dancing and making many signs of friendship.... At length one of them, pointing up to the sun with his hand, would presently strike his breast so hard that we might hear the blow. This he did many times before he would any way trust us. Then John Ellis, the master of the *Moonshine*

... struck his breast and pointed to the sun after their order, which when he had divers times done, they began to trust him.... We threw our caps, stockings and gloves, and such other things as then we had about us, playing with our music, and making signs of joy, and dancing. So, the night coming, we bade them farewell.[1]

What I love about this passage is that in every sense, we are on the cusp of Canada – of the geographical edge of the continent, of those first mysterious encounters between two different worlds. Canada is about to happen, and nothing would be the same again.

Davis's journey sounds very jolly. Musicians. Caps in the air. "Signs of joy and dancing." It's a sort of Elizabethan gay cruise. But the days previous had been awful: north winds and ice, the air "so foggy and full of thick mist that we could not see the one ship from the other".[2] On this and later journeys, the chronicler will struggle to pin down where they are. He names everything he sees: Mount Raleigh, Cape Dyer. But generally they are nowhere, lost in the ice and fog, unable to land, subject to random encounters which sometimes go well. All there is for the most part is a vastness one is constantly coming up against. And that vastness is Canada.

I want you to keep that vastness in mind, because I think it sets a standard we need to hold on to. Davis's is a world-changing cultural encounter. I would like to think that in some small way, committed as we are to commemorating such encounters, museums in Canada caught something of its impact. Indeed, I would like to suggest that in some big way we ought to do so.

It's a good moment to be asking a question very much like Davis and his crew must have been asking. Museums in Canada – and in most parts of the world – are at a crossroads right now. Money is tight, government support is being reined in, public pressure is questioning the needs of

---

1. "The first voyage of Master John Davis, undertaken in June 1585, for the discovery of the north-west passage. Written by Master John Janes, merchant, sometimes servant to the worshipful Master William Sanderson", in David 1981, pp. 335–36.
2. David, p. 334.

culture over basic social services. There is a mood of retrenchment. We're at sea, the fog is rolling in, it's cold. And we have to decide: do we turn back, or do we sail on?

In Canada the risks are evident. Given the country's enormous size, museums can easily retreat into provincial isolation, doing less for less with fewer staff and fewer visitors. Museums can stay home and put the kettle on. No more of that fancy roving about in ships.

I strongly believe that this is exactly what museums must not do. This is the moment for museums to stop thinking small. It's a moment of change, and we need big ideas, bold ambitions and strong leadership. What's holding us back may be something we would class as a virtue: that we know our limits.

It is this, however, that inhibits us. We need to find new ways of working on a larger stage. We need to collaborate more. We need to play out our cultural transactions on a grander scale. Museums need to affiliate themselves with the political, the economic, the global. What we need, in effect, is to look beyond our boundaries, just as Captain John Davis did in 1585. It's terrifying, I fully admit it; there's no knowing where you'll end up. But at the same time, it might just be full of joy and dancing.

I want to put forward a number of ideas that suggest a larger geography for museums. My first will involve South American prize bulls: killing them, eating their tongues, resuscitating them. This suggestion is not for the faint-hearted.

One of the countries that most impresses me with the breadth of its cultural policy is Brazil. This leading light of the BRIC[3] economies has designated 27 festivals, rituals and other practices as being of "cultural significance". The Bumba-Meu-Boi Festival in São Luís do Maranhão takes place in June and July. It blends Portuguese, African and Indian elements into a theatrical dance pageant. A number of characters are involved, including a faithful *rancheiro*, his pregnant wife who has a hankering for bull's tongue, and some shamans known as *curandeiros*. John the Baptist turns up – and

---

3. Brazil, Russia, India and China, countries that international economists generally agree are at a similar stage of economic development.

of course an ox, which dies but is brought miraculously back to life with the power of drumming.

Brazil is one of 154 signatories to UNESCO's Convention for the Safeguarding of the Intangible Cultural Heritage.[4] Six of its cultural practices appear on UNESCO's register, but internally, the country's National Institute of Historic and Artistic Heritage is committed to supporting a wide range of intangible heritage, from cheese-making in the mountains of Minas Gerais to the Bumba-Meu-Boi Festival to Jongo, a dance form invented by Bantu communities in southeast Brazil. Jongo combines music and improvisational poetry. It probably derives from traditional Angolan guessing games known as *jinongonongo*.

The UNESCO register of intangible culture is impressive: acupuncture in China, Himalayan theatre in India, polyphonic male singing in Corsica, fishing rituals in Mali. It is marvelously generous in its understanding of what culture is. That what people do, what they believe, how they feel, are caught up in any number of representative acts. It is culture beyond the museum, passed down from generation to generation. Intangible culture shows the living interaction between communities and their environments, and celebrates the strong sense of identity inevitably bound up in its practice, particularly for indigenous groups.

Support for intangible culture worldwide is moving in two directions. One is bringing that culture in: registering such practices – "collecting them", if you will – to ensure they are recorded and preserved.[5] There are many excellent examples across the globe.[6] Without them, so much is lost.

---

4. See www.unesco.org/culture/ich.

5. Convention for the Safeguarding of the Intangible Cultural Heritage, Paris, October 17, 2003, Article 2(3): "'Safeguarding' means measures aimed at ensuring the viability of the intangible cultural heritage, including the identification, documentation, research, preservation, protection, promotion, enhancement, transmission, particularly through formal and nonformal education, as well as the revitalization of the various aspects of such heritage."

6. UNESCO's own working document "Implementing the Convention for the Safeguarding of the Intangible Cultural Heritage at the National Level: Training and Capacity-building Materials for a Five-day Workshop"

Reading the slender descriptions of travels in the 16th-century, one longs for those cultural encounters to have been preserved. What did it all mean, that jolly dance by Sir John Davis's crew? What did the Inuit make of it in 1585? We can't know, but we can at least apply the lessons of lost history to safeguarding knowledge of events and activities in our own time. It is so much easier today, and museums are in many ways the likely home for so much of what is recorded – from scholarly documentary to instant You-Tube postings. We should make ourselves the archiving experts and find the best ways of doing it.

The other direction for intangible culture focuses on sharing it: knowledge transfer, widening the audience for such practices, sending the variety of the world across the world.[7] It is here where intangible culture intersects so importantly with the larger transactions we need to think about. Festivals such as Carnival in Brazil are key elements to the country's culture, but also to its tourism. In smaller places, they are often the sole means of economic well-being, tied significantly to the marketplace. This can be about producing local commodities for sale, such as lace or bark-cloth or boats[8] – often as a means of fostering economic independence for the communities that produce them. Or it can be about a more general tourist attraction. Cultural publicity has its drawbacks and its dangers, certainly, but with every Pinterest post and traveller's tweet, it is an aspect we cannot be naive about or ignore.

Some countries have not signed up to the UNESCO convention. Canada is one of them. And it puzzles me. We are a country with many fine examples of recording indigenous practices and rituals. It's all the more reason why countries like Canada should be leading the discussion.

(Draft 3.0), April 30, 2011, gives details of projects from around the world, from both within and outside the convention. It includes an example of how policy-making on intangible cultural heritage works at provincial level in Canada. See Newfoundland and Labrador 2006.

7. du Cros 2012, pp. 2–3.

8. From the UNESCO register: Lace-making (Croatia), bark-cloth (Uganda) and boats (Iran).

Canada understands the politics of cultural accumulation – what happens when a culture is taken up? who owns it? how does it move and change and avoid the cliché of fixed representation? No one wants intangible culture suffocating in a box. And Canadians can contribute an enormous amount to answering these questions.

Intangible heritage practices are still in their infancy. But I want to raise their importance now, while it's still easy for us to think about how to mobilize their usefulness. First Nations culture should be Canada's biggest tourist draw. But the primary focus of many First Nations was never material production. Indeed the glory of many indigenous belief systems in the Americas was their light footprint on the land, its invisibility, its harmonious renewal. "Showing" such cultures, in a traditional museum sense, is almost impossible. In museums across the country, we try. But we fail, again and again. It's why the South American bull should inspire us. We need to collect more widely and plug into living practices more effectively. What we need inside our museums is Carnival, Canadian-style.

And there is one further point to make. What constitutes "intangible culture" is even vaster than the examples I mention. It is by no means limited to indigenous communities. It could be what happens in a Macedonian bar in Toronto, of the sort Michael Ondaatje describes so wonderfully in his novel *In the Skin of a Lion*.[9] The immigrant experience is so often one of empty hands, where, in the words of another Canadian writer, Al Purdy, "the shape of home is under your fingernails".[10] How do you capture that shape, where there are no buildings, no artifacts, no possessions, no particular set of things to mark it out? It's hard to imagine a more central preoccupation to many countries, and particularly one like Canada.

---

9. Ondaatje 1988, pp. 36–7. Ondaatje's subplot of the Macedonian Nicholas Temelcoff – one of several immigrants in the novel – charts how the immigrant outsider slowly finds himself "sewn into history" (p. 149), embedded in the story of his new country. Often retrospective when discussing immigrant cultures, it is these new stories we need to capture in museums, the living cultural mix of old and new.

10. Purdy 1996, p. 38.

Purdy was a poet with strong links to Canada's west coast, where the Royal BC Museum resides. In his poem "Trees at the Arctic Circle", he describes his annoyance with some ground willow.[11] (I know. It's a poet's thing.) He complains that these vertically challenged trees (at less than half a metre tall) are not really doing their bit as Canadians. They are not towering Douglas-firs, or big and bold like Bigleaf Maples or Garry Oaks. They don't dominate the horizon. They crawl under rocks and grovel. "And yet", he writes:

> And yet –
> their seed pods glow
> like delicate grey earrings
> their leaves are veined and intricate
> like tiny parkas.

What he finds in them couldn't be more Canadian. And his metaphor shows us everything we need to look for. The overlooked. The hard to see. The evanescent. If this is what we can locate, every visitor to a museum will be enchanted.

A decade ago, Philippe de Montebello, then director of New York's Metropolitan Museum of Art, published an article criticizing blockbuster exhibitions. He wrote:

> These shows are meant to appeal to a public whose range of interests in art ... is relatively narrow. And who but museums are to blame if that is so? If museums continue to spoon-feed the same subjects to [their] public ... then the public will not learn to demand more of museums.[12]

His conclusion makes a brilliant starting point. What else can we offer? How do we expand not just what we do, but the horizon of expectation in ways that will challenge what we do? I think intangible culture is one area that can inspire us. It opens the museum up: different content, having to

---

11. Purdy, pp. 38–40. His ground willow is a passing feature, with just "three months / to make sure the species does not die". Like all overlooked cultures we might seek to preserve, they are struggling for survival.

12. de Montebello 2004, p. 159.

find innovative ways to present it, making us curate differently by bringing in other voices with their own experience and expertise.

And what's useful about this question is that it gets us away from capital expenditure. From the thought that what we need is a better, shinier build-ing, more technology, a bigger car park in order to do more. Yes, we need to preserve our building stock and keep it fit and functional. But we need to think about new ways of *being* a museum. So it's not a pitch for more money, something that cannot fail to wear down even the most persistent among us.

New ways of collecting will throw up new methods as well. What excites me about intangible cultural heritage is not just its scale, but its openness. Almost for the first time, I feel, I can get the people we talk about at the Royal BC Museum into the museum. Not symbols of the people. Or artifacts. Or relics. But people themselves, from every walk of life. And if what we present is more community focused, then how we work in other areas is bound to become more collaborative. Canadian collections hold so much potential for collaborative discovery and display. There's so much we can do to share collections, move them around, compare them. We can break free of fragmented knowledge and tell larger stories. Digitization has made this so much easier, and a lot of the ways of working are coming from the public, working online and creating web pages that are – really, if we're honest – mini museums. We're racing down the digital highway, and it's affecting our other work in really positive ways. Instead of separation, I seem to be finding whole new sets of information and ways to combine things.

It's important to recognize equally that this is a question of research. We perhaps are not rigorous enough in museums and archives about set-ting new research agendas. We react to collections rather than create with them. It seems to me there is an immense prospect for working up much more intricate histories from museum collections. If I'm suggesting a vaster terrain, with new forms of collecting and new ways to collect, then reframing how we do traditional research will be an essential and exciting component of that. Even the culture we know, the culture we've always displayed in cases and catalogues, may have territories yet to explore. At the Royal BC Museum, the collection and archives contain seven million items. It's an intellectual Klondike, and my teams are already panning for gold.

To give you a specific example, one of Brazil's UNESCO-registered practices is Frevo. I don't have a simple word to tell you what it is. It's music, it's dance, it's martial art, it's craft. The music alone derives from military marches, Brazilian tango, square dances, polkas, classical repertoire. The UNESCO adjudicating committee praised Frevo in particular for its syncretism: that wonderful ability to absorb almost anything that matters to its practitioners.[13]

Traditionally, museums have hated mixed cultural forms like Frevo. We're brilliant at isolating cultures in order to explain them. We separate things into distinct categories where they belong, and should stay. Frevo won't do that. It is a poltergeist. No matter where you put it in a museum, it will just change guise and pop up somewhere else.

Mixed forms are so much a part of who we are today, in our increasingly multicultural societies, in our global economic lives (from the shoes we wear to the food we eat), in our online access to communities around the world. Frevo's cultural diversity is a portrait of how we live now.[14] What a wonderful attraction for audiences who need museums to be relevant to their thinking and their experience. If we are to stop seeming old-fashioned to visitors (as we sometimes can), everything we do needs a dash of Frevo.

Articles 19 through 24 of the UNESCO declaration on intangible culture provide for "international cooperation and assistance", including study, training, equipment and standard-setting.[15] It's an active program

---

13. "Frevo constitutes a syncretic artistic expression recognized by the people of Recife as a festive symbol of their identity and continuity and constantly recreated by them in response to changing social conditions". Cited at www.unesco.org/culture/ich/RL/00603 (accessed July 12, 2013).

14. See du Cros on how intangible cultural heritage can break free of being categorized as something old-fashioned, based on traditions and folk memory, by highlighting its ties to present-day cultural diversity.

15. Convention for the Safeguarding of the Intangible Cultural Heritage, Paris, Article 1(d), elaborated in Articles 19–24.

encouraging cultural organizations to look outward, to share knowledge, work together, discover new things. It's very much in the spirit of the International Council of Museums (ICOM). Even for those not working in this area, it is an important indicator of the absolute necessity of working as a global network.

And those global connections are not restrictive: *If you show me your ivory diptych, I'll show you mine.* That's all very well for diptychs. But we're aiming to understand the vastness. One thing we're building through such networks is economic ties – with other countries, with different people, with possibilities we have not even begun to conceptualize. I've mentioned the contribution intangible heritage makes to economic development in many regions. It is one example where cultural policy intersects the wider economy. It gives us influence. It should garner rewards.

At this highest level, what we need in Canada, I would argue, is a cultural foreign policy. Economic. Cultural. Political. One of the remarkable stories of Canada's leadership on the world stage occurred in the Second World War. It was during Poland's occupation by Germany, and a group of about 300 Polish National Treasures was shipped from Poland to Canada for safe storage. They were an amazing array of irreplaceable things: a jewelled sword used to crown Polish kings since 1320; Flemish tapestries; a Gutenberg Bible; a painting by Cranach; a gold tea set; seven saddles; a fistful of original manuscripts by Frédéric Chopin. After a circuitous journey, they reached Canada safely and were moved to various locations in Ontario and Quebec. Some ended up in the vaults of the Bank of Montreal. You can't get much safer than that.

As a Pole in Canada, I love this story. The support for culture. The wider political sympathy at a time of terrible need. It's an impressive historical analogue to Anne Michaels's internationally celebrated novel *Fugitive Pieces*. In that book, a young Polish boy is rescued during an archaeological dig at Biskupin in central Poland. He is almost an artifact himself, the last surviving remnant of his Jewish family, and like the Polish National Treasures, reaches the safety of Canada via Greece.[16]

---

16. Michaels 1997. The book is haunted by rescued treasure. In Toronto, the

What these stories remind us is that troops are not the only international force at our disposal. Cultural diplomacy has its place in how we talk to other nations and build ties with them. In 2010 Polish Senate Speaker Bogdan Borusewicz presented a copy of the Gutenberg Bible to the Canadian Parliament. It was a token of thanks to Canada for helping to safeguard those Polish National Treasures during the Second World War.[17] It is a link neither country is likely to forget and shows with absolute clarity how culture and cultural institutions can be actors on the world stage. If we keep looking out, and show strong leadership, who's to say what culture might not do abroad – in Mali or Afghanistan or Syria.

I've called this paper in part "Knowing Your Limits" because I want to kick that idea into oblivion. Its defeatism, its quiet negativity, its – dare I say it? – Canadian caution hovers in the region of all those class inhibitors so beloved in England, like "knowing your place".

I want museums to know their limits – because limits are interesting places to *start* from, not to end up. Because limits have to be surpassed. Because you need to see what's holding you back in order to progress.

It's about success. Look at how the former governor of the Bank of Canada has leapt out of his box. Mark Carney made the Canadian economy admired around the world during the recent global recession. But rest on his laurels? Keep doing the same thing? Sit back and root for the Edmonton Oilers?[18] No. He's now gone off to rescue the mess that is the British banking system. He worked hard within the limits of what he had to do, then waved goodbye and sailed beyond them. I applaud his courage.

I live in one of the most beautiful places in the world. Victoria, British Columbia, is on the edge of a continent, and the scale of its beauty reminds

---

protagonist, Jakob Beer, will eventually marry Alexandra Maclean, a girl raised on her father's tales of "how his fellow Londoners had carried historical treasures – including the just unearthed Sutton Hoo helmet – into the underground at Aldwych station, to protect them from the bombings" (p. 129).

17. See *Metro Toronto*, May 6, 2010, p. 8.

18. Stewart 2013.

me every day. It's one of the limits of Canada, this vast country that stretches from sea to sea to sea.[19] I feel sometimes as if my museum, the Royal BC Museum, could embrace the whole nation. So much of Canada ends up west – migrating, exploring, venturing over prairie and mountain and glacial lake. But like everyone on the west coast, every day my eye travels out to sea. And I know there's so much further we could go.

---

19. The politics of the Canadian motto, *A mari usque ad mare*, reflects my point. Canada is not just "from sea to sea" any longer. With the political enfranchisement of the northern territories, a third ocean has been added to the Canadian stretch. Who said national limits, however longstanding, however enshrined in language taken from the Vulgate, couldn't be surpassed? (See, for instance, "'To sea' or not 'to sea': That is the question", *CBC News*, March 10, 2006.)

Acknowledgements

Thank you to Gerry Truscott, publisher at the Royal BC Museum, for patiently transforming dozens of papers into a coherent book. I also owe an enormous debt of thanks to all those who helped give birth to the stories contained in these essays, especially Dr Kathryn Bridge, Dr Martha Black, Dr Mark Kilfoyle, Dr Darryl McIntyre, Dr Cathy Ross, Alex Werner, Professor Kate Goodnow, David Spence and Pawel Huelle. Professor Andrew Ciechanowiecki has patiently mentored my thinking over the years, and a number of outstanding chairmen have greatly egged me on, none more so than Rupert Hambro, Michael Cassidy, John Williams, Camilla Mash, Flea Osborne and Michael Hoffmann – to them I am deeply grateful.

About the Author

Jack Lohman is chief executive officer of the Royal British Columbia Museum in Victoria, Canada, and professor in museum design at the Bergen National Academy of the Arts, Norway. He was formerly chairman of the National Museum in Warsaw, director of the Museum of London and chief executive officer of Iziko Museums of Cape Town, South Africa.

References Cited

Alexander, Edward. *Museums in Motion: An Introduction to the History and Function of Museums*. Nashville: American Association for State and Local History, 1979.

Amaral, Aracy. "Stages in the Formation of Brazil's Cultural Profile", *Journal of Decorative and Propaganda Arts* 21, 1995.

Andermann, Jens. *The Optic of the State: Visuality and Power in Argentina and Brazil*. University of Pittsburgh Press, 2007.

Ando, Tadao. "From the Periphery of Architecture" in *Tadao Ando: Complete Works*, edited by Francesco Dal Co. London: Prestel, 1995.

Asmal, Kader. "Making Hope and History Rhyme". *South African History Online*; sahistory.org.za/archive/making-hope-and-history-rhyme. n.d.

Baker, Malcom. "Bode and Museum Display: The Arrangement of the Kaiser-Friedrich-Museum and the South Kensington Response", *Jahrbuch der Berliner Museen* 58, 1996.

Beck, Dimitri. "Afghanistan through Afghan Photojournalists' Eyes", *The Digital Journalist*, February 2005.

Bennett, Tony. *The Birth of the Museum: History, Theory, Politics*. London: Routledge, 1995.

Bethell, Leslie, ed. *The Cambridge History of Latin America*, vol. 10. Cambridge University Press, 1995.

Black, Graham. *The Engaging Museum: Developing Museums for Visitor Involvement*. London: Routledge, 2005.

Bo Bardi, Lina. "The Theory and Philosophy of Architecture". Lecture given at the Visual Arts School, Federal University of Bahia, 1958, reproduced in *Lina Bo Bardi Obra Construida* 2G:23–24 (special issue, Barcelona, 2002).

BOP Consulting. *World Cities Culture Report 2012*. London: Mayor of London, 2012.

Campbell, Louise. "The Phoenix and the City: War, Peace and Architecture" in *Phoenix: Architecture/Art/Regeneration*. London: Black Dog Publishing, 2004.

Campbell, Peter. "At the British Museum", *London Review of Books*, September 20, 2007.

Cattermole, Paul. *Buildings for Tomorrow: Architecture that Changed our World*. London: Thames & Hudson, 2006.

Chittenden, Newton H. *Official Report of the Exploration of the Queen Charlotte Islands for the Government of British Columbia*. Victoria: Government of British Columbia, 1884.

Collins, Peter. *Concrete: The Vision of a New Architecture*. London: Horizon Press, 1959.

Comment, Bernard. *The Panorama*. London: Reaktion Books, 1999.

Commission for Africa. *Our Common Interest*. Report. Harmondsworth, UK: Penguin, 2005.

Cotterell, Arthur. *Chariot: The Astounding Rise and Fall of the World's First War Machine*. London: Pimlico, 2005.

da Costa Leitão Vieira, Ana Maria. "The São Paulo Immigrants' Memorial: Fields of Research and Challenges in the 21st Century", *Museum International* 59:1/2:233/234, 2007.

Damase, Jacques. *Carriages*. Translated by William Mitchell. London: Weidenfeld and Nicolson, 1968.

David, Richard, ed. *Hakluyt's Voyages: A Selection*. London: Chatto & Windus, 1981.

de Montebello, Philippe. "Art Museums, Inspiring Public Trust" in *Whose Muse? Art Museums and the Public Trust*, edited by James Cuno. Princeton University Press, 2004.

Dickens, Charles. *Bleak House*. Harmondsworth, UK: Penguin, 1996.

DMCS (Department of Culture, Media and Sport, UK). "Code of Practice for the Care of Human Remains in Museums". Policy draft, 2004.

du Cros, Hilary. *Intangible Cultural Heritage, Education and Museums*. Hong Kong: UNESCO Arts in Education Observatory for Research in Local Cultures and Creativity in Education, 2012.

Edugyan, Esi. *Half-Blood Blues*. Toronto: Thomas Allen Publishers, 2011.

El Shabrawy, Charlotte. "Naguib Mahfouz, The Art of Fiction, no. 129", *The Paris Review*, no. 123, 1992.

Epstein, Jacob. *Let There be Sculpture: The Autobiography of Jacob Epstein*. London: Readers Union, 1942.

Espinosa y Tello, Josef. *A Spanish voyage to Vancouver and the north-west coast of America: being the narrative of the voyage made in the year 1792 by the schooners Sutil and Mexicana to explore the Strait of Fuca*. Translated by Cecil Jane. London: Argonaut Press, 1930.

Fielding, Henry. *Amelia*, edited by Martin C. Battestin. Oxford: Clarendon Press, 1983.

Findlen, Paula. "Renaissance Collecting and Remembrance" in *Museums and Memory*, edited by Susan A. Crane. Stanford University Press, 2000.

Fowler, Marian. *Blenheim: Biography of a Palace*. London: Viking, 1989.

Fox, Celina. *Lord Mayor's Coach*. London: Museum of London, 1990.

Frampton, Kenneth. *Tadao Ando: Light and Water*. London: Birkhäuser Architecture, 2003.

Franck, Klaus. *The Works of Affonso Eduardo Reidy*. Translated by D.O. Stephenson Reidy. New York: Frederick A. Praeger, 1960.

Freyre, Gilberto. *The Portuguese and the Tropics*. Lisbon: Executive Committee for the Commemoration of the Fifth Centenary of Prince Henry the Navigator, 1961.

Frye, Northrop. "Silence in the Sea" in *The Bush Garden: Essays in the Canadian Imagination*. Toronto: House of Anansi Press, 1971.

Gehry, Frank. *Gehry Talks: Architecture and Process*. London: Thames & Hudson, 1999.

Gibbs-Smith, Charles. "The Fault is in Ourselves", *Museums Journal*, 1964.

Girouard, Mark. *Cities and People: A Social and Architectural History*. New Haven, Connecticut: Yale University Press, 1985.

Gissen, David, ed. *Big and Green: Toward Sustainable Architecture in the 21st Century*. New York: Princeton Architectural Press, 2003.

Glancey, Jonathan. *New British Architecture*. London: Thames & Hudson, 1989.

Grimely Kuntz, Paul. *Alfred North Whitehead*. Twatne's English Authors Series. Boston: Twayne Publishing, 1984.

Group for Large Local Authority Museums. *Museums and Social Inclusion*. Department of Museum Studies, University of Leicester, 2000.

Guardian, The. "Hail Siza", *The Guardian*, January 26, 2009.

Hall, Stuart. "Negotiating Architecture" in *David Adjaye Houses: Recycling, Reconfiguring, Rebuilding*, edited by Peter Allison. London: Thames & Hudson, 2005.

Harbison, Robert. *Reflections on Baroque*. London: Reaktion Books, 2000.

Heaney, Seamus. *Human Chain*. London: Faber & Faber, 2010.

Herzen, Aleksander. *My Past and Thoughts: The Memoirs of Aleksander Herzen*. London: Chatto and Windus, 1924.

Hodgins, Jack. *The Invention of the World*. Agincourt: Macmillian, 1977.

Hooper-Greenhill, Eileen. "The Museum in the Disciplinary Society" in *Museum Studies in Material Culture*, edited by J. Pearce. Leicester University Press, 1989.

Hubbard, Phil. *City*. London: Routledge, 2006.

Hudson, Kenneth. *A Social History of Museums: What the Visitors Thought*. London: Macmillan, 1975.

Huelle, Pawel. *Mercedes-Benz*. Translated by Antonia Lloyd-Jones. London: Serpent's Tail, 2005.

Huelle, Pawel. *Castorp*. Translated by Antonia Lloyd-Jones. London: Serpent's Tail, 2007.

Huelle, Pawel. *The Last Supper*. Translated by Antonia Lloyd-Jones. London: Serpent's Tail, 2008.

Hughes, Kathryn. "A Museum is not an iPod", *The Guardian*, January 20, 2007.

Hume, Christopher. "City's New Architecture Frees Toronto the Timid", *Toronto Star*, November 28, 2009.

Hyde, Vernon. *Baroque and Rococo: Art and Culture*. London: Laurence King, 1999.

ICOM (International Council of Museums). ICOM Statutes and Articles, *ICOM News* 57:2, 2004.

Isozaki, Arata. *Four Decades of Architecture*. London: Thames & Hudson, 1998.

Jenkins, Barbara. "Toronto's Cultural Renaissance", *Canadian Journal of Communication* 30:2, 2005.

Josephson, Michael. *Preserving the Public Trust: The Five Principles of Public Service Ethics*. Bloomington, Indiana: Unlimited Publishing, 2005.

Kostof, Spiro. *The City Shaped: Urban Patterns and Meanings Through History*. London: Thames & Hudson, 1991.

Kowalski, W.W. "Restitution of Works of Art Pursuant to Private and Public International Law". *Hague Academy of International Law, Recueil des Cours* 288, 2002.

Kreps, Christina. *Liberating Culture: Cross-cultural Perspectives on Museums, Curation and Heritage Preservation*. London: Routledge, 2003.

Krishnamurti, Jiddu. *Freedom from the Known*. Bramdean, UK: Krishnamurti Foundation Trust, 1969.

Kroetsch, Robert. "Disunity as Unity: A Canadian Strategy" in *The Lovely Treachery of Words: Essays Selected and New*. Toronto: Oxford University Press, 1989.

Kunsthistorisches Museum Wien. *The Collections and Carriages of Schönbrunn: Carriages and Horses at the Court of Vienna*. Vienna: Kunsthistorisches Museum Wien, 1995.

Lenclos, Jean-Philippe, and Dominique Lenclos. *Colours of the World: A Geography of Colour*. Translated by Gregory P. Bruhn. New York: W.W. Norton, 1999.

Leszkowic, Pawel, and Tomasz Kitlinski. "*Miłość i demokracja. Rozważania o Kwestii Homoseksvalnej w Polsce.*" *Poznan*, 2005.

Levine, Robert M. *The History of Brazil*. London: Pelgrave MacMillan, 2003.

Lohman, J., and K. Goodnow, eds. *Human Remains and Museum Practice*. Paris UNESCO Publishing; London: Museum of London, 2006.

Lopès, Maria Margaret. "*Le Rôle des Musées, de la Science et du Public au Brésil*", in *Les Sciences Hors d'Occident au XXé siècle*, vol. 5: *Sciences et Développement*, edited by Martine Barrère. Campinas, Brazil: Instituto de Geociencias – Unicamp, 1996.

Lopès, Maria Margaret, and Irina Podgorny. "The Shaping of Latin American Museums of Natural History, 1850–1990", in *Osiris*, 2nd series, vol. 15: *Nature and Empire: Science and the Colonial Enterprise*. Chicago: Orstom, 2000.

Louyot, Anne. *São Paulo en Mouvement*. Paris: Editions Autrement, 2005.

Lowry, Glenn. "A Deontological Approach to Art Museums and the Public Trust" in *Whose Muse? Art Museums and the Public Trust*, edited by James Cuno. Princeton University Press, 2004.

Mahjoub, Jamal. *Travelling with Djinns*. London: Vintage, 2004.

Mainstone, Rowland J. *Hagia Sophia: Architecture, Structure and Liturgy in Justinian's Great Church*. London: Thames & Hudson, 1988.

Margalit, Avishai. *The Ethics of Memory*. Cambridge and London: Harvard University Press, 2002.

Marsden, Jonathan, and John Hardy. "'O Fair Britannia Hail': The 'Most Superb' State Coach", *Apollo*, February 2001.

Martin, James. "The Role of Cathedrals in the 21st Century". *Docstoc*; www.docstoc.com/40690685/the-role-of-cathedrals-in-the-21st-century. May 28, 2010.

McNeil Bertrand, Jennifer. "Public Funding for Arts and Culture in Canada", *Suite101*; http://suite101.com/article/public-funding-for-arts-and-culture-in-canada-a240611. May 24, 2010.

Michaels, Anne. *Fugitive Pieces*. London: Bloomsbury, 1997.

Michell, George. *The Royal Palaces of India*. London: Thames & Hudson, 1994.

Ministry of Culture. National Museums Policy. Brazilia: Ministry of Culture, 2007.

Morris, Jane. Untitled article in *The Guardian*, July 2002.

Museums, Libraries and Archives Council. *"Access for All" Toolkit: Enabling Inclusion For Museums, Libraries And Archives*. London: Museums, Libraries and Archives Council, 2004.

Musgrave, Susan. "Entrance of the Celebrant" in *Selected Strawberries and Other Poems*. Victoria: Sono Nis Press, 1977.

National Museum of Denmark. "Utimut-Return: The Return of More than 35,000 Cultural Objects to Greenland". Copenhagen: National Museum of Denmark, 2004.

Newfoundland and Labrador, Government of. *Creative Newfoundland and Labrador: The Blueprint for Development and Investment in Culture*. St John's: Government of Newfoundland and Labrador, 2006.

Norberg-Schulz, Christian. *Late Baroque and Rococo Architecture*. London: Faber & Faber, 1980.

OMA/AMO and Rem Koolhaas. "Junkspace" in *Content*. Cologne: Taschen, 2004.

Ondaatje, Michael. *In the Skin of a Lion*. Markham, Ontario: Penguin, 1988.

Ottomeyer, Hans. Introduction to *I.M. Pei: The Exhibitions Building of the German Historical Museum Berlin*, edited by Ulrike Kretzschmar. Munich: Prestel Verlag, 2003.

Parker, Richard. "From Conquistadors to Corporations", *Sojourne Magazine*, May-June 2002.

Parry, J.H. *Trade and Dominion: European Overseas Empires in the 18th Century*. London: publisher unknown, 1974.

Pecchio, Giuseppe. *Semi-Serious Observations of an Italian Exile During his Residence in England*. London: publisher unknown, 1833.

Pickering, M. "Repatriation, Rhetoric, and Reality: The Repatriation of Australian Indigenous Human Remains and Sacred Objects". Paper delivered to Australian Registrars Committee Conference, Melbourne, October 8–9, 2001.

Purdy, Al. "Transient" in *Rooms for Rent in the Outer Planets: Selected Poems 1962–96,* selected and edited by Al Purdy and Sam Solecki. Madeira Park, BC: Harbour Publishing, 1996.

Rajan, Mira. "A Time of Change in the United Kingdom", *Media & Arts Review*, 2002.

Ramsey, Nancy. "Chronicling the History of their Afghan Sisters", *New York Times*, November 16, 2004.

Reed, Dimity, editor. *Tangled Destinies*. Canberra: National Museum of Australia, 2002.

Reichl, Christopher A. "Stages in the Historical Process of Ethnicity: The Japanese in Brazil, 1908–88", *Ethnohistory* 42:1, 1995.

Reynolds, Simon. *Retromania: Pop Culture's Addiction to its Own Past*. London: Faber & Faber, 2011.

Rochon, Lisa. "Complex Backed by Aga Khan will Bring New Life to Urban Neighbourhoods", *Globe and Mail*, May 28, 2010.

Rogers, Richard, and Philip Gumuchdjian. *Cities for a Small Planet*. London: Faber & Faber, 1997.

Roosevelt, Theodore. *Through the Brazilian Wilderness*. New York: publisher unknown, 1914.

Rosenberg, Eugene, and Richard Cork. *Architect's Choice: Art in Architecture in Great Britain since 1945*. London: Thames & Hudson, 1992.

Royal Archives, London, UK. *A Journal of the Most Material Occurrences in the Department of the Master of the Horse during the Reign of His Majesty King George III*. DB 1a.

Said, Edward. *Out of Place: A Memoir*. New York: Vintage Books, 1999.

Sandberg, Mark. *Living Pictures, Missing Persons: Mannequins, Museums and Modernity*. Princeton University Press, 2003.

Sebald, W.G. *On the Natural History of Destruction*. Translated by Anthea Bell. New York: Random House, 2003.

Sepúlveda dos Santos, Myrian. "The New Dynamic of Blockbuster Exhibitions: The Case of Brazilian Museums", *Bulletin of Latin American Research* 20:1, 2001.

Sepúlveda dos Santos, Myrian. "Museums Without a Past: the Brazilian Case", *International Journal of Cultural Studies* 6:2, 2003.

Sepúlveda dos Santos, Myrian. "Representations of Black People in Brazilian Museums", *Museum and Society* 3:1, 2005.

Sewing, Werner. "Movement and Transparency" in *I.M. Pei: The Exhibitions*

Building of the German Historical Museum Berlin, edited by Ulrike Kretzschmar. Munich: Prestel Verlag, 2003.

Sherman, Daniel J. "Objects of Memory: History and Narrative in French War Museums", *French Historical Studies* 19:1, 1995.

Slaby, Alexandra. *Making a Single Case for the Arts: An International Perspective*. Research report for the Canadian Conference for the Arts, October 2008.

Slessor, Catherine. *Contemporary Architecture*. Victoria: Images Publishing Group, 2004.

Soros, G. *The Age of Fallibility: The Consequences of the War on Terror*. New York: Public Affairs, 2006.

Staal, Gert, and Martijn de Rijk. *IN side OUT / ON site IN: Redesigning the National Museum of Ethnology, Leiden, The Netherlands*. Amsterdam: Bis Publishers, 2003.

Stanyhurst, Richard. "The History of Ireland" in *The Chronicles of England, Scotland and Ireland* (1577) by Raphael Holinshed. London: Henry Denham, 1587.

Stewart, Heather. "Mark Carney: Bank Governor's Journey from Wilderness to Heart of the City", *The Guardian*, June 13, 2013.

Swirnoff, Lois. *The Colour of Cities: An International Perspective*. New York: McGraw-Hill, 2000.

Thomas, Audrey. *Intertidal Life*. Toronto: General Publishing, 1986.

Underwood, David. *Oscar Niemeyer and the Architecture of Brazil*. New York: Rizzdi, 1994.

UNESCO. *Museum International*, no. 202 (November), 2002.

Venturi, Robert. *Complexity and Contradiction in Architecture*. New York: Museum of Modern Art, 2002.

Venturi, Robert, and Denise Scott Brown. "Mess is More" in *Urban Visions: Experiencing and Envisioning the City*, edited by Steven Spier. Tate Liverpool Critical Forum, vol. 5. Liverpool University Press, 2002.

Wackernagel, Rudolf H., ed. *Wittelsbach State and Ceremonial Carriages: Coaches, Sledges and Sedan Chairs in the Marstallmuseum Schloss Nymphenburg*. Stuttgart: Arnoldsche Art Publishers, 2002.

Wealthclick. "Philanthropy at the Cutting Edge". *Wealthclick*; wealthclick.com/philanthropy/good-practice/philanthropy-at-the-cutting-edge, 2013.

Wiseman, Carter. *The Architecture of I.M. Pei*. London: Thames & Hudson, 1990.

Wordsworth, William. *The Prelude*. London: Oxford University Press, 1965.

Work Foundation. "Staying Ahead: The Economic Performance of the UK's Creative Industries". Report. London: Department for Culture, Media and Sport, 2007.

Young, James. "The Veneration of Ruins in the Landscape of Holocaust Memory" in *Architourism: Authentic, Escapist, Exotic, Spectacular*, edited by Joan Ockman and Salomon Frausto. Munich: Prestel Verlag, 2005.

Zeiger, Mimi. *New Museum Architecture: Innovative Buildings from Around the World*. London: Thames & Hudson, 2005.

Zukin, Sharon. *The Culture of Cities*. Oxford: Blackwell, 1995.

Zukin, Sharon. "Space and Symbol in an Age of Decline" in *Re-Presenting the City: Ethnicity, Capital and Culture in the Twenty-First Century Metropolis*, edited by Anthony D. King. London: Macmillan, 1996.

Zweig, Stefan. *Brazil: Land of the Future*. Translated by Andrew St James. New York: Viking Press, 1943.

Index